Affect and POWER

Affect
and
POWER

Essays on Sex, Slavery, Race, and Religion
in Appreciation of Winthrop D. Jordan

Edited by David J. Libby, Paul Spickard, and Susan Ditto
Foreword by Charles Joyner
Introduction by Sheila L. Skemp

University Press of Mississippi
IN AFFILIATION WITH THE DEPARTMENT OF HISTORY,
UNIVERSITY OF MISSISSIPPI

www.upress.state.ms.us

The University Press of Mississippi is a member of the Association of American University Presses.

Copyright © 2005 by University of Mississippi
Published by the University Press of Mississippi in affiliation with the Department of History, University of Mississippi
All rights reserved
Manufactured in the United States of America

Print-on-Demand Edition
⊗
Library of Congress Cataloging-in-Publication Data

Affect and power : essays on sex, slavery, race, and religion in appreciation of Winthrop D. Jordan / edited by David J. Libby, Paul Spickard, and Susan Ditto ; foreword by Charles Joyner; introduction by Sheila L. Skemp.—1st ed.
    p. cm.
  Includes bibliographical references and index.
  ISBN 1-57806-769-3 (cloth : alk. paper)
    1. United States—Race relations. 2. Slavery—United States—History. 3. Slavery—Political aspects—United States—History. 4. Sex role—United States—History. 5. Sex—United States—History. 6. United States—Religion. 7. Christianity—United States. 8. United States—Civilization. I. Jordan, Winthrop D. II. Libby, David J., 1969– III. Spickard, Paul R., 1950– IV. Ditto, Susan.

E184.A1A355   2005
305.8′00973—dc22   2004022119

British Library Cataloging-in-Publication Data available

CONTENTS

Acknowledgments   vii

Foreword   xiii
  CHARLES JOYNER

Introduction   xvi
  SHEILA L. SKEMP

I. SEX
The Erotic South
  Civilization and Sexuality in American Abolitionism   3
  RONALD G. WALTERS

Ministerial Misdeeds
  The Onderdonk Trial and Sexual Harassment in the 1840s   25
  PATRICIA CLINE COHEN

Stallions in the Churchyard
  Sexuality and Privacy in Rural Mississippi   44
  SUSAN DITTO

II. SLAVERY
Relations Which Might Be Disastrous
  Natchez Indians and African Slaves in French Louisiana   67
  DAVID J. LIBBY

Christ in Chains
  *Slavery's Negative Impact on the
  Conversion of African American Slaves*   84
  DANIEL L. FOUNTAIN

III. RACE

What's Critical about White Studies   107
PAUL SPICKARD

Lester Young
Master of Jive   126
DOUGLAS HENRY DANIELS

Holding Center Stage
*Race Pride and the Extracurriculum at
Historically Black Colleges and Universities*   141
PATRICK B. MILLER

IV. RELIGION

"Blessed Are the Peacemakers"
William Jay and the Drive for International Arbitration   161
STEPHEN P. BUDNEY

Max Weber in New England   170
CHARLES L. COHEN

Notes   183

Contributors   222

Index   225

ACKNOWLEDGMENTS

Winthrop D. Jordan is a giant among American intellectuals. As one of the contributors to this volume wrote in another context, just as every basketball player wishes he or she could be like Michael Jordan, so every United States historian wishes he or she could be like Winthrop Jordan. His writings are rich in imagination, scrupulous of documentation, and gloriously phrased. They have garnered all the honors available to a member of his profession. No historical writer in the second half of the twentieth century cast a larger shadow than Winthrop Jordan. No one writing on race, sex, or slavery in American history is without debt to Winthrop Jordan.

The authors of the essays in *Affect and Power* owe Win Jordan debts that are more personal than those of other scholars. He has been a north star to us, each and all, when we were graduate students at Berkeley and the University of Mississippi, and through the decades as we have gone about our lives and careers. Those who know Jordan's scholarship will see the stamp of his mind on our work. Few of us have ever written anything formal without hearing Win's voice in our heads, urging us toward more scrupulous scholarship and sharper prose. More importantly, we never cease to admire his example and strive, however imperfectly, to follow it. If we manage to listen carefully to the sources from which we draw, if we succeed in writing prose that is clear and vigorous, then those virtues are due in no small part to Win Jordan's guidance.

Beyond the scope of intellectual lineage, we nearly all owe even more private debts to Win and his partner in life, Cora Miner Jordan, a steel magnolia if ever there was one. Not only when we were students but also later in our lives, to this very day, they can always be counted upon for wise counsel and unflagging support. During crises, they have taken us in, listened to our hopes and fears, encouraged us, and sent us back out to do our best in the world. They mourn our losses with empathy and patience and celebrate our successes with exuberance and pride.

This volume was born in the spring of 2002. A group of Jordan's former graduate students gathered in Oxford, Mississippi, to hold a *festschrift* and celebrate our mentor. We met, many of us for the first time, and talked—swapping stories about Win and telling each other about our work. We benefited from the hospitality of the History Department of the University of Mississippi, where we convened around a seminar table, students once again, with Win at the helm. We enjoyed a fine and memorable party at Win's and Cora's home, and before we left Oxford we purposed together to write a book of essays in appreciation (Win's Quaker equalitarianism and utterly unjustified but nonetheless sincere humility would not allow us to say "in honor") of Win. *Affect and Power* is that book.

Several people have earned thanks from this volume's editors. Among them are Robert Haws, chair of the University of Mississippi Department of History, Craig Gill, Editor-in-Chief at the University Press of Mississippi, Hon. William F. Winter, Cora Jordan, Mott Jordan, Ted Ownby, Anne Hardgrove, Sheila Skemp, Charles Joyner, and each of Win's former students who participated in the Mississippi *festschrift* and contributed their writing. Publication was made possible by support from the Ventress Order of the University of Mississippi Alumni Association and the University of Mississippi's Department of History. Without these people and institutions, the book would not have come to be. Our thanks must go, most of all, to Winthrop Jordan. Win, as the Japanese say, we have *on* for you: a debt that cannot be repaid, one that binds us together for the ages.

One of the more gifted among us, Chuck Cohen, wrote a poem—a biographical verse—to our mentor and friend for the occasion of our *festschrift* weekend in Oxford. As good poems do, it speaks from and to all our hearts. The editors are grateful to Chuck for allowing us to include it here.

To Win, on his Career

I see you sitting in a book-strewn room—
Semi-subterranean and suffused
with sweet tobacco smoke—meditating
on the veneniferous bonds of race,
Ancient attitudes engendering
Cruel intimacies among blacks and whites.

The past comes easily to one whose blood
Retains corpuscular remains of Boston

Brahmins, Yankee merchants, and Puritan
grandees, lineages tracing to the
long-faced governor whose quill lined out
God's blueprint for the City on a Hill;
So easily, as well, when venerable
objects keep one company:
a Federal-era banjo clock whose tocks
keep time in parallel centuries,
its nineteenth-century mechanism
clicking out the new millennium;
The chairs Lucretia Mott in Quaker order
set around her table;
                        and the bell
that Wendell Phillips tolled to warn the planters
how in binding slaves they bound themselves to hell.

So strong a thrust of genes and culture
could have predisposed you to expound
New England's classic themes:
                        God's controversy
with his Saints, so near to heaven, yet
so far from grace, condemned by their humanity
to sin with predetermined constancy;
The Revolution brewed by ersatz Mohawks
preferring to steep their tea in brine and
overthrow their king than forsake liberty;
The growth of mills whose industrial magic
conjured bolts of cloth from rushing rills,
metal looms, and blushing farmers' daughters;
Tall ships unloading oil and ambergris
while widows mourned their Ahabs lost at sea;
And transcendentalism, extolling
nature's sublimity, human self-reliance,
and Boston, the universe's hub.

Yet when facing two career paths
diverging in a yellow wood, you took
the one less frequented by Bay State scribes

and (in imagination) quit the realms
where long-haired men and short-haired women vilified
the master race immersed in languid sin
to journey South, awed by its febrile charms
and flagrant cultural perversity—
The abolitionist's fascination
for an ancient adversary. Intent
on laying bare the enslaving psyche,
you came to show abiding interest
in the souls and mores of black folk,
a calling augured in an old aunt's notes
of Negroes singing in the cotton fields,
her sketches catching Dixie's vivacity,
however fraught with clanks of antique irons.
This southward turning to retrace ancestral
pilgrimages added to the family
romance with sun-struck people slave and free
another chapter.

Your work conveys the trauma of America's misfortune:
Freedom's progress straight-jacketed at birth
by prejudices culled from early modern
Europe's naturalizing chains of being,
actualizing chains for beings deemed
to worship pagan gods, live savage lives,
and flaunt miscolored skins.
                           The ties that knot
the races to each other also chafe
the nation's conscience and arrest its heart:
The white man's burden is the black man's burden,
The black man's burden is the white man's shame,
and the net result of these perceptions
carried forward centuries and bruited about
with scientific rigor and righteous
ignorance is a covert fear
that slaves are plotting mayhem: fouling wells,
destroying tools, stealing themselves, re-routing

produce into a truly black market,
and—utmost horror—sneaking into
the holy of holies, the white man's bed,
there to cozy mistress and cave in her
husband's head. Black thrusting over white
The antidote for white over black.
The thought is father to the deed, and from
such nightmares sprang conspiracies of slaves—
real and fancied—executing fatal plots
and tumulting—a wish more often treason'd
than acted out, the plot dispatched (the plotters too)
and all caught up within conspiracies of silence,
whites invoking their right not to know.

The genius of your scholarship derives
From your tenacious seizing of the obvious,
The data so conspicuous by its
Banality that others pass it by
without a thought. This commonsense approach
Not commonly pursued you taught your students,
Pressing them to grasp the blatant fact
While simultaneously instilling
An aptitude to ask the curious query:
When did stars descend on Alabama?
When did little skirts adorn piano legs?
What was Dolly Madison's I.Q.?
these questions, prologues to circuitous
investigations, instigated
Archive rambles not meant to find arcane
Particulars, but to actuate
Imagination, creativity,
And a mind to find significance in
Oddball bits and pieces. Such pedagogy
Evoked your graduate brood's respect,
As did your amiableness our nurture,
Men and women equally committed
To mother you through personal upsets

Never advertized by you but witnessed
Nonetheless by caring hearts delighted
To return some petty tribute to repay
Your tutelage and magnanimity.

I see you sitting in a book-strewn room,
A true historian's historian.

Charles L. Cohen

FOREWORD

CHARLES JOYNER

I first met Winthrop Jordan in the spring of 1978 in the baggage claim area of the airport in Toronto. We were waiting for the shuttle to Waterloo, where Michael Craton had organized a large international slave studies conference. In the airport, on the shuttle, and throughout the conference, we discussed slavery, in particular slave culture and slave language, in which he was very interested. Win strongly encouraged my effort to combine the ethnographer's preference for spatial concentration with the historian's commitment to study change over time in a single slave community.

His reassurance heartened me; for while he was still a young man when I first met him, he was already a star in the historical profession. He was a professor of colonial history at the University of California, Berkeley, having joined the faculty in 1963 after completing his undergraduate work at Harvard College, earning graduate degrees at Clark and Brown Universities, and being awarded a postdoctoral fellowship at the Institute of Early American History and Culture at Williamsburg, Virginia.

His first book, *White Over Black: American Attitudes Toward the Negro, 1550–1812*, had been an instant success.[1] It appeared at a time when American society was preoccupied with the question of race relations. Typically, scholars argued the question according to ideology rather than evidence. Winthrop Jordan's evidence in *White Over Black* was substantial and significant, and his impressive range of sources served as the cornerstone upon which he constructed a more expansive, more sophisticated, and more convincing explanation of the rise of American racism than any of his predecessors. The young author had created a masterpiece in his first book, and it won the Bancroft Prize, the Parkman Prize, the Ralph Waldo Emerson Award, and the National Book Award in history and biography. The profession quickly and deservedly hailed *White Over Black* as the ultimate authority on early American racial attitudes.

After teaching in the history department at Berkeley for two decades, Jordan joined the faculty at the University of Mississippi in 1982, where he became William F. Winter Professor of History and F. A. P. Barnard Distinguished Professor of Afro-American Studies.

We saw each other briefly at academic meetings over the next few years. We renewed our friendship in earnest in the spring of 1987, when I became a Ford Foundation Visiting Professor of Southern Studies at the University of Mississippi. I enjoyed my semester in Oxford immensely. In my seminar on slavery I encountered the impressive students that Win had helped to attract and train at the University. To say that they were well prepared is to understate; they were veterans of Winthrop Jordan's course in historiography. In many ways I felt that my seminar was merely one stage in an ongoing seminar they had begun before I arrived and would continue after I had gone. Many of the members of the seminar have gone on to successful and productive careers in history.

Since I arrived at the University of Mississippi fresh from a visiting professorship at Berkeley, we eagerly shared recent news of Win's old friends and former colleagues, often over meals at some of Oxford's fine array of restaurants. Not least of the attractions in Oxford was the opportunity to meet Win's vivacious wife Cora, an attorney and a native Mississippian with a background in the Civil Rights Movement.

Our friendship continued at historical meetings and conferences in Oxford and in Myrtle Beach. Win and Cora hosted my participation in the Porter Fortune Symposia on "Cultural Interaction in the Old South" and "The South and the Caribbean." I hosted Win's participation in conferences on "Large Questions in Small Places" and "Southern Writers of Fact and Fiction" at Coastal Carolina University.

Winthrop Jordan has maintained a lifelong intellectual commitment to the study of race relations in the United States and the Caribbean. That commitment has been expressed not only in *White Over Black*, but also in such works as *The White Man's Burden: Historical Origins of Racism in the United States*, brilliant articles such as his "American Chiaroscuro: the Status and Definition of Mulattoes in the British Colonies," and his "Modern Tensions and the Origins of American Slavery." It was a major theme in the textbook he co-authored with his friend Leon F. Litwack, *United States: Conquering a Continent* and *United States: Becoming a World Power*.[2]

His first masterpiece was *White Over Black*. His second was *Tumult and Silence at Second Creek: An Inquiry into a Civil War Slave Conspiracy*.[3] The breadth of his wisdom in *White Over Black* was matched by the depth of his insight in *Tumult and Silence*. In the former he had labored long in the archives attempting to master an exhaustive body of evidence. In the latter he pondered long and deeply the meaning of cryptic and clandestine scraps of evidence he discovered in 1971. They were transcripts of testimonies by slaves interrogated by a council of slaveholders that pointed toward a slave conspiracy near Natchez during the spring and summer of 1861. The conspiracy was verified by neither speeches, pamphlets, newspapers, nor government documents. After a twenty-year search for additional evidence, Jordan supplemented these tantalizing and frustrating fragments with context from a Federal Writers Project interview with a former slave in the 1930s, plantation records, diaries and letters, census records, and a lifetime's immersion in the primary and secondary sources of slavery.

Already renowned as one of the most eloquent writers in profession, Jordan employed a very different style in his new book from the one he used earlier. His tone in *White Over Black* was erudite, urbane, witty, and judicious, ranging easily over centuries of Anglo-American intellectual history. In *Tumult and Silence* the tone was sober and brooding, tragic and profoundly moving, deeply rooted in the sights and sounds of Adams County, Mississippi, in the spring and summer of 1861.

Tumult and Silence, like *White Over Black*, was warmly received and enjoyed brisk sales. David Brion Davis, reviewing the work in the *New York Review of Books*, called it "one of the most remarkable feats of detective work achieved by a modern historian."[4] The book earned Win a second Bancroft Prize, making him only the second author in the history of the award to receive that honor twice.

Win's books and articles are, of course, a major part of his legacy, because people who never met him directly are empowered to embrace the world of ideas, to evaluate claims of truth and virtue as intellectual and rational beings rather than depend on their senses and appetites alone. But his scholarship is only a part of his legacy. The historians he has trained and mentored at Berkeley and the University of Mississippi are also part of his legacy. Their own essays grace this volume, casting their own shadows. But they too are only a part of his legacy. It also includes family and friends, good times shared and remembered, and his special ability to inspire his students, his colleagues, and his friends to strive to do our very best.

INTRODUCTION

Sheila L. Skemp

At the annual meeting of the Organization of American Historians, in the Spring of 1998, an overflow crowd gathered to honor the thirtieth anniversary of the publication of Winthrop Jordan's magisterial work, *White Over Black*. Many of us old folks remembered where we were when the book first appeared, as we marveled at the impact it made on the profession then—an impact that continues to have reverberations even today. Younger scholars joined the conversation, acknowledging that their comprehensive exam lists invariably include *White Over Black* as a "must read." Audience members and panelists alike commented on the book's merits and their memories of reading it in graduate seminars or undergraduate courses. The panel continued in an appropriately academic fashion, until a young woman stood up and asked to be heard. She was from the Caribbean island of Dominica, and had first encountered *White Over Black* as a young woman. The book, she said simply, changed her life. It was the first thing she had ever read that enabled her to understand herself, who she was, and what her relationship to the rest of the world was all about. The book, moreover, moved her to become a historian, so that she, too, could join a community that asked the right questions and, at least on occasion, arrived at the right answers. Most historians would give anything to know that just once their work has had a profound—and positive—effect on someone's life. Winthrop Jordan experiences that sense of satisfaction more often than most of us.

As this compilation of essays indicates, Win attracted and influenced a diverse and talented group of graduate students over a forty-year career, at the University of California at Berkeley and at the University of Mississippi. A glance at the table of contents tells the story. The topics of these essays range from the seventeenth to the twentieth century, from Puritan New England to the music of jive master Lester Young. They deal with sexuality, slavery, race, and religion, and their authors all owe a great deal to the gentle yet demanding oversight of Win Jordan. Very few historians at major universities would be comfortable directing dissertations on such a wide array of subjects. Many only accept students who are little more than pale imitations or clones of themselves. By contrast, Jordan's intellectual breadth, his curious mind, his rigorous approach to the discipline made it possible for him not only to attract talented students but to allow them to pursue their own interests, to listen attentively to the voices of the past, and to share the results of their work with the rest of us.

At the University of Mississippi, before his official retirement in June 2004, the process inevitably began with Jordan's legendary seminar—an introduction to the discipline, a requirement for every M.A. student in the Department of History, and an experience no student will easily forget. Curiously, it is a very difficult, almost impossible process to describe. The course was a mélange of historiography and history, with a bit of methodology and a small dose of theory thrown in for good measure. Every class was different. There were invariably a few books that Jordan had in mind for each new group, but after that the course could and did go in any direction, depending upon the interests of the students themselves. The course syllabus was sketchy and open-ended. Assignments varied from year to year. Students were often bewildered in the beginning, not knowing quite what to make of this class where the professor sat back, listened, asked a pointed question or two at appropriate places, and forced them to take charge of their own education.

If they craved direction, however, they got more than they asked for when Jordan returned their first papers. Few students were quite prepared for the meticulous lessons in grammar, word usage, and scholarly interpretation to which he subjected them. Fewer still were happy when they had to re-write their papers. But virtually no student left that seminar without a real appreciation of the English language or a healthy respect for the *Oxford English Dictionary*. And they all left knowing more than even they realized about the life of the mind and the profession they hoped to call their own.

If Winthrop Jordan's former students have one thing in common, it is this: they all go to the sources. Jordan does not have a great deal of patience for faddish theories or even for historiographical debates. Perhaps it is his Quaker faith that leads him to eschew arguments with other historians and instead to listen respectfully to the lessons his historical subjects can teach us. He teaches his students to have an open mind about just what those voices from the past are saying. No matter how relevant his own work is, Jordan never allows his own political or ethical agenda to interfere with his reading of the sources, and he urged his students to put their own preconceived notions aside as well. When their work led them in new directions and they arrived, often despite themselves, at unexpected conclusions, no one was more delighted than Jordan to discover that common wisdom is neither infallible nor particularly wise.

When Jordan wrote *White Over Black*, no university had begun even to contemplate creating a women's studies program. Gender studies had not yet appeared on the horizon. That makes the book's analysis of the connection between race and sexuality in America all the more remarkable. It is hardly surprising that many of his students have been drawn to work in the history of sexuality, largely due to Jordan's own brilliant example.

Ronald G. Walters, in "The Erotic South: Civilization and Sexuality in American Abolitionism," casts the abolitionist impulse after 1831 in gendered terms. Abolitionists such as Theodore Dwight Weld and William Lloyd Garrison, he says, were deeply suspicious of slavery in large measure because they feared the corrupting effect that absolute power had on any human being. For "abolitionists, the distance was not great from lust for power to mere lust." They believed that the South's slave society created an environment that gave free rein to man's sexual nature, thus creating a dangerously erotic and sensual environment where carnal restraint was known only by its absence. Many abolitionists found such an environment especially frightening because they knew how difficult their struggle to conquer their own sexuality continued to be. They were convinced, furthermore, that the "sin" of the South endangered the entire nation. Their vision of America's future depended, ultimately, upon the eradication of slavery everywhere.

Had Walters's abolitionists read Patricia Cline Cohen's "Ministerial Misdeeds: The Onderdonk Trial and Sexual Harassment in the 1840s," they would have found ample proof of the connection between power and sexuality. Cohen examines the case of the Right Reverend Benjamin T. Onderdonk, Episcopal Bishop of New York, who was tried by an ecclesiastical court for what, in today's world, would be called sexual harassment. No such concept, no such language existed in 1844 when the trial took place. Supporters and opponents of Onderdonk were puzzled by Onderdonk's behavior. While he did not engage in actual intercourse with any of the women he harassed, he accosted his victims in public places, often when their husbands were in the vicinity. Many people found it impossible to understand why these respectable women waited years before coming forward with their stories. Nor did they understand why no male protector had rushed to defend the women. Onderdonk's supporters assumed that the allegations against him were a smokescreen for a real religious agenda. Significantly, only when a Philadelphia almanac interpreted the Onderdonk controversy through the lens of a blackface parody, did the Bishop's behavior become comprehensible. In the "negative figuration of blackface, immature and inappropriate fondling could be seen now to be an end in itself." Black women, in the North as well as in the South, were obviously fair game for white men's fantasies.

If some Americans wanted to control what they saw as rampant sexuality in the antebellum era, yeomen farmers in Mississippi did not appear worried about such a plague until the end of the nineteenth century. Making excellent use of a wide variety of sources, including architectural plans, state laws, diaries, and letters, Susan Ditto contends that attitudes toward sexuality had profoundly changed in Mississippi by the turn of the twentieth century. "Stallions in the Churchyard: Sexuality and Privacy in Rural Mississippi" argues that the state's yeomen lived a pre-modern existence throughout most of the nineteenth century. Members of farm families were evidently not bothered by a lack of privacy in their homes. Patriarchs ruled. Farm wives were part of the "ovarian economy." Their value as biological producers of a large number of children, members of a rural workforce, remained unquestioned. No one imagined that young women were chaste or passionless. Adultery and seduction were crimes against male dominance, threatening the economic power fathers and husbands had over their own households. By the end of the century, however, old attitudes were beginning to change. Ditto's before-and-after picture of Mississippi's yeomen provides evidence of that change, even as it makes an effort to explain it. She also reminds historians that class as well as race mattered in the South, and that historians will ignore class realities only at their peril.

Not surprisingly, many of Jordan's students are drawn—if at times only tangentially—to the topic of slavery. Jordan's own *Tumult and Silence at Second Creek: An Inquiry into a Civil War Slave Conspiracy* examined—in meticulous and exhaustive detail—evidence for the existence of a slave conspiracy in Adams County, Mississippi, in 1861. The book gave Jordan his second Bancroft Prize. David J. Libby also studies the Natchez area, but he looks at the region as it existed a century before the county's slave conspiracy took place. Libby's "Relations Which Might Be Disastrous: Natchez Indians and African Slaves in French Louisiana" examines the ethnic and racial relations that characterized colonial Natchez long before England, and later the United States, assumed power there. French, Africans, Choctaw, and Natchez all existed together uneasily in the area. In his richly textured analysis, Libby examines the complexities of the region's racial and ethnic divisions, the effect those divisions had on the development of race-based slavery, and the impact that the presence of Africans had on the events leading to the demise of the French settlement in Natchez. Africans and Indians took advantage of an unstable and precarious order in French Louisiana, defending their own interests and—at least momentarily—exerting some control over their own lives.

The slaves in Daniel L. Fountain's "Christ in Chains: Slavery's Negative Impact on the Conversion of African-American Slaves" enjoyed much less autonomy. They were, however, at least able to say "no" to the version of Christianity that their white owners favored. Slavery, argues Fountain, did not create a hospitable environment for Christianity. Owners carefully monitored all slave activity, and made sure that the lessons their chattels learned in church did not threaten the peculiar institution. Thus, many slaves simply refused to attend Christian services, and those who did attend were highly critical of the message they heard from white ministers. As a result, contact with religious instruction was "the exception rather than the rule for most slaves."

If some of Jordan's students have been drawn to a study of American slavery, others are intrigued by issues of race and identity. Three of the essays in this volume reflect Jordan's interest in race as a phenomenon that is not merely *constructed* but that has a real and abiding impact on the lives of all humans.

Paul Spickard's "What's Critical About White Studies" reflects the author's ability to think cogently and critically about current approaches to the study of race. More than simply a balanced and nuanced analysis of "whiteness studies run amok," it argues, at least implicitly, that the racial paradigm that Win Jordan explicated with such care, wit, and grace in 1968 is still relevant today. Moreover, Spickard reminds those who would claim otherness for themselves that the experience of black Americans has been—and continues to be—fundamentally different from the experience of members of other ethnic groups.

In "Lester Young: Master of Jive" Douglas Henry Daniels examines the cultural meaning of Young's unique use of slang in the 1930s and '40s. Daniels argues that such language bound musicians together, giving them shorthand means of communicating with one another and excluding others from their conversations. Paradoxically, however, because the argot could be easily learned by non-musicians, jive invited "hip black folk and whites" to become part of the musicians' conversation and their community. Interestingly, Daniels's perspective owes its inception to Jordan's seminar in U.S. Colonial History at Berkeley. That seminar helped him appreciate the importance of language and the value of culture to any full understanding of the past.

Patrick B. Miller's fascinating study, "Holding Center Stage: Race Pride and the Extracurriculum at Historically Black Colleges and Universities," discusses the meaning of extracurricular activities to African American students at segregated black colleges and universities. Even when they imitated the activities of students at white colleges and universities, African American students were determined to shape those activities in ways that enabled them to preserve their own heritage. More socially aware than their white counterparts, many black students viewed even their most frivolous pastimes as training for individual uplift and as "temples for the cultivation of race pride and social change." Whether they formed Greek societies or engaged in sports or forensics, they always found themselves working both with and against the dominant culture.

Not all of Win Jordan's students have focused on slavery or race. Jordan received a doctorate at Brown University where he was trained as a colonial historian, an identity he has always cherished. He was a fellow at the Institute of Early American History and Culture before accepting a position at Berkeley, and has served on the Institute's advisory council and as a member of the *William and Mary Quarterly*'s editorial board. Thus it is altogether fitting that some of his students have done their work in early American history. Two of those students have focused on religion, another topic that Jordan finds personally and intellectually compelling.

Stephen P. Budney's essay, "Blessed are the Peacemakers: William Jay and the Drive for International Arbitration," is a case in point. It traces the intellectual roots of the antebellum peace movement and the call for "stipulated arbitration" of all international disputes. Budney recognizes the centrality of religion to the peace movement, while arguing that, at least in the case of William Jay, there were also other—more personal—forces at work. It was John Jay's controversial treaty with England, Budney argues, that provided the starting point for his son William's interest in world peace.

Like many reformers of his day, William Jay linked his support for world peace to other reforms, including—most importantly—the cause of anti-slavery. Both causes appealed to Jay's sense of Christian morality and his republican ideals. According to Budney, Jay and men like him advocated pacifism and abolitionism because they were "mandated by God," as well as because they "permitted men to focus upon business matters while they nurtured their morality."

"Max Weber in New England," by Charles L. Cohen, revisits the much-maligned "Weber Thesis" in a piece that should be required reading for all graduate students in early American History. It provides us not simply with a deftly drawn examination of Puritan historiography, but with a witty and trenchant analysis of the Weber thesis itself. Weber mostly got it wrong, says Cohen. He did not understand the implications of predestination. He confused socio-economic cause for effect. Yet, despite all that, Weber's insights are occasionally on target, and the thesis remains worth visiting, even today.

The scholar from the Caribbean whose life was changed when she read Win Jordan's *White Over Black* is not alone. Indeed, it is fair to say that Jordan's scholarship, his teaching skills, and his own rare personality have all acted to touch the lives of his students—and his colleagues—throughout the years. This volume stands as a testament to his work as scholar, teacher, and friend. It is a testament, as well, to the deep personal and professional esteem and affection in which all who know Winthrop Jordan hold him.

Part I

SEX

THE EROTIC SOUTH
Civilization and Sexuality in American Abolitionism

RONALD G. WALTERS

American antislavery sentiment took a very different turn after 1831. Whereas early abolitionism accepted a gradual end to slavery, after 1831 immediate emancipation became the goal and abolitionism became a passion driving men and women into lifelong reform careers. Yet slavery was not new in 1831—it had been present for nearly two centuries. And slavery did not suddenly become evil in 1831; by abolitionist logic it had been sinful all along. Still, a number of northern whites who had little direct contact with the institution joined blacks in becoming acutely aware of it, so much so that they felt compelled to seek its instant destruction. There is a mystery here, a need to account for the rise of a particular kind of anti-slavery sentiment at a particular moment in time. The problem, however, is not fully to be resolved by a search for direct "causes" of post-1830 abolitionism. There is the related, perhaps prior, task of charting antislavery's form, a need to determine why it seized upon certain issues while ignoring others, why its images were so compelling to whites who might well have ignored slavery, and why those who accepted abolitionism's call also drifted into a striking and novel variety of other reforms.

Historians attempting to assess the antislavery impulse have sometimes seized upon the doctrine of "disinterested benevolence," a product of 1820s revivalism and an encouragement to engage in good works as proof of salvation. Yet such benevolence was anything but emotionally disinterested, as at least one person possessed by it realized. Jane Swisshelm, herself a prominent abolitionist and feminist, cited the zealous commitment of William Lloyd Garrison, pioneer of post-1830 abolitionism. "It is necessary to his existence that he should work," she wrote, "—work for the slave; and in his work he gratifies all the strongest instincts of his nature, more

3

completely than even the grossest sensualist can gratify *his* by unlimited indulgence."[1] Jane Swisshelm revealed more than she imagined by setting up an antithesis between William Lloyd Garrison and the "sensualist." Antislavery was not simply a result of sexual fears or sexual repression (these, like slavery, existed well before 1831); but antislavery after 1831 gained direction and force from changing, culturally-determined attitudes about sex, attitudes that merged with other assumptions to make conditions in the South appear uncomfortably applicable to the North, attitudes that both shaped perception of the problem and guided reformers to a new set of answers in the half-century after 1830, ultimately helping bridge the distance between immediate emancipation and a postwar world in which fit and unfit were presumed to struggle for survival.

Charles K. Whipple described slavery as "absolute, irresponsible power on one side, and entire subjection on the other." Like virtually all abolitionists he grounded his objections to the institution on this relationship of utter submission and total dominance between bondsman and master. There were, of course, other kinds of emphasis possible. Earlier humanitarian reform stressed slavery's suffering and cruelty but, no matter how useful examples of these might be in stirring sentiment, most post-1830 abolitionists finally denied that ill-treatment was what made bondage so terrible. Theodore Dwight Weld, after combing southern newspapers and exhausting eyewitnesses for horror stories about slavery, asserted that atrocities were not the institution's most basic feature. The "combined experience of the human race," he thought, proved that such "cruelty is the spontaneous and uniform product of arbitrary power. . . ." Abuse was only an effect of submission and dominance. Even those who began by looking at slavery in still another way, in terms of "the chattel principle," came around (like Weld) to a definition that was neither economic, nor institutional, nor based on specific treatment. "Slavery is the act of one holding another as property," a correspondent to the *Philanthropist* declared, adding "or one man being wholly subject to the will of others." In his mind slavery (as a property relationship) resolved itself into a matter of power just as surely as it did for Whipple or Weld.[2]

Slaveholders were not reluctant heirs to their authority, according to abolitionists. So driving was the urge to dominate that it outdistanced all other possible motives, including greed. Garrison thought "the master-passion in the bosom of the slaveholder is not the love of gain, but the possession of absolute power, unlimited sovereignty." Abolitionists maintained that slaveholders were not peculiar in their failings but rather that they demonstrated what all people should beware of in themselves. C. K. Whipple and Theodore Dwight Weld, after detailing in their different ways slavery's devastating effects, each reminded readers that the danger was not confined to white southerners. "No human being, is fit to be trusted with absolute, irresponsible power," claimed Whipple. "If the best portion of our community were selected to hold and use such authority [as masters possess], they would very soon be corrupted." "Arbitrary power is to the mind what alcohol is to the body; it intoxicates," Weld believed. "It is perhaps the strongest human passion, and the more absolute the power. The stronger the desire for it. And the more it is desired, the more its exercise is enjoyed. . . . The fact that a person intensely desires power over others, *without restraint*, shows the absolute necessity of restraint."[3] Humankind might have an innate moral sense and might at times be molded by race or environment, but abolitionists were at bottom certain that man also had a deeply implanted drive to tyrannize over others, a drive that required constant vigilance and suppression.

If the slaveholder was not unique in lusting after power, then neither was slavery the only example of coercion and "arbitrary power" disturbing to abolitionists. Few were as extreme as Abby Kelley Foster, who took her nonresistant principles to the point where, an amazed visitor reported, she was "very conscientious not to use the least worldly authority over her child."[4] Other abolitionists, even those less dogmatic (or foolhardy) than Mrs. Foster, were outraged by the tyranny of preacher, politician, corrupt public opinion and institutions.[5] Slavery might be a special case because of its magnitude and because it followed racial lines, but the principle could appear elsewhere. Antislavery politicians attempted to persuade white northerners that the Slave Power endangered their own liberties, not merely the slave's. Abolitionists likewise warned that arbitrary authority did not stop with master and chattel. "Who is safe?" asked Henry B. Stanton in 1836. "Can you confine the operations of this principle to the black man?"[6] Suppression of white civil liberties and stories of whites sold into slavery were reminders that you, in fact, could not do so.

Slavery, then, stood as the distillation of the malevolence lurking in the breast of humankind. The institution, Lydia Maria Child decided, "concentrated the strongest evils of human nature—vanity, pride, love of power, licentiousness, and indolence"—all stemming from man's unrestrained will to dominate. Yet Americans of an earlier generation had also been suspicious of man's ability to wield authority. Such hostility appeared at the time of the American Revolution and it had even then been applied to slavery. John Woolman, almost a lifetime before Garrison's career began, argued against the institution because "so long as men are biased by narrow self-love, so long an absolute power over other men is unfit for them." John Adams, in 1765, could write of "the love of power, which had been so often the cause of slavery."[7] But, deep as fear of power had been among the Revolutionary generation, it took on new life after 1830. In addition to bearing an invigorated affinity to a romantic age's individualism, it regained vitality among antebellum whites who seemed to be losing control over their own destinies, as middle-class moralists well might be in an industrializing nation where the political system was passing into the hands of uncouth men. A disturbing concept of "power" was also, by the 1830s, coming to fit into a new web of associations that ensnared some of the deepest and most mysterious forces abolitionists believed to be in all men. These included the deepest, most mysterious, most fearful force of all: human sexuality. For abolitionists the distance was not great from lust for power to mere lust.

Abolitionists did not dwell "excessively" on sexual misconduct in the South; their writings have little merit as pornography. For centuries, moreover, whites imagined (and cultivated) erotic potential in interracial contact. This imagining, nevertheless, could be organized into more than one pattern of perception, and antislavery propaganda is distinctive for directly reversing a prevalent assumption by presenting white men, not black men, as sexual aggressors. Early in his career Garrison set the tone. He was accosted by a slaveholder who posed American racism's classic question: "How should you like to have a black man marry your daughter?" Garrison replied that "slaveholders generally should be the last persons to affect fastidiousness on that point, for they seem to be enamoured with amalgamation."[8] The retort was unanswerable and persisted down to the Civil War. It was, in part, simply fine strategy, pointing both to obvious hypocrisy and a very real consequence of slavery.

Abolitionists did not stop with this simple and expedient formula. They did not argue that white males were always the sexual aggressors. Gerrit Smith believed planters would not fight an insurrection effectively because they would be too "busy in transporting their wives and daughters to places where they would be safe from that worst fate which husbands and fathers can imagine for their wives and daughters." George Bourne pondered "What may be the awful consequences, if ever the colored men by physical force should attain the mastery?" He decided "If no other argument could be adduced in favor of immediate and universal emancipation, that single fact is sufficient. Delay only increases the danger of the white women and augments the spirit of determined malignity and revenge in the colored men." Abolition would lead to forgiveness and to sexual security for white women as well as female slaves.⁹

Rape, however, was only one form of sexual retribution abolitionists foresaw bondsmen exacting upon the master class. Louisa Barker believed black women lured young slaveholders into illicit attachments as a way of lessening chances that the favored slave might be sold and to destroy the master's constitution through physical overindulgence. Still another writer argued that "women who have been drawn into licentiousness by wicked men, if they retain their vicious habits, almost invariably display their revenge for their own debasement, by ensnaring others into the same corruption and moral ruin." This placed on female slaves much responsibility for stirring the sensuality of their masters, for degrading the slaveholder as they had been degraded. But there were even more horrifying prospects: lasciviousness, in the abolitionist imagination, did not stop with white men and black women enticing each other. "Were it necessary," John Rankin stated primly, "I could refer you to several instances of slaves actually seducing the daughters of their masters! Such seductions sometimes happen even in the most respectable slaveholding families." It was impossible for white girls always to "escape this impetuous fountain of pollution."¹⁰

Comments like these, besides titillating the imaginations of genteelly horrified readers, touched the South at a sensitive point—its image of itself and of its women. They also moved the argument from the idea that whites were sexual aggressors to the more comfortable position (for whites) that blacks represented sensuality after all. Yet the key to understanding antislavery rehetoric is not in any particular aspect of the relationship between race, slavery, and sexuality, although emotional associations concerning interracial sex undoubtedly played their part. It is in a generalized sense that the South was a society in which the sexual nature of man (and here the gendered pronoun is especially appropriate) had no checks put upon it.

"Illicit intercourse" was embedded in the very conditions of southern life, abolitionists believed. For the master "the temptation is always at hand the legal authority absolute—the actual power complete—the vice a profitable one" if it produced slaves for market ". . . . —and the custom so universal as to bring no disgrace. . . ." In addition, the planter, who had others to work for him, could be indolent and this had a "very debasing" effect on "less intellectual minds." Consequently such men "are driven by it to seek occupation in the lowest pleasures." John Rankin felt that "we may always expect to find the most confirmed habits of vice where idleness prevails." Making matters worse, there was scandalous nudity among slaves. One author, using the apt pseudonym, "Puritan," was appalled that "not only in taverns, but in boarding houses, and, the dwellings of individuals, boys and girls verging on maturity altogether unclothed, wait upon ladies and gentlemen, without exciting even the suffusion of a blush on the face of young females, who thus gradually become habituated to scenes of which delicate and refined northern women cannot adequately conceive. As if that were not enough, abolitionists believed that free and easy association between slave children and white children on the plantation spread the depravity of the back cabins to the big house once again. "Between the female slaves and the misses there is an unrestrained communication," southern-born James A. Thome explained to the American Anti-Slavery Society. "As they come in contact through the day, the courtesan feats of the over night are whispered into the ear of the unsuspecting [white] girl and poison her youthful mind."[11]

In its libidinousness the South resembled other examples of utter depravity and dissolution. Thome informed an audience of young ladies that "THE SOUTHERN STATES ARE ONE GREAT SODOM" and his account was seconded by another abolitionist who had lived in Virginia and Maryland. "The sixteen slave States constitute one vast brothel," the *Liberator* declared in 1858. Twenty years earlier the *Pennsylvania Freeman* spoke of the "great moral lazarhouse of Southern slavery. . . ." Thomas Wentworth Higginson decided that, compared to the South, "a Turkish harem is a cradle of virgin purity." Henry C. Wright preferred comparison with New York's notorious Five Points district, much to its advantage, of course.[12] Like Sodom, brothels, or a harem, the South appeared to be a place in which men could indulge their erotic impulses with impunity.

Yet, according to abolitionist logic, there must be retribution. It could be physiological since—by nineteenth-century assumptions—sexual excesses ultimately destroyed body and mind. Planters, according to Mrs. Louisa Barker, exemplified the "wreck of early manhood always resulting from self-indulgence." They were "born with feeble minds and bodies, with just force enough to transmit the family name, and produce in feebler characters a second edition of the father's life." Mrs. Barker's comments were consistent with the way other abolitionists viewed the South and with the way her contemporary middle-class Americans viewed sex, but they were almost unique in antislavery literature, although the character of the languid but erratic planter was not.[13] The more usual form of retribution predicted for southern licentiousness was social.

There was a sense among some abolitionists in the 1830s, as immediate emancipation sentiment among them began to take hold, that (in the words of James G. Birney) "from causes now operating, the *South* must be filled in a few years, with blacks and, it may be, that in our lives it will be given up to them." Birney, in a letter marking his public renunciation of colonization as a solution to slavery, detailed the "alarming rapidity" with which the process was operating in his native Kentucky. "In the midst of their oppressions, and in spite of them, the colored population of the South is rapidly increasing," wrote A. A. Phelps in 1834. "Like the Israelites in Egypt, the more they are afflicted, the more they multiply and grow. . . ." Maintain slavery, John Rankin warned, and you will "increase their [slaves'] numbers, and enable them to overpower the nation. Their enormous increase beyond that of the white population is truly alarming." Liberation, however, would disperse blacks and make their population growth "proportionate to the rest of the nation." LaRoy Sunderland quantified the increase, using censuses through 1830, and was not convinced that it all came from promiscuity among slaves. "That the blacks should increase faster than the whites, is easily accounted for," he remarked dryly, "from the fact, that the former class are increased by the latter, but the blacks cannot increase the whites."[14] Such statements seem to have decreased in time and with additional censuses (although complaints about licentiousness persisted), but they and fears of imminent insurrections glare luridly from early abolitionist propaganda, twin expressions of a belief that the South faced an overwhelming chastising event, that white dominance might in turn become submission.

There were, of course, wonderful propaganda advantages here. The issue of miscegenation forever dogged the antislavery movement and by stressing southern licentiousness abolitionists could turn on their accusers.

They could speak of the slave system's "dreadful amalgamating abominations" and argue that such would "experience, in all probability, a ten fold diminution" with emancipation. They could go as far as Elijah Lovejoy and claim "one reason why abolitionists urge the abolition of slavery is, that they fully believe it will put a stop, in a great and almost entire measure, to that wretched, and shameful, and polluted intercourse between the whites and the blacks, now so common, it may be said so universal, in the slave states."[15] Yet propaganda advantages—if they were the only consideration—would have been greater had abolitionists not also insisted, as they did at times, that "the right to choose a partner for life is so exclusive and sacred, that it is never interfered with, except by the worst of tyrants. Garrison, with his usual tactless boldness, even asserted perfect racial equality and concluded that "inter-marriage is neither unnatural nor repugnant to nature, but obviously proper and salutary; it being designed to unite people of different tribes and nations, and to break down those petty distinctions which are the effect of climate or locality or situation. . . ."[16] Such frontal assaults on antimiscegenation sentiment, if nothing else, show that sexual attitudes were not something merely to be played upon as instruments to achieve social power.

Instead, what abolitionists wrote about southern sexuality must be put in relation to nineteenth-century assumptions and to conditions in the North that gave urgency to concern for licentiousness, as well as in relation to other reform interests of those involved in the antislavery crusade.

It was possible for abolitionists to perceive the South as a society given over to lust not simply because miscegenation occurred under slavery. After all, erotic activity between master class and bondsmen did not originate in 1831 (nor did disgust with southern morals—New England Federalists a generation before had that in abundance). And miscegenation may well have been decreasing at the very time it became a staple of antislavery propaganda.[17] Nevertheless, antebellum northern sensibility about the subject was sharpened by presuming an interchangeability between power and sexuality, by believing that man's nature, if unchained, exhibited fearsome and diverse urges to dominate and possess. Sexuality therefore seemed to exist in the master-slave relationship itself (or, rather, in man himself) not just in the South, which was only an archetype. One abolitionist noted that "Clerical Slave-Holding in Connecticut" some years before had resulted in a "constant illicit intercourse" between ministers and their female slaves. In other words, it could happen anywhere—even with clergymen and even in Connecticut.[18]

Portions of the abolitionists' view had historical validation: some human beings have always turned tyranny into erotic pleasure (and vice versa). But belief that social submission and dominance inevitably lead to sexual license had wide currency in nineteenth-century America. Victorian pornography, for instance, exploited situations of power and powerlessness more than the contemporary variety does and probably more than ancient bawdy literature generally did. In one nineteenth-century classic the action took place in a harem where "The Lustful Turk," a darkly sensual being, literally reduced women (even good English women) to sexual slaves. His power was both political and erotic, and his desires were as unchecked as they were varied. This was strikingly similar to antislavery images of the South and the slaveholder, a similarity increased when one of the lustful Turk's victims made a speech attacking slavery as "the most powerful agent in the degradation of mankind," a charming bit of abolitionism amidst depravity. In more respectable Victorian circles it was thought that servants, another class of underling, were both sexually corrupted and agents of corruption, a matter that later attracted the attention of Sigmund Freud.[19]

A similar sense that subordination engendered debauchery shaped contemporary anti-Catholic diatribes. George Bourne, an early and important abolitionist, doubled as a Catholic-baiter and found his careers easily reconciled. He pictured the South as an erotic society where whites "have been indulged in all the vicious gratifications which lawless power and unrestrained lust, can amalgamate. . . ." Much the same, he believed, prevailed in another closed society, the convent. There, in Bourne's imagination, the priest's absolute power and unchecked erotic energy replaced the planter's and the seduction and seductiveness of nuns replaced female slaves.[20]

Enough southern sensuality existed to fuel the minds of people like Bourne; but in antislavery propaganda southern sensuality, as much as anything, illustrated a general and not very lovely principle abolitionists held to be true about humans and what possession of power did to them. "We know what human nature is: what are its weaknesses, what its passions," the *Philanthropist* asserted confidently, as it remarked upon the plantation's potential for depravity.[21] Plantations—a moralist's equivalent for the settings of pornographic novels—were simply places where the repressed could come out of hiding. Abolitionists saw both what was actually there—sexual encounters occurred—and what associations of power with sex prepared them to see.

The abolitionist critique's intensity was not just a matter of these associations, nor was it a simple matter of recognizing that sexuality could flourish under slavery. After all, neither power nor sexual opportunity is innately fearsome: some people relish both. The existence of licentiousness and arbitrary will, however, helped abolitionists define the South, slaveholders, and slavery in such a way that they became symbols of negation, opposites against which to measure what was good and progressive. That measurement necessarily reflected a number of firmly held judgments about what human beings and society should be.

In 1839, unconsciously forecasting the insight of a later and more famous Victorian moralist, Theodore Dwight Weld wrote that "Restraints are the web of civilized society, warp and woof." James G. Birney, musing to his diary in 1850, decided: "The reason that savage & barbarous nations remain so—& unrighteous men, too—is that they manage their affairs by passion—not by reason. Just in proportion as reason prevails, it will control & restrain passion, & just in proportion as it prevails, & passion diminishes nations emerge from ignorance & darkness & become civilized." Here was a feeling that civilization, if not its discontents, depended on curbing what another abolitionist called "the fatal anarchy of the lowest passions."[22]

These passions were not exclusively sexual. Birney would not have argued that "savage & barbarous nations" governed themselves by erotic means. But sex was clearly among the most formidable components of the "animal nature" that was to be subdued before humans could be counted as civilized. Theodore Parker decided when a man "is cultivated and refined, the sentiment [of love] is more than the appetite [of sex]: the animal appetite remains but it does not bear so large a ratio to the whole consciousness of the man as before. . . ." The proper gentleman, like the proper lady, triumphed over sensuality. Sarah Grimké, emerging from a different tradition of gentility from Parker's, agreed with his estimate. It was impossible for men and women to enjoy the relationship God intended until "our intercourse is purified by the forgetfulness of sex. . . ." This resonated, almost as a linguistic pun, with an older, basically biblical, tradition holding (as restated by Beriah Green) that "All visible slavery is merely a picture of the invisible sway of the passions."[23] In the minds of Christians, slavery had always borne with it imputations of sin and human willfulness, but it took the nineteenth century, and a millennialistic nation, to transfer these ancient associations from slave to master and to impose upon them a drive for "civilization" and for (what was virtually the same thing) control, particularly control of the inner and lusty man.

Slavery was a guidepost, marking the outer limits of disorder and debauchery; but abolitionist perceptions of human failings neither began nor ended with the South's peculiar institution—reformers defined their own moral responsibilities in much the same terms they applied to slaveholders and other sinners. "And how is slavery to be abolished by those who are slaves themselves to their own appetites and passions?" Beriah Green asked. The *Emancipator* noted "the common acceptance of things" in which "men deem themselves the most happy when they can the most easily set aside known prohibitions and indulge in certain propensities." It contrasted this with the "early propagators of the religion of the cross" who had "no animal passions to gratify" as they went to martyrdom. The lesson was unmistakable: those who would do good must first conquer themselves.[24]

The courtship of Theodore Dwight Weld and Angelina Grimké, a veritable orgy of restraint, revealed that reformers were willing to practice what they preached. Weld regarded his emotions for Miss Grimké as a challenge to be overcome. "It will be a relief to you," he triumphantly assured Angelina in March 1838, "to know that I have acquired perfect self-control, so far as any expression or *appearance* of deep feeling is visible to others." She earlier chided him for carrying things too far. "Why this waste of moral strength?" she asked. But she likewise thought of civilization as a repression of mankind's deeper and more mysterious forces. She responded ecstatically upon finding how elevated Weld's views of courtship were, how similar to her own, and how unsensual. ". . . I have been tempted to think marriage was sinful, because of what appeared to me almost invariably to prompt and lead to it," she wrote. "Instead of the higher, nobler sentiments being first aroused, and leading on the lower passions *captive* to their will, the latter seemed to be lords over the former. Well I am convinced that men in general, the vast majority, believe most seriously that women were made to gratify their animal appetites, *expressly* to minister to their pleasure. . . ." The couple's control extended beyond courtship. A few years after their marriage, James G. Birney visited them, remarking to his diary, with a touch of envy, "Their self-denial—their firmness in principles puts me to shame."[25] The Welds, their passions correctly ordered, settled into a long and gently loving life together.

Abolitionists not only controlled their own passional natures, and sought to control the South's, but they also detected more general threats that they again frequently put in terms of rampant sexuality. "There is not a nation nor a tribe of men on earth so steeped in sexual pollution as this," Henry C. Wright thought. Thomas Wentworth Higginson saw the mass of men "deep in sensual vileness" while William Lloyd Garrison attacked a colonizationist not simply for his views on slavery but also for refusing to believe that "licentiousness pervades the whole land." William Goodell credited the South with an especial licentiousness, but the baneful influence did not stop there. Instead it "pollutes the atmosphere of our splendid cities, and infects the whole land with the leprosy of Sodom." Less metaphorical, Stephen Pearl Andrews flatly stated that "Prostitution, in Marriage and out of it, and solitary vice, characterize Society as it is."[26] The South might lead in debauchery but the sin itself jeopardized the North as well.

Once problems were defined in such a way—as loss of moral control and consequent growth of licentiousness—then perception and real conditions fit neatly together, with dire implications for the nation. Southern sensuality, and southern "barbarism," confirmed abolitionists in their fears about what unbridled human nature could produce anywhere. Even the South's economic state provided proof, because most abolitionists saw northern industrial growth as a sign of advancing civilization. It might require moral guidance, but it was a sign of progress that was not appearing below the Mason-Dixon line—time and again antislavery propaganda pictured the South as an economically backward region, building neither factories nor railroads, seldom even paying its debts. Progress could not long continue in a region where men could not control themselves. Only with destruction of the master's arbitrary power and restoration of moral restraint on all southerners could the South develop spiritually and economically; only with strengthened restraint could the North continue to develop. Here abolitionism drew directly upon change in northern society, taking it to be both a cause for anxiety and a means of weighing the South's lack of progress, its failure to share the benefits of nineteenth-century civilization.

There were, however, less direct consequences of industrialization, and these would likewise reinforce abolitionist images of southern depravity and imply specific cures for general social evils. At first glance some of these consequences seem far removed from slavery since they touched society's most pervasive institution—the family. Although the relation between antebellum family change and economic change is still something of a puzzle, family patterns in America clearly altered from 1800 onward. The birth rate dropped steadily but appreciably throughout the nineteenth century, particularly in the northeast where both industrialization and reform impulses were strongest. And the household appears to have been declining in economic functions: fewer goods were made in it as a wider variety of products were factory-produced and store-bought; men increasingly commuted to work; and middle-class women seemed to be losing their most apparent economic roles—no longer contributing in obvious ways to the family enterprise, purchasing products rather than making them, and using immigrant servants to tend fewer numbers of children than those their mothers bore.[27]

What the family lost in economic value it gained in moral prestige, standing in the antebellum period as the center for instruction in virtue. Gamaliel Bailey, echoing his contemporaries, declared the family to be "the great primal institution, established by the Creator himself, as the first and best school for training men for all social relations and duties."[28] There were good reasons why abolitionists like Bailey and others eager for moral guidance in a time of flux would look to the family. No other social institution seemed as reliable. American Protestantism divided into rival denominations, the fragments co-operating briefly during revivals, then going their separate, bickering paths. No single clergyman served the community; no one church dominated the landscape. Jacksonian America's political system was even more bewildering because, so moralists thought, it played to the basest instincts of the voter, rewarding demagoguery rather than respectability and virtue. Changing though the family was, there was no other safe haven for morality in a decentralized society in times of great change.

And so, in yet another way, southern sexuality focused what was a matter of immediate concern among abolitionists: the nature of relationships within the home. Because the slaveholder lacked restraint on his erotic energy, antislavery propaganda assumed he "totally annihilates the marriage institution."[29] Not only did the master fail to sanction or respect marriage among slaves, but also his uninhibited lustfulness meant he did not honor his own marriage vows, destroying family relations among whites as well as blacks. Everything in the abolitionist imagination converged to see the South lacking a stable family life, robbing it of the basic mechanism of social control, confirming it as the antithesis of order and civilization. There is no evidence that southern family instability was increasing in the 1830s, nor did abolitionists claim it was. The difference was that by 1830 the family itself was a matter of both anxiety and hope. Anxiety found confirmation in the southern way of life, with its disdain for the one certain moral guardian, the family.

Antebellum sexual attitudes, merging with objective conditions and with ideas about power and civilization, guided abolitionists as they looked southward. But in many of their beliefs abolitionists were hardly unique. Antislavery moved to much larger rhythms of public concern. If abolitionists worried about licentiousness and the decline of order, so did those who opposed them in anti-antislavery mobs, fearful that emancipation would upset conventional social relations and promote miscegenation. If abolitionists threw much of their faith for moral training upon the family then, it has to be said, so did defenders of slavery, who portrayed their supposedly patriarchal institution as an alternative to decay of personal ties in the North.[30] It would be a mistake, nevertheless, to dismiss patterns of thought as unimportant because they appeared among otherwise very different people, used for different purposes. Concern for human sexuality, and equation of civilization with its suppression, was too general to be a direct cause for the rise of antislavery. Rather than make abolitionism inevitable, it fostered a certain kind of abolitionism; it ensured that some northerners enmeshed in change would be able to see certain things in the South that earlier generations either had not seen or had taken far more lightly. There was, moreover, another kind of importance to assumptions abolitionists applied to southern behavior, particularly to southern sexuality: these were threads radiating outward, forming a web of reform commitment much larger than antislavery alone, extending beyond the death of slavery itself.

Abolitionists seem crankish, or quaint, for the various fads and reforms they drifted into. Yet many of these auxiliary causes fit the same mold as antislavery, indicating that abolitionists were driven as much by a generalized desire to control the "animal nature" standing between man and civilization as they were by a specific quarrel with the South, which was only the worst of offenders, the logical extension of human depravity. Time after time abolitionists turned their guns toward the same lack of restraint in the North, or in individuals, as they imagined in the South. In numerous and occasionally subtle ways they betrayed how much of their vehemence stemmed from a pervasive fear that man (and in this they primarily did mean "man") was giving in too easily to his passionate self. The most frequent attacks of this sort probably were reserved for tyranny of the bottle over human self-control. But despite near universality of temperance sentiment among abolitionists, they also found spectacular examples of sin in northern sexual immorality, a more literal surrender of man's "higher" qualities (his civilization) to the body's claims than alcoholism.

Abolitionists devoted themselves to sweeping back "the wild sea of prostitution, which swells and breaks and dashes against the bulwarks of society." Almost coincident with the rise of antislavery was a Moral Reform movement designed to curb prostitution and to promote purity. It had appeal at antislavery centers such as Oberlin and Western Reserve, and many abolitionists became involved in the efforts of one of Moral Reform's chief promoters, the Reverend John McDowall. McDowall's spicy account of sexual depravity in New York City brought tremendous criticism on his sponsor, the local Magdalen Society, and particularly on Arthur Tappan, a prominent member as well as a future president of the American Anti-Slavery Society. A successor to the Magdalen Society, called the American Society for Promoting the Observance of the Seventh Commandment, drew upon abolitionists for its officers. Beriah Green was president; three abolitionists, including Weld, were vice-presidents. Others, Joshua Leavitt and William Goodell among them, were on the executive committee. Lucretia Mott's support of an organization to redeem fallen women was dampened only by her discovery that it did not offer its services to blacks.[31]

Some abolitionists were convinced that things were drastically wrong even with the institution designed to contain erotic impulses. "The right idea of marriage is at the foundation of all reforms," Elizabeth Cady Stanton decided in 1853. Amidst her suggestions for change was the complaint that "Man in his lust has regulated long enough this whole question of sexual intercourse."[32] Henry C. Wright produced a work on *Marriage and*

Parentage that attacked "THE UNNATURAL AND MONSTROUS EXPENDITURE OF THE SEXUAL ELEMENT, FOR MERE SENSUAL GRATIFICATION" within marriage. He presented as ideal two husbands able to "control all their passional expressions." Stephen Pearl Andrews preached an individualism that bordered on Free Love—except he argued that a liberalization of marriage and divorce practices would actually "moderate the passions instead of inflaming them, and so . . . contribute, in the highest degree, to a general Purity of life. . . ."[33]

So sinister seemed man's erotic nature that it would not be satisfied with the brothel and marriage bed. Abolitionists grasped odd times to warn against the "secret vice" of auto-eroticism. Lewis Tappan interrupted a biography of his brother to urge readers to warn their children that "youthful lusts" could lead to "idiocy, insanity, disfigurement of body, and imbecility of mind." Garrison used the *Liberator* to review a book entitled *Debilitated Young Men*, taking occasion to rail against "the dreadful vice of Masturbation." The vice apparently was prevalent enough, and dreadful enough, to call forth veiled words of warning from Harriet Beecher Stowe and her sister in a book for homemakers they coauthored.[34]

All of this put a terrible burden on the erotic offender. The prostitute spread disease and misery; the lustful husband blighted his wife and transmitted sins to his unborn child; and the masturbator faced self-destruction. One did not even have to be consciously lustful to be harmed by his sexuality. Theodore Dwight Weld badgered his son, suffering both from a mysterious lethargy and an apparently unstimulated loss of semen, by warning "All authorities agree that this drain upon the seminal fluid will lead ultimately to "*insanity* or *idiocy*."[35]

Such beliefs may have bordered on conventional wisdom; certainly abolitionists were not the only people to think that sexual excess caused insanity and other frightening ills. But abolitionists fit such attitudes into a pattern of social concern, characterized by anxiety over eroticism, North and South. A major part of the pattern resulted from an antebellum turn to find the key to reform within human beings—not just within mankind (for others had done that too), but in humankind's physical nature. A feeling in Jacksonian reform that man's animal self had to be conquered in favor of the immaterial being came around, in circular fashion, to the body once more. Control and liberation were to be found in the same place. Victory lay in the enemy's camp after all—within ourselves.

Some ways of reaching that camp were more promising than others. Controlling mankind's sensual nature implied certain strategies, if one accepted the terms of antebellum culture. For one thing, the path was cleared for women to participate more openly in reform causes than they had previously. As the middle-class woman withdrew from direct and obvious economic support of the family it became common to invest her with other virtues; she was, it seemed, also removed from worldly crassness, more spiritual by nature and by position than man, less sensual. Sarah Grimké, late in life, made explicit what had more commonly been implicit in the antislavery crusade from the beginning. "Woman is innately man's superior," Grimké thought, a belief related to her assumption that "the sexual passion in man is ten times stronger than in woman." Under the right order of things, William Goodell believed, woman serves man as "the chastiser of his desires." Sarah Grimké's sister, Angelina, knew where this argument led, writing of women that "it is through their instrumentality that the great and glorious work of reforming the world is to be done." Of course, it can be a dubious blessing to be presumed morally superior—it places shame on sexual impulses and guilt on failure to produce social change. Sarah Grimké, for instance, felt that female asexuality made women more culpable in sexual transgressions than men, and other abolitionists concluded from woman's moral power that "American mothers are responsible for American slavery." Yet there was a powerful justification for female activity here, and the point that women had a special role in the drama of redemption was conceded by male abolitionists, even relatively conservative ones who never brought themselves to support the Woman's Rights Movement that grew out of antislavery.[36]

A drive to control man's animal nature had other implications for antebellum reform besides providing middle-class women a rationale for social action and helping them articulate their own very real grievances. Virtually simultaneous with the rise of antislavery were still more attempts to subdue licentiousness—less obvious than the Moral Reform movement and less rooted in genuine social evils than antislavery and Woman's Rights. Chief among these peripheral causes was health reform, exemplified by Sylvester Graham, whose memory lives in the Graham cracker. Graham, and others like him, sought to purify the body and heal it of infirmities through proper diet. Graham's regimen, which seemed laughable or repulsive to many Americans at the time, found adherents among abolitionists, and not just among Garrisonians (who had a susceptibility to fads). Non-Garrisonians like Henry B. Stanton and Lewis Tappan also found the Graham system persuasive and Oberlin greeted Graham and a fellow dietary reformer, William A. Alcott, with initial enthusiasm. In its heyday the Graham system had as loyal followers such staunch immediate emancipationists as the Welds, Sarah Grimké and William Goodell. LaRoy Sunderland claimed he owed his life to Graham's diet. Amasa Walker merely achieved regularity from it.[37]

There was also a considerable interest among abolitionists in exercise and gymnastics, programs that, like proper diet, helped in bringing the body under control and in preventing it from interfering with man's spiritual nature. Theodore Dwight Weld had been a missionary for the manual labor school idea before he turned to antislavery. This was a plan to mix education and work, both for financial reasons and to put body and spirit into right relation. After his career as an abolitionist had virtually ended, Weld taught in Dio Lewis's gymnastic institute—where William Lloyd Garrison sent at least some of his children and where the Welds themselves sent the son who exhibited signs of excessive loss of seminal fluid. Charles Follen, an early and beloved abolitionist, had been among the first to bring German physical culture ideas to the United States. Although Follen died tragically before Thomas Wentworth Higginson entered the movement, Higginson proved to be his spiritual heir, managing (in New England culture) to glide from antebellum reform to the late nineteenth century's "vigorous life." So persuasive was Higginson's campaigning for exercise that his efforts, according to one abolitionist, produced an outburst of ice-skating in Worcester, Massachusetts, that earned the title "Higginson's Revival."[38]

Such activities seem innocent and innocuous enough, and, like dietary reform, they aimed at an improvement in the quality of life. All that they were. But connected with dietary reform and advocacy of exercise was the familiar drive to subdue man's physical, particularly his sexual, being. Health reformers like Graham and William A. Alcott wrote extensively on the terrible effects of sexual excess and presented proper diet as a means of suppressing erotic impulses. Propagandists for physical culture such as Dio Lewis and Russell Trall likewise counseled sexual control and likewise saw their programs as a way of achieving it. "A vigorous life of the senses not only does not tend to sensuality in the objectionable sense," Higginson claimed in an essay on gymnastics, "but it helps to avert it."[39] Dietary reform and the cult of exercise, like antislavery, focused upon humankind's erotic nature in order to overcome it.

This was where it led, the concern for excessive sexuality that found some of its more lurid justification in southern licentiousness and lack of civilization: the other side of fear of man's physical being was a belief that properly understanding it could lead to salvation. The other side of barbarism was true civilization. Certainly Grahamites and gymnastics enthusiasts aimed at a kind of redemption, a freedom from the body's infirmities and corrupt desires. Given the right social engineering, it might even be possible to turn those same desires to the task of regeneration—regeneration of the race, if not the individual. Garrison's tutor in perfectionism, John Humphrey Noyes, produced the clearest example of this in his Oneida Community, where a form of contraception was practiced, as well as plural marriage, in hope that "scientific combination" might be "applied to human generation." The result, Noyes believed, would be increasingly perfect children.[40]

Few, if any, in the antislavery movement were willing to take their ideas to Oneida's extreme. Yet abolitionists of various sorts did accept Noyes' assumption that regulation of sexuality might go beyond mere suppression of licentiousness and become an active force for human betterment. Henry C. Wright, as usual, wandered as far along the way as any abolitionist Wright believed that all kinds of antenatal influences shaped human development; that diseases, alcoholism, and parents' attitudes at the time of conception were passed on to children. Wright, however, realized possibilities, as well as dangers. If ungoverned sexuality had power to destroy, then, properly regulated, sexuality also had power to produce better men and women. People simply had to use sex wisely, for progress rather than gratification. Wright, ever a visionary, believed, "To the LAW OF REPRODUCTION will human beings, in the future of this world, look as the one great means to expel disease from the body and soul."[41] Like Wright, Elizabeth Cady Stanton believed such traits as drunkenness descended to children, and she was impressed by an essay entitled "Cerebral Dynamics" because it "shows so clearly that children are the victims of the vices and excesses of their ancestors." Stephen Pearl Andrews envisioned a time when marriage relations might be changed so that a woman could "accept only the noblest and most highly endowed of the opposite sex to be the recipients of her choicest favors, and the sires of her off-spring, rejecting the males of a lower degree." He suggested "by this means, Nature has provided for an infinitely higher development of the race."[42]

This was eugenics and hereditarian thought only in embryonic form. There was, in the antebellum period, no real sense that biological laws might have humankind in an inescapable iron grip. Even phrenology, which asserted that character was irrevocably revealed in configurations of the skull, allied itself with hygiene, exercise and an interest in the environment. James G. Birney, in his philosophical meditations, thought that "a large, or well developed brain & head" might be partly the product of "early training & sufficiency & good nourishing food." Birney's speculations were consistent with those of professional phrenologists, who tied their craft to ways of improving skulls already in existence and of realizing their full potential, rather than to consigning inferior ones to genetic hell.[43] The mechanisms and social pressures for eugenics were not available before the Civil War; birth control (another attempt to regulate sexuality, dating from the 1830s) was bound up with fears of promiscuity, not with postbellum fears of white "race suicide"; racialist thought attacked the human unity abolitionists preferred to believe in; and Darwinism lay in the future when Wright, Elizabeth Cady Stanton and Stephen Pearl Andrews formulated their attitudes into convictions.[44] Concern for licentiousness, symbolized most spectacularly by the erotic South, was not, however, the product of a universe completely different from that of postwar America. In their drive to control humankind's animal nature, particularly sexuality, abolitionists were part of a continuum from romantic reform, with its emphasis on the individual, to middle-class moralists at the century's end who valued certain kinds of individualism, but who ultimately cast their faith and anxieties onto race and reproduction.

This was a continuum from religiously-based perfectionism to physical perfectionism, from enthusiasm to eugenics. Standing mid-way along it, abolitionists sought to reconcile both ends with each other as well as with human equality. Physical salvation, in these pre-Darwinian days, could not be just a matter of biological necessity. It was God's mandate, not evolution's, that made man's task on earth, according to Theodore Parker, "to unfold and perfect himself, as far as possible, in body and spirit." There was a transition, nonetheless, when Harriet Beecher Stowe, who bore with her the great revival's seed, exclaimed that "Perfect spiritual religion cannot exist without perfect physical religion."[45]

Abolitionism began, and ended, with humankind. It began with a call for individual outrage and repentance and ended with the Yankee schoolmar'm carrying civilization southward. It sought to liberate men and women and, at the same time, to control man, to make him moral, eventually to direct his most fearful energies toward his salvation. Abolitionists were not alone in their preoccupations. They were very much children of antebellum America, less unique in their anxieties and hopes than in the embodiment they found for those anxieties and hopes. The problem of why certain individuals became abolitionists while others, of similar backgrounds, did not is a task for those who can untangle personal motivation. Equally important to understand is the function antislavery played for abolitionists. For them, slavery summed up discontents that were social, personal, and far more general than the South's peculiar institution. The erotic South, like the inhuman and exploitative North of proslavery propaganda, was less a real place than an organizing principle, a culturally planted reference point measuring the dreadful rush of antebellum change. To their credit, antislavery and allied reforms were still too optimistic, perhaps too naïve, to see man, even at his most beastly, as imprisoned by biology. There was hope among antebellum reformers that human nature could be overcome, that civilization depended on a struggle within man, not a struggle among men.

Yet there was a transition. Younger abolitionists drifted elsewhere after the war. The Garrison children absorbed Darwinism. Moncure Conway went to England, to a friendship with Herbert Spencer and to another kind of revelation. "Darwin's discovery made a new departure in my pilgrimage necessary," he exclaimed. Elizabeth Cady Stanton, shortly after the Civil War, declared that Herbert Spencer's popularization (and socialization) of Darwin achieved the grand objective of "teaching us to lose sight of ourselves and our burdens in the onward march of the race." Nearing the end of his days, Parker Pillsbury, one of the oldest abolitionists, took satisfaction in Loring Moody's career. Moody had been general agent for the pioneer organization, the Massachusetts Anti-Slavery Society. He went from there to the Society for the Prevention of Cruelty to Animals, and then to "a similar association in behalf of poor children." Yet, according to Pillsbury, Moody's "last labor was doubtless most important of all in his life of nearly seventy years. He originated and organized *The Institute of Heredity*, perhaps, viewed in all its aspects and relations, the most important enterprise to universal human well being of the nineteenth century."[46] The distance from sentimentalism to evolution could be bridged in a lifetime; it was no farther than the erotic South was from Oneida perfectionism. Among antebellum reformers it was the distance between humankind's moral nature—the universal human being who could be trusted to behave correctly when not corrupted by arbitrary power—and mankind's animal nature, the passionate creature needing to be kept tightly under control, the physical being over whose body civilization was to triumph.

MINISTERIAL MISDEEDS

The Onderdonk Trial and
Sexual Harassment in the 1840s

PATRICIA CLINE COHEN

In late 1844, the Right Reverend Benjamin T. Onderdonk, Episcopal Bishop of New York, was brought to trial before an ecclesiastical court of his peers on nine counts of "immoralities and impurities" committed against Episcopal women. Followed with intense interest by the public and covered with rapt attention in the secular and religious press, the Onderdonk case generated a best-selling trial report and a heated pamphlet war, focusing sharply on questions of correct gender deportment between ministers and female parishioners. To his supporters, Onderdonk was a man wrongfully accused by enemies within his church who really opposed his theological politics. To his antagonists, the bishop was a powerful man who abused his position to prey on women within his circle. The Onderdonk controversy has all the hallmarks of what today would be called a case of sexual harassment. But lacking a concept of sexual harassment to frame the issues, commentators on both sides of the case remained perplexed and at odds about how to interpret Onderdonk's intimate touches.

The story unfolded in a place and time already alert to serious charges of misconduct by the clergy. News of an apparent epidemic of clerical vice oozed from the presses in antebellum America, from the urban penny newspapers to the respectable secular and religious papers. Several features of the sociology of antebellum religion promoted a climate of fear about increased sexual temptation. The rapid growth of denominations in the wake of the Second Great Awakening created space for irregularly trained ministers to make their way in the world; lax educational and licensing requirements inevitably allowed an occasional charlatan to move into a position of trust. An adversarial denominational press stood ready to publicize questionable behavior as a way of discrediting the competition.

The emotional style of the evangelical movement further encouraged an atmosphere conducive to sexual disorder. Evangelism often brought passion and sensuality to the fore in a spirituality that manifested itself in ecstatic moments, altered states of being, uncontrolled weeping, or speaking in tongues. Camp meetings and all-night revivals provided a new kind of mixed-sex social space where older rules of gender deportment might be held to less rigidly. Emotional religion allowed for more unrestrained touching, embracing, and general physical intimacy among adherents than did the traditional orthodox churches. Even among those staid denominations, the renewal of religious fervor and the necessity to compete with charismatic clerics inevitably led to a greater cultivation of ministerial showmanship. Some men might ease into the presumption that their spiritual magnetism, displayed so dramatically in the pulpit, betokened sexual magnetism as well.

Whatever the causes, antebellum religious leaders were coming to realize that sexual temptation posed an important occupational hazard for clergymen. No other male occupation offered such easy proximity to women. Protected by an assumption of unimpeachable morality, ministers could approach strange women in public without benefit of introduction; for other men, this was rude or risky forwardness. ("Ah, your parsons know the way to the women! Would that I did!" wrote an envious young bachelor in his diary on an Erie canal boat trip in 1833, upon observing a minister approach some likely young women and propose a checkers game.)[1] Ministers were entitled to converse with women about intimate matters in private spaces—the parlor, the sickbed room, the minister's study. They were supposed to be above the ordinary temptations of life; but some succumbed to sin.

The Onderdonk case, however, was sharply different from the several dozens of tales of ministerial misconduct retailed in the press. No actual sex crime—seduction, rape, attempted rape—was ever alleged. The behavior that the women complained of was universally regarded as inappropriate; there was no possible innocent interpretation for a man's burrowing his hand into a woman's neckline and fondling her naked breast. But in context, the behavior made no sense to the 1840s commentators, because Onderdonk pursued his frontal assaults in public places, when male protectors of the women were nearby. His defenders were thus sure that some less intimate act of tenderness had somehow been misconstrued.

Rarely, before the twentieth century, have such minute, gendered interchanges of body language been the subject of so much discussion in print. Not surprisingly, the trial report created a sensation. The entire transcript was published in a 330-page soft cover book within three weeks of the verdict. At least a dozen pamphlets debated the case, as did local and national news publications. The fullness of the testimony and its wide distribution allowed a throng of people to participate in defining, interpreting, rationalizing or condemning sexual harassment.

Two themes dominated the public discussion. One focused on the women's testimonies and the inappropriate familiarities. Why did the women not complain at the time? Why did their male relatives fail to defend them? What could the Bishop have possibly had in mind? Under what circumstances could a man presume a woman's willingness to engage in intimate touching? As so often happens in modern sexual harassment cases, questions were raised about the encouragement some of these women might have given the Bishop.

The other significant and weighty subject of discussion was the issue of warring factions within the Protestant Episcopal Church. The presentment for trial came in November of 1844, just one month after the most searing General Convention the Episcopal Church had ever witnessed in America, where the controversy over the English "Oxford Movement" erupted. The struggle pitted High Church adherents against Low Church defenders, the former group advocating a Romanizing move in the direction of Catholic doctrine and especially liturgy.[2] The debate turned on symbolic ritual acts: the lighting of candles, kneeling at the mention of Jesus's name, the color of the surplice worn, facing the congregation or not. Bishop Onderdonk was on record as a strong supporter of the High Church (or Puseyite) position, a minority view in American Anglicanism. The bishop's supporters claimed that the morality charges were a smokescreen for a sinister ulterior plot to oust the bishop and divest the church of Catholic leanings.

The modern experience of adjudicating sexual harassment grievances suggests that the two motives to unseat Onderdonk were not mutually exclusive, as commentators in the 1840s thought. Women who suffer sexual harassment often get heard more quickly and clearly when the harasser already has acquired powerful enemies on other grounds. The theological dispute, then, could well have been an important precondition that enabled the charge of immorality to be taken seriously. And of course, to some, the two objections were not completely unrelated: ornate High-Church ritual and aberrant sexuality could be seen as dual manifestations of an aristocratic posture now under attack by an increasingly bourgeois American Episcopalianism.

Onderdonk's defenders would naturally never agree that elaborate liturgy had anything to do with sexual irregularities. They insisted that a theological attack was being mounted under the guise of spurious and scandalous charges. And there was some foundation for this view. In the complicated religious and political terrain of antebellum America, gendered ideas were often invoked as a strategy to distill debates and simplify disagreements. Stereotypes of masculinity and femininity tend to be widely shared in a culture and can thus be used as a kind of shorthand to make accessible other, more complicated ideas. For example, depicting the concept of Liberty as a white woman in revolutionary-era political cartoons conveyed in a glance the idea that liberty was vulnerable to attack and in need of male protection. Fundamental ideological tensions between the emerging political parties of Andrew Jackson and John Quincy Adams in the 1828 election become readily accessible to voters in the famous campaign fight over Jackson's alleged adulterous marriage.[3] And impugning the masculine honor and sexual purity of a clergyman was a quick way to bring him down.

The difficulty in the Onderdonk case was that using stereotypes of masculine and feminine behavior did not simplify things. Gendered behaviors lay at the heart of the case; they were not metaphors for larger questions of character. But they eluded quick comprehension. Onderdonk did not fit the mold of a lecherous man out to seduce a woman; the women also behaved unintelligibly according to 1840s notions of female delicacy, by keeping quiet for years. Without a vocabulary of sexual harassment, of the intricate interrelations of sex and power, commentators of the 1840s were at a loss. Ultimately, only one interpretive strategy succeeded: a translation of the Onderdonk phenomenon into blackface, where racist stereotypes distilled and simplified the complex issues the Episcopalians struggled with. Where gender metaphors no longer sufficed, racial metaphors worked.

In order to capture the perplexing nature of the incident with its gendered and racialized configurations, we must first reconstruct the players and the stage and hear the testimony of the women themselves. Then we will turn to the contested explanations and interpretations, nearly all offered by men, from lawyers and clergy to acknowledged libertines and the jokester-creators of "Black Under-Donk-En Doughlips; or, De Feelin Deacon." The celebrity of the Onderdonk case derived from its famed centerpiece personality—the Bishop of New York; but this was far more than a seamy tabloid story of an individual public figure's fall from grace. Its richness derives from its resonance with complex public attitudes about sexuality, gender and race that preoccupied antebellum America.

Benjamin T. Onderdonk, 53, was born in New York City of an old Long Island Dutch family. Both he and his brother Henry attended Columbia University and became ordained ministers in the Protestant Episcopal Church. He married at 22, fathered seven children, and spent his whole career in New York City. Onderdonk was an ambitious leader, and in 1830, at the relatively young age of 39, he was consecrated Bishop of New York. His brother Henry rose to be Bishop of Pennsylvania in 1836.[4] Both men were articulate and powerful proponents of the High Church party; both made enemies.

In the fall of 1844, the controversy over the Oxford Movement erupted at the Episcopalian convention in Philadelphia. Tense delegates hammered out a set of new procedures governing dismissals of bishops. Henry Onderdonk had recently been persuaded to resign his bishopric on grounds of habitual intemperance. Within a month, the new procedures were invoked against Benjamin Onderdonk, and in December the trial to unseat him on nine charges of sexual immoralities opened in New York City.

The first woman to testify was the daughter of an Episcopal minister who had known the Bishop since her childhood. Onderdonk came to Syracuse in June 1837 to ordain her newlywed husband, Clement Moore Butler. The couple met him in Ithaca and drove all night with him in a two-seat wagon, the 20-year-old Mrs. Butler in the back seat with the Bishop, and her husband and the driver in front. According to Mrs. Butler, Onderdonk had had too much to drink, and as the sun set, he became unusually attentive, which alarmed her.

He first put his arm around my waist and drew me towards him; this he repeated once, perhaps twice. He had often done this when I was unmarried,

*and I had permitted it, although always disagreeable to me; because I believed
him incapable of wrong. At this time, however, I removed his hand each time,
because I saw that he was not himself. I was exceedingly fearful lest our driver
should discover it. . . . The bishop persisted in putting his arm about me, and
raised his hand so as to press my bosom. I then rose and withdrew the arm from
behind me, and laid the hand upon his knee, and said to him in a raised tone
of voice . . . that a Bishop's hands were sacred in my eyes, and that his were particularly so, because they had been laid upon the heads of many I loved in confirmation, and were about to be laid upon my husband's head in ordination. He
made but little answer, but for some little time let me alone.*

Mrs. Butler hoped it was just the alcohol and that the bishop meant no
intentional insult. But

*while sitting in thought, I found he was again moving: I waited to see whether
he might not be merely steadying himself in his seat, as the roads were rough,
when he suddenly and violently again brought his hand upon my bosom, pressed
and clasped it. In some horror I struck the hand with all my force, and he withdrew it; but immediately grasped my leg in the most indelicate manner.*[5]

This was too much; Mrs. Butler clambered into the front seat onto her
husband's lap and whispered her fears to him. Mr. Butler got the impression the bishop had actually lifted her skirt and touched her naked leg. At
a rest stop he and his wife debated what to do. Mr. Butler, very agitated,
wanted to confront the man, but Mrs. Butler, mindful of the ordination
ceremony just hours away, counseled silence.

Under oath, Mr. Butler confirmed his wife's story. He coldly avoided
the bishop after his ordination. He divulged his painful story to other ministers only after hearing rumors of similar incidents. His wife broke her
silence by confiding in her sister-in-law, a close female friend, and later her
father, who did not believe her. The Butlers' complaint constituted two
counts: undue familiarities and improper inebriation.

The third formal charge against Onderdonk involved an unknown
woman, about 25, who shared a stagecoach with him in upstate New York
in 1838. Also on board was another minister, a reluctant witness who now
clearly wished to minimize the incident. Onderdonk, he testified, had put
his hand over the woman's on her armrest. She blushed and withdrew the

hand, but the bishop took it a second time. At the next stop the woman disembarked before reaching her stated destination. The witness observed the woman's discomfort but rejected the notion that Onderdonk had impure motives: "in a notoriously bad man such conduct would have been indicative of a bad design; but it did not occur to me, nor do I think, that the Bishop had any impure or lustful desires towards this woman." Nevertheless, the clergyman was sufficiently uneasy that he mentioned the event to another minister, whence the story spread.[6]

The next witness was Helen Rudderow, who had shared an eight-block ride from church to her home with the bishop in 1841, when she was 29.

> *We had not proceeded very far from the church, when Bishop Onderdonk put his arm around my neck, and thrust his hand into my bosom: this he continued to do. I was very much surprised and agitated, and would have jumped from the carriage, had it not been for exposing him to the Rev. Mr. Richmond [then driving]. He kept repeating the offense until we reached home, where he was to dine with us.[7]*

Careful questioning elicited the information that his hand was well below her neckline on her naked breast, under her shawl. Remarkably, the bishop continued to converse with Mr. Richmond all the while. Once home, Helen sought out her sister. "I entreated her to go down and entertain him, as the family were not yet prepared to do so; she consented, upon condition that I should follow as soon as I could sufficiently compose myself." Jane Rudderow greeted the bishop in the drawing room, whereupon he led her to the sofa and there "thrust his hand in my bosom." Jane backed away, but the bishop attacked her again, withdrawing only when a sister-in-law entered the room moments later. Jane said she did not cry out, because her brothers were close by in the hall: "I was fearful for his personal safety, and did not expose him for the sake of the Church." Significantly, both Helen and Jane thought first of protecting him.

Jane's ordeal was not over. Despite great "fright and astonishment," she and Helen sat through a midday meal with Onderdonk and the family, remaining mostly silent while their mother chattered on with the distinguished guest. After dinner the bishop twice more maneuvered to be alone with her for just a few seconds and again plunged his hand inside her neckline, she testified.

The sisters commiserated with each other that day and told a sister-in-law a few weeks later. But they waited six months to tell their mother, and did not tell their brothers at all until they were called to produce affidavits in late 1844, for fear that the brothers would deliver "an ignominious if not bloody vengeance."[8]

The next charge against Onderdonk was dropped when the complainant, a young governess, suddenly refused to cooperate. Her pre-trial affidavit recalled a meeting five years earlier, when the bishop steered her aside in a Westchester garden and suddenly put his hand into her bosom.[9] Her refusal to testify underscores the difficulty these young women had withstanding close questioning by sharp trial lawyers about deeply embarrassing incidents before a roomful of Episcopal bishops, including of course Onderdonk.

The last witness was Charlotte Beare, wife of the Rev. Henry Beare of Bayside, Long Island. Like Mrs. Butler, Mrs. Beare was a recent bride in 1842 when the bishop accosted her. Mrs. Beare sat next to Onderdonk in a carriage on their way to her husband's church, with her mother-in-law and nephew in front. When the bishop put his arm around her and pressed her bosom, she shrank away from him. She told her husband soon after, who tersely advised her to keep civil but distant.

Onderdonk accompanied them home for dinner. There, in the presence of her mother-in-law, the bishop lifted Mrs. Beare's chin and kissed her, calling her "my daughter." The young wife reflected that "I had too much confidence in him to suppose that he would offer me an insult in my own house."[10] Yet she was unsettled and wary. Hours later, in another carriage ride with the husband and nephew in the front seat, Mrs. Beare came under assault:

> *The Bishop put his arm around my waist; then raised it, and put it across the back of my neck; he thrust his hand into the neck of my dress, down in my bosom. I threw his hand from there; he immediately put it upon the lower part of my person. I pushed it aside from there, and he then with the other hand repeated the same upon the other side of my person; but removed it towards the centre of my person.*[11]

The carriage was in the lane at the Beare's house at this point, and the wife alighted and sought her husband's help. He still counseled caution: "say no more now; let us join the family, and have our evening devotions." The bishop stayed the night, and Mrs. Beare kept her distance. Except for her husband, she told no one of her concerns until eighteen months later, when she confided in three aunts.[12]

These, then, formed the substance of the first eight charges against Bishop Onderdonk. The ninth and last was a dark hint of a continuing pattern of immorality: "that at sundry times . . . [he] has impurely and unchastely laid his hands upon the bodies of other virtuous and respectable ladies, whose names have come to the knowledge of the said Bishops, so that he is of evil report within the limits of the said Diocese."[13] The sense of a larger field of victims was aptly conveyed in a pamphlet by Rev. James Richmond, who drove with Helen Rudderow and the bishop, and who, it develops, played a key role in marshaling all of the witnesses' affidavits and orchestrating their testimonies.

> *Where is the presbyter who walked on the banks of the Hudson, and related to a fellow clergyman that gross insult to his family, (worse than any on the trial,) which will yet be dragged to the light, unless all parties make up their minds to abandon so forlorn a hope as this man's restoration? Where is the lady in Bond-street who related to me her daughter's refusal to be confirmed these four years? Where the bevy of young ladies on Long Island who declared, if the spiritual father was coming, they could escape by wearing dresses high in the neck? . . . Where is the other young lady on York Island, who long refused to be confirmed, and at last actually tittered, as she went up, at the sad and yet ludicrous idea, that he might make a mistake, through old habit?*[14]

If it was true that a bevy of young women on Long Island shared lore about the bishop's unusual interest in necklines, we are here tapping into a collective female response to sexual harassment in the 1840s: the girls practiced avoidance, deterrent dress, and sororal humor, assuaging individual embarrassment by a shared knowledge of the bishop's habitual behavior. Evidently such girls were unwilling to be witnesses, however; they did not appear at the trial.

The four women witnesses together constituted the first interpretive gloss on Onderdonk's strange behavior. Singly, each woman reported confusion and disbelief; each kept quiet for fear of bringing dishonor on their bishop and their church. The married women put their husbands' careers first. The Rudderow sisters feared their brothers would seek vengeance. Mrs. Beare's husband was at first unreceptive to her concern, and Mrs. Butler's father, himself a minister, flat-out refused to believe her. So the women confided in trusted females and abandoned the idea of correcting the bishop. Together, at the trial, their individual experiences still perplexed them, but their conviction of Onderdonk's immorality was validated by knowing that three other woman had been through the same experience.

Lawyers were the next in line to attempt a coherent account of the puzzling actions. Onderdonk opted to hire top professional lawyers, not customary in church trials, and the presenting bishops were forced to follow suit. Lawyers brought their sense of constitutional rights and legal wrongs to the case; evidence was held to a strict standard, and undermining the women's credibility became the prime defense strategy. The charge involving the unknown woman on a stage was immediately tossed out, since no one could name the woman. The ninth charge, of a broad pattern of immoralities and general "evil report," was similarly dismissed for lack of sworn evidence. What was left were four women, testifying to events many years in the past.

The lawyers' main defense strategy invoked gender stereotypes: none of the women had responded as an insulted woman of true virtue. None summoned help, even though help was nearby. Mrs. Butler's concern to keep quiet for the sake of the driver was dismissed as ludicrous beyond belief. Much was made of the Butlers' confusion as to whether the bishop's hand was on top of or under her skirt, suggesting they had not gotten their concocted story straight. Maybe, the lawyers postulated, the jolting of the carriage on the bad roads out of Ithaca fully accounted for Mrs. Butler's complaint. Mrs. Beare had only to lean forward and tug on her husband's sleeve when she apprehended the bishop's hand moving up her leg; Jane Rudderow could have leaped from the couch and run to her brothers in the hall.

What is more surprising, the lawyers said, was that the women continued to be civil to him. Why would Helen Rudderow send Jane down to be alone with him? How could they possibly dine with him, as did Mrs. Beare? Helen Rudderow even visited him months later in a delegation of young women pleading support for a charitable activity, a point established at great length in the trial. Why had all of these victims failed to complain in a timely fashion?

The defense lawyers' narrative of uncredible women in the end did not persuade. The presiding bishops found Onderdonk guilty on a vote of eleven to six. Apparently it was hard to imagine a conspiracy of perjury large enough to encompass all the ministers, wives, and parishioners who had testified. On the question of punishment, the vote was also eleven to six, this time eleven voting for indefinite suspension of the bishop from his duties, while six voted for the harsher sentence of complete deposing from office. (The six who had voted for acquittal and lost now shifted their votes to the lesser penalty of suspension.) The Diocese of New York was put into ecclesiastical limbo, its leader suspended from all priestly functions but still technically occupying the office.

The verdict in, the pamphlet war began, each of the dozen writers—mostly clerical leaders—vying with the last to impose a credible account on the evidence. While the trial had limited itself to the women's allegations of immoralities, the pamphlets opened up the ulterior theological motives.

Bishop Onderdonk, silent at the trial, produced his own carefully crafted "Statement of Facts." He avoided comment on the women's particular charges, except to say that it was his impression that Mrs. Butler was unwell and had gratefully leaned on him in the carriage out of Ithaca. The charges were all very old, brought up now as a conspiracy against him instigated by Rev. James Richmond, in revenge for a bad letter of recommendation Onderdonk had once written for him.[15]

James Richmond in his two pamphlets denied any personal grudge, just as he denied that animosity over High Church/Low Church differences formed his motive. Sexual sin was his chief concern. Richmond had driven the carriage with Helen Rudderow in 1841, uneasy about what was going on behind him—but too timid to turn and look. After hearing rumors of the bishop's unchaste attentions to other women, he returned to the Rudderow home in 1843 and boldly asked the women pointed questions. Richmond quoted a letter he wrote to his brother that year, warning that Onderdonk's indecencies were "now a matter of notoriety in the female portion of the Diocese, here, there, and everywhere. I know no man whom I would watch *so closely, every minute* in my house. No lady is safe from the grossest, most palpable, and almost open insult."[16]

Soon thereafter, at a dinner party of ministers and deacons, Richmond turned the conversation to "Pope Benjamin I," hinting at his intemperate, licentious ways. The other diners became instantly tense; some cautiously asked him what he meant, while others called "order! order!" to shut him up. "I looked through my fingers, and said to one and another, 'you know'; '*you know*,' and some of them did know." A nearby cleric said darkly to another: "'Don't ask him . . . for he will tell you.'"[17]

To challenge that obstinate denial at the highest levels of church hierarchy, Richmond commenced gathering women's stories and securing agreements to testify. Most turned him down, he reported; this countered the complaint of Onderdonk supporters that the women witnesses were insufficiently modest. With good reason, women were reluctant to go public, for their own reputations were called into question. One writer tried to be kind, claiming that Mrs. Butler and Mrs. Beare, "ardent and impulsive" brides presumably in the fresh bloom of sexual awakening, might well misinterpret affectionate gestures that they would have innocently accepted when unmarried. Recall, this was intended to be a defense of the bishop—that his accusers confused his pure caresses with the preliminaries of lovemaking, simply because they were delicately ripe for sex.[18]

Much harsher treatment of the women came from a New York literary writer editorializing in the *New York Evening Mirror*. Nathaniel P. Willis set out "A Man of the World's View of the Onderdonk Case."

> *In our opinion, no modest woman has ever been outraged by such liberties as are charged upon the Bishop. . . . Every man knows—and the most vicious man knows it best—that no woman is ever invaded till the enemy has given a signal from within! . . . We declare our belief that no woman whose virtue is above suspicion, was ever insultingly spoken to—far less, insulting touched—by a man in his senses. . . . The look of surprise only, with which the first shade of a questionable sentiment is met by a completely pure woman, is enough to arrest, and awe from his purpose, the boldest seducer.*[19]

Profligate men all over New York City, Willis knowingly reported, were laughing to think that a woman could be surprised when a man put a hand on her breast. Worse still, Willis declared that clergymen everywhere would of course sympathize with Onderdonk, because of "the caressing character of the intercourse between the clergy and the women in their parishes whose affections are otherwise unemployed." Worldly men all knew that ministers frequently took advantage of affection-starved women.

Indignation greeted Willis's article. The secular press castigated him as a vulgar libertine who had libeled all of American womanhood. Willis's essay provoked a sharp reply from female pens as well, from the women editors of the bi-monthly *Advocate of Moral Reform* who had thus far steered clear of the Onderdonk case. To think that a look of surprise alone was sufficient to deter harassment was ridiculous, the editors wrote. Willis was in effect saying that women, not men, were to blame for sexual sin.[20]

The inexplicable failure of the victims to raise an outcry seems to have been the sticking point for many commentators. An anonymous pamphlet, by "Spectator," produced the most closely reasoned analysis of the complex power dynamics at work. As individuals, he pointed out, the women must have feared their accusations would not be believed; even four together testifying under oath were still met with skepticism. With no possibility of official redress, they took the only other path: avoidance and aloofness.

"Spectator" had a grasp of what prevented harassed women from complaining. But he could not explain the bishop's conduct; no one could, because of a persistent resort to the models of courtship or sex crimes as the context for interpreting his actions. One Onderdonk supporter, the Bishop of New Jersey, dismissed the alleged acts of immorality by simply asking, "What was to come of it?" With people all around, the bishop could not have intended to carry his misdeeds any further, so even if he touched a breast, there was no true evil intent. *The Churchman*, the official national publication of the Episcopal Church, urged the faithful to absolve the bishop because his sins were "comparatively light."[21] Even "Spectator" assumed that sexual intercourse was the ultimate goal of a man with roving hands. "Every body . . . knows that seduction is insidious in its beginning, gradual in its progress, and because insidious . . . and gradual, the more sure in its end. It always begins in 'passages that lead to nothing' in the eyes of its victims."[22]

Feelings ran high on the Onderdonk case precisely because it was hard, in the 1840s, to create a narrative that accounted for the bishop's conduct and the women's silence. To the bishop's High Church supporters, the only explanation that made sense was a conspiracy by theological opponents. His normally affectionate manner toward women had been misinterpreted; whatever he had done, he had no ultimate evil intent to seduce or rape. From the victims' point of view, the story was equally puzzling. How could such a touch be anything but immoral? Why would he touch them without trying to do more? Why would he take such a risk with people nearby? The ambivalent outcome—removing Onderdonk from duty without removing him from his bishop's office—perfectly reflected the bafflement religious leaders felt.

Framing the events through the lens of modern sexual harassment concepts helps bring several features of the case into focus. The four women, widely separated in location, each reported a very similar experience, suggesting a pattern of behavior indulged in by the bishop. He had enormous institutional power over his victims, and, as importantly, over their male relatives. He picked virtuous churchwomen—wives of ministers, single women active in church circles—to make sure of their allegiance to the larger entity of the church. He picked wives of young clergymen at precisely the point of their husband's greatest vulnerability to pressure, the moment of ordination or of grand visitation. Onderdonk's preference for apparently risky situations, with male protectors close by, actually ensured silent acquiescence from his victims. If no one had been within earshot, the women would have been freer to complain to him, to push him away, to make a scene. But these women well understood the cultural pressure for male protectors to respond with violent anger, and they thus feared for their bishop's safety and by extension the reputation of the church.

Onderdonk probably had no intention to seduce or rape; the quick, unauthorized plunge into forbidden territory carried a sexual charge and enhanced his sense of power over the women. His thrill was to touch naked bosoms in crowds and get away with it. Over many years, he had gotten away with it, by picking his moments and victims carefully. During the years of rumors, his fellow clerics deliberately looked the other way; they really hoped James Richmond would not tell them anything unpleasant at that rancorous dinner party. Women told their war stories chiefly to other women, rarely to men, and never to authorities, knowing that the outcome of telling would be bad for them and bad for the church they respected.

But not everyone was baffled. Cynics and libertines in New York's night spots had a laugh over Onderdonk's scandalous plight. The *Herald* reported that at intermission at Niblo's, a popular New York City music hall on Broadway, four or five copies of the Onderdonk trial report were seen circulating through the audience and made the basis of choice humor.

One mild joke that did make it into print told of a fancy evening party where the gas lights went out all of a sudden. "Ladies, don't be afraid, the Bishop is not here!" called out a man's voice in the darkness, "followed by an ungenerous burst of laughter."[23]

Nathaniel Willis, the self-appointed spokesman for libertine men, found the bishop's actions completely comprehensible: affection-starved women subtly but surely invited his caresses. A somewhat different humorous take on the libertine world-view was offered by George Thompson, a racy fiction writer and some-time radical social critic, who devoted a chapter to licentious clergymen in his 1848 book *New-York Life*. Thompson characterized Onderdonk as "a man so full of wine and lust— a high liver, a full eater of flesh, and a man of fleshly lusts, which war against the soul." Women were innocent victims of such men, Thompson claimed. Evil ministers easily seduced young women into believing that pleasing God and pleasing the minister were closely related undertakings. They knew how to excite tender feelings, both religious and sexual, in young women: "So far from a sin, it seems to be an act of duty and of piety to submit to his desires, and when the object is once accomplished, the reward is a devout blessing and thanksgiving, that removes every scruple of conscience and the pleasing duty of comforting a beloved pastor is performed as an act of religious merit." In Thompson's view, unscrupulous men under the camouflage of clerical robes took advantage of incredibly naive girls, who remained naive even after sexual favors were cleverly coaxed out of them. As absurd as that seems, Thompson's fantasy spoke to a deep and abiding male desire, even among libertine men, to maintain an illusion of female sexual innocence.[24]

The most interesting and on-the-mark social commentary interpreting the Onderdonk case took the form of a blackface parody of the bishop's carriage rides. It appeared in an 1845 scurrilous Philadelphia almanac, titled "De Darkie's Comic Al-Me-Nig." The illustrated story, "Black Under-Donk-En Doughlips; or, De Feelin Deacon," recounted in exaggerated Negro dialect the tale of a buggy driver who drove Deacon Doughlips to a purity meeting along with another clergyman and his wife. First the driver hears sounds "berry much like niggar lips comin in contact." He turns and sees the Deacon kissing the clergyman's wife. Next he hears the sound of a dress coming undone, and beholds "a sample ob dark under-donkation to parfection: dar was Mrs. Frogpaw's bare black beautiful bosom fast in de Deacon's boff hands, an his black fist war worken its way along like a black snake under de loose bark ob a gum tree." The text and accompanying illustration make clear that the black clergyman in the front seat looks on the whole scene of his wife and the bishop with full approval. The woman, in contrast, looks utterly astonished.[25]

The almanac, of course, was the production of whites for a white audience, just as blackface minstrelsy in theaters of the 1840s involved whites speaking to other whites using the semantics of race. The mediation of race transposed the bishop's behavior from the realm of privileged, religious whites—where it seemed to make no sense—to the realm of black burlesque and broad comedy, where infantile jokes and wishes could be given full expression. Rendering the Onderdonk story in blackface allowed white men to indulge in the forbidden fantasy of touching a woman's breast at will and without punishment. The female victim as black woman is understood to be open game for sexual attack; no system of patriarchy protects her, as it would a white woman. This black woman victim has a husband, to be sure, but he looks on with approval and enjoyment, since the conventions of blackface exaggerate his prurient sexuality, along with his dialect and facial features.

In the world of privileged whites, men could not touch women disrespectfully as a social rule, and if they did, male relatives were supposed to spring to the women's defense. Even harboring the thought of such an invasive action was so foreign—forbidden—to white commentators in the Onderdonk case that they could not imagine why the bishop might do it in actuality. In the negative figuration of blackface, immature and inappropriate fondling could be seen now to be an end in itself, an infantile compulsion and not a preliminary to serious seduction or courtship as might be expected from a grown man. The child-like and stupid black caricatures served to mark Onderdonk's behavior as child-like and stupid, a giving way to an impulsive urge that most men in real life would quickly censor were they even to allow the thought to creep into their heads. "Deacon Under-Donk-En" revealed the sexual fantasy for the forbidden thrill that it was. The racial inversion played off of an ambivalent identification some whites felt for blacks and black culture in the 1840s, a potent mixture of fear, ridicule, and desire. The caricature also expressed a sense of cross-race male solidarity at the expense of women: the almanac story invited masked men, white or black, to take delight in a sexual insult to

BLACK UNDER-DONK-EN DOUGHLIPS;
OR, DE FEELIN DEACON.

Ya, ya, ya! by smash, I blebe dar's no more human natur any more, when a bit o' women natur am about, for all our Deacon's am getting so fat dat de spiritual feelin am all smashed out ob 'em like de yolk out ob geese egg, an dar all flesh like ebery oder boddy else. Fader Miller am been about, all de preachers am takin toll ob de fair black sheep ob dar flock. Dar's only last Octember I went to drive de Rev. Doctor Frogpaw down to de purity night meetin house, when dey took a notion to stop for Deacon Dough-lips on de way, an earry him down to de meetin at de same time. Well, de Deacon got in de bugbee, an Doctor Frogpaw gib him his seat along side of Mrs. Julep Frogpaw ob course, and took a seat next behind me, so as he could look me face to face in de back, an tell me which way to drive. Now somehow or todder how, as soon as de Deacon got to de bugbee, I tought dat he smelt berry loud ob dat little house below de cider press, an his two eyes walked out like de risen moons; so tinks I, I'll jist keep one eye behind my back, for I'se berry lately had a berry loud suspicion ob dese he black sheep Well, as we war gwan along de road, I seed sebral wery queer sounds dat look berry much like niggar lips comin in contract; I turned boff eyes around, an smash me up into corn cakes, if de ole Deacon wasn't biting de tallest kind ob a buss from de innocence an dullifferous forbidden lips ob Mrs. Julep Frogpaw. Well, I drove on a little furder, an I soon heered furder sights; I tought dat I seed de bosom ob de dress crack an come apart, an look around some more, an oh, bullglory an seductionation, if I didn't dar behold a sample ob dark underdonkation to parfection: dar was Mrs. Frog-paw's bare black beautiful bosom fast in de Deacon's boff hands, an his black fist war worken its way along like a black snake under de loose bark ob a gum tree. I gib Dr. Frogpaw a wink wid de corner ob my elbow, and he turned right around backwards, an dar he seed de hull sight for nothin,—a Deacon's hand on a new edition ob de bible,—a she nigga's bosom; de hosses laughed, I fainted in exprise, as de Doctor called de Deacon a most feel-in fader; an de next ting I he red ob, was dar making up a purse ob money as a reward for his feeling so fur into de bosoms an hearts ob de black flock.

Figure 1: Courtesy of the American Antiquarian Society

women. This is why the black woman in the illustration must look surprised and scared—a reversal of the prevailing stereotype of black women's freer and easier sexuality, usually invoked to justify sexual advances. The thrill of the Onderdonk grab relied precisely on the fact that the victim felt great consternation and distress.

Bishop Onderdonk was suspended from office but his friends in the New York diocese refused to turn him out completely. He continued to occupy the bishop's house near Trinity Church and to draw his full bishop's salary. He attended church daily and led the procession to communion. He ceased all social life, rarely left his house, and retired from church politics. The confusion occasioned by having a suspended bishop finally led to the appointment of an interim bishop, and the death of this substitute in the late 1850s prompted Onderdonk's supporters to try, yet again, to have the suspension lifted. But the Convention of Bishops refused, and in 1859, the cleric died, unrepentant and officially unforgiven. His supporters installed an elaborate marble memorial, with an unintentionally multi-valent symbol chiseled on it, depicting a "serpent darting his venomous fangs at the bishop," in the All Saints' Chapel in Trinity church.[26] On-lookers and mourners could wonder whether the serpent represented the external enemies (the snakes) who drove the man from power or the internal temptations of serpentine sexuality that bedeviled him.

The power of the Onderdonk case to amaze, in 1845 as surely now, is that it emerged in the midst of one of the most traditional, hierarchical, and ritual-bound religious institutions in America. Theological controversy for the Episcopalians involved struggles over minute details of ritual; the new and "radical" opinion lay with the High Church proponents, who wanted more symbolic punch in their liturgical arrangements. This was not a religion turned topsy-turvy by democratizing forces.

Americans in the 1840s were more prepared to find altered gender relations and aberrant sexuality among the liminal, anti-ritual, democratic religious groups pioneering on the margins of the major denominations. The religious upheavals of the antebellum period opened the doors to divergent styles of gendered interactions between a largely male clergy and an increasingly feminized congregation. Some of these new movements forged deliberately new styles of sexuality—the Oneida Community, the Shakers, and the Mormons, to name three very distinct examples.

Fragmentation lessened the possibility for institutional oversight and control. Irregular ministers had the irregular lives, insisted the religious press; it was most comfortable to isolate unbridled sexuality on the margins of society.

But when the figure of the clerical seducer emerged in the highest pillar of respectable society, different explanations had to be invoked. For his low-church opponents, Bishop Onderdonk's sponsorship of neo-Catholic symbolism was congruent with his sexual lust in that both were expressions of an indulgent sensuality—the man who ate rich foods during Lent and argued for opulent surplices also had fleshly desires he could not control. They framed their explanation in terms of undisciplined desire; but they could not fully comprehend the peculiar form his desire took, the quick and compulsive grab, that seemingly accomplished so little and yet incurred such risk.

But in the frame of modern understandings of sexual harassment, a pattern takes shape. The bishop preferred a church that maximized hierarchy and consolidated lines of authority to the top, one that contained women and men congregants within ritual forms. Elaborate liturgy distanced the minister from the congregation and operated as a symbolic language to express social arrangements honoring status and privilege. Individual congregants did not have individual voices within his institution, and so they found it hard to speak back to authority figures. Onderdonk's compulsion to grab breasts was at heart idiosyncratic and unrelated to any aspect of religion, but his insistence on a vast privilege and power inherent in a clerical elite gave him scope and cover to indulge with a remarkable degree of security his intimate frontal attacks. His authority and eminence became his safety net, giving him a sense of entitlement to do as he did and assuring him that no one would ever believe him capable of it. And it very nearly worked.

STALLIONS IN THE CHURCHYARD

Sexuality and Privacy in Rural Mississippi

Susan Ditto

Among a group of laws Mississippi legislators enacted in 1892 to regulate "obscenities" including profanity, possession of "indecent" pictures or literature, and indecent exposure, was an act forbidding the keeping of a stallion or jackass within one hundred yards of a church.[1] A generation or two earlier, breeding stock only raised the hackles of the law when they ran astray and aroused questions regarding ownership and branding rights.[2] Why would lawmakers who already had their hands full circumventing the fourteenth and fifteenth amendments to the Constitution, redesigning the state flag to include a prominent Confederate symbol, giving bombastic, race-baiting speeches, and promoting an extractive New South economy make room on their legislative agenda for the sex lives of farm animals? Many of their constituents—the rural descendents of yeoman farmers who had domesticated the southern frontier—were accustomed to thinking about sexuality in terms of production, reproduction, and duty. By the turn of the twentieth century, however, the state's leading citizens were pioneering a new agenda. From Mississippi's courthouses and pulpits emerged concerns over threats to female sexual purity, the innocence of children, and the privacy of families. In addition to public rhetoric, one can witness these changing values in the material culture of yeoman farmsteads. As both white women and ungelded horses receded from the landscape, the vernacular farmhouses of rural Mississippi grew to include a telling innovation—private bedrooms.

Nineteenth-century farm families were not in the habit of concealing their sexuality behind closed doors. In the summer of 1861 Sarah Wadley,

44

a teenaged girl whose family lived for a time near Vicksburg, Mississippi, described their home as "a long low building divided at one end by a partition into two rooms, the end room . . . is occupied by Mother, Father, George and the baby . . . the room in which I am now writing is appropriated to Miss Mary, Eva, Lory and I, besides Rose who sleeps on the floor and Georgie's puppy who cannot bear the cold night air and is therefore obliged to be taken into our room. These are its occupants during the night, its our sitting room in the day."[3] Although Sarah found these living arrangements "amusing," the size and composition of the Wadley household and the uses of space by its members were typical of the homes of "Southern country people" before the 1880s.[4]

Like the Wadleys' home, most rural houses in mid-nineteenth century Mississippi consisted of two rooms. One was the hearthroom, also known as the sitting room, the family room, or the "room we lived in." It was the physical and psychological center of domestic culture and the multifunctional locus of many different activities including, as in the case of Sarah Wadley, writing in diaries. The other room, sometimes called a "bed room," was used less extensively during the day. As Wadley's diary suggests, neither room conformed to the standard of individual ownership and personal privacy that characterize bedrooms in our modern understanding of the space. For the 28 percent of rural Mississippi families who lived in single pen houses, where the hearthroom was the one and only room, personal space was even more a state of mind than a physical domain.

Mississippi's two-room farmhouses were crowded and diverse places. In 1860, the average yeoman household in Mississippi had six members, slightly above the state-wide average of 5.8, and well above the steadily declining average of northern bourgeois families. Fully one quarter of yeoman households in Mississippi contained eight people or more and many held upwards of ten.[5] In Monroe County, Mississippi, D.Y. Palmer, whose land and all other worldly possessions amounted to no more than $2000 in value, shared a home with his wife and twenty other dependents.[6] Evidence from probate inventories taken in the early-to-mid century suggest that Mississippi families of median wealth owned an average of only 2.5 beds. This includes mattresses which lay on the floor and trundle beds which could be rolled out of sight during the day.[7] According to Sarah Wadley's diary, the room in which she slept contained two beds for five people and a dog.

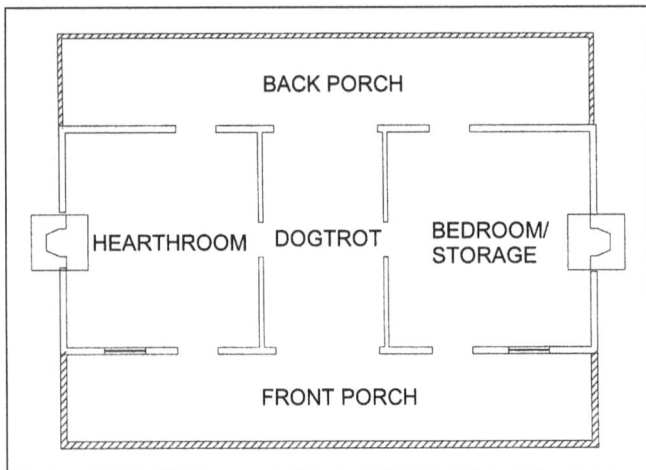

Figure 1: Typical Yeoman Farmhouse, 1830–80

In the complex household Sarah Wadley described, "Miss Mary" was actually a pet name for Sarah's younger sister, but some 25 percent of yeoman Mississippi households in 1860 contained free white adults who were not a part of the householder's immediate family. Although most of these unrelated adults were male farm laborers, about one fifth of them were women such as unmarried sisters and widowed mothers. A somewhat smaller percentage of households contained children who belonged to neither the household head nor to any other resident adults.[8] Evan and Lory may have been Sarah's cousins or other relations, or at least one of them may have belonged to Rose. Rose, whose subordinate status may be inferred from the fact that she was obliged to sleep on the floor, was probably a slave.[9] We can only guess whether her pallet on the floor was more or less comfortable than the sleeping arrangements afforded George's dog. One thing, at least, is certain. In the Wadley household, as in many others in rural Mississippi, where one slept did not necessarily reflect one's familial relationships, nor did consanguinity always determine with whom one shared a bed.

Neither were beds in the Wadleys' house divided strictly by age or gender. Sarah's parents shared their room with two members of the next generation, George and "the baby." The infant's gender, which Sarah does not even mention, was less important than its age and hence its need to be frequently fed and otherwise cared for. The commonality with which mothers put their infants and toddlers to bed beside them is evidenced in the small number of yeoman households that contained cribs or cradles as well as the large number of children whose lives were snuffed out by suffocation.[10] George, the only boy in the household (besides the infant whom, as it happens, was male), may have preferred not to sleep in a room full of females, or perhaps his parents acquiesced to pleas from Sarah and the other girls to not have their four-year-old brother underfoot. Whatever the motives for the Wadleys' sleeping arrangements, personal intimacy for the married couple was apparently a secondary consideration, if in fact it was considered at all.

In the nineteenth-century rural South, household heads usually slept in the room in which the entire family occupied most of its time. This use of space may have reflected practical concerns, such as a desire to continue to work or socialize in the hearthroom while other members of the family slept, or a desire to remain literally at the center of all domestic activities day and night. It may also have suggested status. The man or woman whose bed lay nearest the hearth, winter or summer, symbolically claimed dominion over that space and all that it lit, warmed, or fed. In contrast, children slept wherever there was space, sometimes being forced to move from bed to bed or from one room to another in order to make room for a guest or invalid.[11]

Personal privacy, companionate marriages, efforts to prolong the innocence of childhood, the separation of men's and women's spheres, and the institutionalization of private bedrooms in middle class homes were all part of the Cult of Domesticity that enveloped Victorian America. Scholars have linked the movement toward more private sleeping spaces in many homes outside the South to "the family's desire to present itself as middle class or as rising on the social ladder by [ironically] making a show of privacy."[12] Mid-nineteenth-century advice columnists insisted that separate bedrooms for parents and children and for children of different sexes were as essential as maternal vigilance in preventing young boys and girls from "encountering prematurely the seductive wiles that the wicked world will be sure to throw around them."[13]

In 1856, one housing reformer made explicit the parallels between the home and marketplace, calling for each room in the house, like each member of the family, to have its own clearly defined role and function. "Merchants find the classification of their goods indispensable, or separate rooms for different classes of things" he argued "and why [is] not this principle equally requisite in a complete house?"[14] Adolescents, many believed, should have their own rooms in order to help foster personal independence, a cherished trait among competitors in the new, market-oriented economy. Midwestern farmers hoped that private bedrooms would encourage young adults to remain on the farm instead of running off to the city.[15]

On the southern frontier, neither "seductive wiles," city lights, nor capitalist competition was of immediate concern. For the yeomanry, independence required the collective effort of a household head and all his dependents rather than individual autonomy. The southern version of republican ideology revolved around households that valued women primarily for their ability to be fruitful and multiply and children for their labor.[16] Whereas increasing concern for privacy among non-southern middle-class families saw a concomitant rise in affection toward children and between married partners, southern yeoman farmers continued to view marriage and child-rearing as an essentially economic enterprise. As *The Rural Southerner* quipped in 1871, "Love has been defined as the insane desire to maintain somebody else's daughter."[17]

Yeoman self-sufficiency relied enormously upon women and children. Both farmers and the village merchants who traded in the byproducts of household production were well aware that "all economy was 'domestic economy'."[18] When asked whether his family had ever kept any servants or slaves, a yeoman farmer's son from middle Tennessee responded "no onley white ones and they was my Fathers children."[19] In addition to housework, textile production, and gardening, farming women and children bore primary responsibility for poultry and dairy production and the tending of other small livestock, all of which were essential to their family's ability to support itself.

Women's biological production—what might be called the *ovarian economy*—was every bit as important as the work of women's hands.[20] The number of acres a yeoman farmer could cultivate and the general prosperity of his household largely depended upon the number and age of his children.[21] While many women outside of the South experimented with birth control in an attempt to limit the size of their families, southern white women remained veritable baby factories. A typical yeoman farm wife bore her first child toward the end of her first year of marriage and continued to

produce an infant every two years or so until menopause, physical inca-
pacity, or death prevented her from contributing any longer to the ovarian
economy.[22]

Lawmakers in frontier Mississippi carefully protected the power of
fathers over their domestic workforce. In 1822, five years after Mississippi
became a state, the "taking" of a female child under age fourteen with her
own consent but "against the will of the father, mother, or guardian . . .
with an intent to seduce, deflower, or contract matrimony" could get six
months to a year in prison for her paramour.[23] The key to this offense was
not the law's disdain for the deflowering of a young maiden so much as the
culprit's violation of parental rights to approve the marital choices of their
offspring. For a woman or girl to assume control over her own sexuality
was to rob her male guardian of his prerogative over it. Other statutes bol-
ster this interpretation. An act passed in 1839 outlawed the marriage, concubinage, or prostitution of a female under age fourteen "without parental
consent."[24] The penalty for this offense was twice that set earlier for simply robbing a girl of her virginity. The latter law reflected even less concern
for the virtue of young women and an increase in parental authority, in
that it implicitly gave parents (meaning fathers) the power to approve or
disapprove not only the seduction and marriage but, theoretically at least,
even the concubinage or prostitution of their thirteen-year-old daughters.

Rape, by far the most emotionally charged sexual act in the nineteenth-
century South, combined issues of power and sexuality into one potent
package. The word rape comes from the Latin word *rapere*, meaning "to
take by force" or to kidnap, suggesting a long-standing association
between parental authority and the sexuality of female children. From the
Territorial Act of 1807 through the 1830s, rape in Mississippi consisted of
the "defiling of any maid, widow, or wife contrary to her will." Rather than
simply making it unlawful to violate any woman, the law defined potential victims of rape as only those women whose identities were subsumed
under that of a man other than their assailant. A maid was some man's
daughter. A widow was his mother, and a wife was the mother of his children. Presumably, it was open season on divorcees, spinsters, and other
women who did not fit into one of these three dependent categories.
So crafted, the law revealed a definition of rape as primarily an assault
on a family's honor and the dominion of a husband or father over control
of a woman's body rather than a violation of her own right to do so.[25]

In 1839, Mississippi legislators made some interesting changes to the state's rape law. That year, state law defined rape as "carnally and unlawfully knowing a female child under the age of ten years or by forcibly ravishing any woman of the age of ten years or upwards." Public acceptance of the idea that a ten-year-old female was a "woman" capable of consenting to sexual intercourse with a man reveals a pre-modern regard for female children as virtually the same as female adults. The penalty for "child stealing" in 1839, without any explicitly sexual intent but presumably for the purposes of procuring the child's labor, was several times more severe than the penalty for child marriage or prostitution.[26] Together these laws sent the unmistakable message that extracting work from children was far more important than protecting them from sex at an early age.

On the yeoman farmsteads of Mississippi, sexuality was ever present. In 1860, the Mississippi landscape was positively overrun with domesticated animals. Almost every family owned at least one horse or mule, there were about as many cattle as people, and pigs outnumbered humans by more than two to one.[27] This meant that understanding the role of the rooster in the henhouse or the relationship between the bull in the field and the cow in the barn was second nature to all rural Mississippians. Given the southern custom of "turning out" livestock onto the open range to graze or forage—and breed—as nature would allow, reproduction was as visible a part of the environment as the production of cotton or corn. Yet one did not have to stray far from the home to learn the facts of life. Procreation was a natural, observable, and eminently desirable fact of life indoors as well.

Breastfeeding provided a common avenue for imparting some of this sexual knowledge to children. In spite of the modern mythology surrounding the prevalent use of wet nurses by antebellum slaveholders, the overwhelming majority of elite southern white women breast fed their own infants. One may surmise that virtually all non-slaveholding white women, who were physically able, did so as well. Census evidence further supports this supposition. Depending on how often and for how long an infant was nursed, breast-feeding could limit female fertility to one birth about every two years. Children of farming families recorded in the population census of 1860 tend to be spaced at least two years apart, with infant and child mortality accounting for most of those siblings separated by appreciably larger gaps. Since children who survived infancy were normally weaned at the end of their first year, the average woman of childbearing age had a respite of only one or two months every other year during which she was not either pregnant or nursing.[28] Growing up amid this cycle of gestation and lactation, older children were as cognizant of the generative role of their mother's body as they were of the fact that their own milk came from the family's cow.

In households where children shared sleeping quarters with their parents, childhood familiarity with sexual activity was especially common.[29] As we have already seen, in the two-room houses of typical Mississippi farmsteads, couples often shared a room, if not a bed, with some of their children. Antebellum traveler Frederick Law Olmsted complained that, during his visits to the backcountry, he often spent the night in the same bed as one of his unpretentious hosts. The practice clearly offended Olmsted, but the custom was second nature to common farmers.[30]

The material impossibility of obtaining physical privacy, along with the productive and reproductive realities of rural life, inevitably exposed rural young people to sex at an early age. Each night, in homes that slept an average of three people per room and which contained fewer than half as many beds as occupants, infants were suckling at their mothers' breasts and future siblings were being conceived, while older brothers and sisters, visiting relatives, and possibly even a stranger like Frederick Law Olmsted, lay close by.

Some quite public, socially accepted methods for allowing young people to express their own sexual energy centered around the annual harvest celebration known as the corn shucking. As its name implies, a corn shucking was a work-sharing ritual in which friends, neighbors, and relations gathered together after a successful harvest to pull the husks off of ears of corn. In addition to consuming drams of corn liquor, singing "corn songs," and competing in corn-shucking contests, there was an important sexual element to the corn shucking. During the actual shucking, any young man who uncovered a red ear of corn won the right to kiss the woman or girl of his choice.[31]

Actually obtaining a kiss often involved chasing, and no doubt grabbing and holding the lucky female until one had received his reward, but the appeal of this ritual went beyond minor foreplay. Why was kissing associated with red corn? We can only speculate. For one thing, red ears were obviously rare, as was probably the opportunity to forcibly kiss a woman or girl in front of her friends and family. Also, the color red represents the menstruation that marks the passage of a young girl into womanhood, as well as the female blood that often accompanies the loss of virginity. Southern white men also relished any excuse for competition, and the red-ear ritual provided an opportunity to assert one's virility in the presence of one's male companions. Some men were known to stack the deck, so to speak, by bringing a red ear with them to a shucking and whipping it out at an opportune moment.[32] The corn cob itself, particularly in the hands of a man pursuing an eligible woman, presents a strong phallic image. In his novel *Sanctuary*, William Faulkner employs a sinister version of the cob-as-phallus in the rape of Temple Drake. More humorous tales of women simulating sex with corn cobs and similar objects like candles, bananas, bottles, and even snakes or eels are widespread in southern folklore.[33]

Another sexually charged ritual associated with corn shuckings, barn-raisings, and other communal activities was a game known as "shaking the cat." Quilting bees were common pastimes for women while the men in their company were engaged in work sharing. After a quilt was finished, young unmarried women might gather around, each gripping a corner or side of the quilt. Then someone would throw a cat onto the center of the quilt while the young women shook their arms vigorously. The cat, a symbol of both virginity and old maidenhood as well as composure and self-control, would be obviously distressed by this commotion and head for the nearest way out of there, much as a young woman might fear her first sexual encounter or might hope to be saved from the prospect of spinsterhood. The girl to whom the cat ran first was proclaimed the next to marry.[34]

The significance of these rituals lies not in their sexual implications alone but in the attitudes of rural nineteenth-century folk toward them. Because young people engaged in these games with the encouragement or at least permission of their parents, they show an apparent acceptance—even eager anticipation—of the fact that lost virginity was an eventual consequence of youthful flirtation. Further, the delight that spectators took in red ears of corn and shaken cats shows the levity, rather than puritanical severity, with which the antebellum yeomanry approached youthful sexuality. Finally, as harvest rituals, these customs show the connections yeoman families drew between natural cycles of agricultural production and human reproduction.

Members of societies so oriented to production and reproduction have historically not tried to repress individual sexuality, but have in fact encouraged it as a duty and a joy.[35] Although there is little direct evidence for the "joy" of marital sex on the southern frontier, laws and court cases offer evidence of the duty of procreation. In cases where married couples were either unable or unwilling to propagate the species, law makers and state courts did their best to encourage marital fertility. The failure of self-working farmers and aspiring planters to marry and produce heirs made the enormous effort required to carve a farm out of the wilderness ultimately pointless if not physically impossible and threatened the long-term success of new settlements. For these reasons, the production of free labor who would later become legitimate heirs to the results of that labor was an extremely high priority.

Mississippi legislators passed the state's first law regarding divorce in 1822.[36] The code provided only three causes for which a divorce could be granted: impotence, desertion, and adultery. In citing only these grounds, legislators were attempting to use legalized divorce to support family ties rather than to weaken them.[37] Like Quakers, Baptists, and other Protestant denominations that sanctioned divorce in order to allow the godly to "separate from the ungodly and to join the regenerate," proponents of divorce in early nineteenth-century Mississippi could have argued that their intent was to allow the fruitful to separate from the unfruitful and to join a productive household.[38] The cotton and corn of yeoman farms was sown from the seeds of marital duty. By allowing for divorce in cases of impotence, for example, state legislators ensured that a fertile woman would not go to waste. After obtaining a divorce from her impotent husband, she could then remarry and conceive the children that would provide her new husband with much needed labor, her family with heirs, and the community with citizens.

Divorce on the grounds of desertion stemmed from much the same rationale as impotence. If a husband, or wife, left home without returning at all for five years, his or her spouse could be considered a widow or widower. In 1822, five years was an interminable amount of time in the pages of the Farmer's Almanac or according to the ticking of a woman's biological clock, and seemed ample time for an abandoned husband or wife to wait before resuming the activities of a productive (and reproductive) household. By the 1850s, the waiting period for a divorce on the grounds of desertion had been reduced to three years. Still, the court was not disposed to play fast and loose with one of its most vital institutions. When, in 1851, Elizabeth Gaillard sought a divorce after her husband had deserted her for three years, the court found that during that time her husband had returned for a period of ten days after which the couple had separated again. Reluctant to dissolve a potentially productive union, the jurors decided to deny Elizabeth's plea for freedom until at least three years had passed from the time of the attempted reconciliation.[39]

As with impotence and desertion, divorces for adultery were intended to assure the production of legitimate progeny. When the inheritance of a family's hard-won property was not at stake, the law dealt with adultery strictly as a deviant sexual act separately under "An Act for the Punishment of Crimes and Misdemeanors." Under that act, proven adulterers were levied a fine of anywhere from $100 to $500.[40] "Buggery" could be fined under the same statute, but neither anal intercourse nor sex with livestock was apparently grounds for divorce. Homosexuality and bestiality violated socially accepted sexual ethics, but neither necessarily interfered with the economic mission of the family, and thus were not considered worthy of terminating an otherwise productive marriage.

Three quarters of a century later, this view had changed only subtly. In 1905, Frances E. Crutcher sued her husband George T. Crutcher for divorce after having discovered his "addiction" to "improper intimacy . . . with the male sex."[41] Her attorney argued that, although not strictly adultery since the sexual act "practiced by the defendant [was] with his mouth", the crime known as "pederasty" was "infinitely more wrong and greater cause and surely more destructive of the . . . objects of the marital relation."[42] The court recognized that George Crutcher's actions caused his wife "mental suffering to the extent of affecting her health, and would give rise to serious apprehension of communication of disease in case of the continuance of cohabitation."[43] Her health, it would seem, was of greater concern to this judge than any idealistic notions regarding the importance of companionate marriage. Since cruelty had become an accepted cause for divorce by the early 1900s, the court granted Frances Crutcher's plea, yet the court's opinion betrayed an enduringly traditional view of the objects of wedlock, stating that "unnatural practices of the kind charged here . . . would make the marriage relation so revolting to her that it would become impossible for her to discharge the duties of wife, and would defeat the whole purpose of the relation."[44] Whatever other duties Frances Crutcher may have performed, her primary duty as the court saw it was to have sex with her husband since the "whole purpose of the [marriage] relation" was to produce children.

Even when it involved a human female, adultery on the part of men was not greeted with enormous trepidation. In 1851, for example, Phebe Armstrong sued her husband for divorce because of his adulterous affair with a Mrs. Tubbs, which had been "a subject of notoriety in the neighborhood for several years." George Armstrong did not deny the affair and in fact claimed Mrs. Tubbs' oldest child as his own, sending her to school and "otherwise manifesting a deep interest in her." Phebe, who had been aware of the other woman for some time, forgave her husband and even agreed to "take the little girl (meaning the child he had by that woman) and do for it as if it were her own."[45]

The betrayal of an adulterous husband meant private grief or public humiliation and perhaps venereal disease for his wife but did not often mean the end of her marriage. Divorcing wives frequently accused husbands not only of adultery but also of additional transgressions such as drinking, swearing, gambling, or violence. If the injury to her pride or other offenses of her wayward husband were great enough, a wife might want to leave, but most rural farm women had nowhere to go nor the means to get there. As the subordinate of the two parties, the woman, her children, and their property were under the complete control of her husband. Legal wrangling could, and often did, take years to resolve, during which time she would be forced to manage alone. Divorces were also costly, and the outcome was by no means certain. Women of limited means had little choice but to put up with a husband's philandering.

After enduring "extreme ill treatment" by her husband, being thrown out of her home, and told that she was "no longer his wife," Phebe Armstrong still "begged to be permitted to remain." Yet, her husband ordered her off his property, despite the fact that she had no means of supporting herself, and threatened to beat her again if she ever returned. The local Chancery Court granted Phebe a divorce plus alimony. George appealed, citing that his wife had condoned his adultery.[46] The appeals court ultimately decided in Phebe's favor, declaring that the doctrine of condonation did not apply in her case or in fact in the case of most women. "A woman," the court reasoned, "may submit to necessity." Wives were expected to put up with behavior in a husband that a man would not permit in a wife. "Her want of control over him; the difficulty she may find in quitting his house, or withdrawing from his bed . . . renders it not improper that she should, for a time, show a patient forbearance." She "has not the same guard over his honor," the Court continued, "has not the same means to enforce the matrimonial vow—his guilt is not of the same consequence to her."[47] In this ironic ruling, the court simultaneously granted a woman both personal and financial independence while under-scoring the imbalance of sexual power that characterized marriage in southern frontier society.

As the court in the case of *Armstrong v. Armstrong* implied, men's adultery was far less threatening than women's. In southern evangelical churches, disciplinary committees censured men five times more fre-quently than women and for a wider variety of offenses. Adultery was the one crime for which evangelicals singled out women for harsher scrutiny. Disciplinary committees charged women with sexual offenses more often, and their punishments were more severe. Churches nearly always banished adulteresses from their membership, and, unlike all other manner of sin-ners, even those unfaithful wives who repented and reformed usually found their former brothers and sisters unforgiving.[48] Because men con-trolled church disciplinary committees, as they did civil courts, it stands to reason that these bodies viewed affronts to patriarchal power as among the most heinous of crimes. Female adultery was, at its core, a challenge to the control of white men over the reproductive capability of their wives. "Why is adultery punishable at all?" one attorney rhetorically asked. "Simply because it is an invasion of social right, and the disturbance of the course of descent."[49]

Both law and custom encouraged men to behave, literally, like masters in their homes. Phoebe Kenley complained in 1838 that her husband forced her to endure "ill treatment and abusive language" until she felt compelled to take refuge in the home of relatives. One can almost hear the condescension in the voice of the judge as he informed Phoebe that the court would not protect her from "mere austerity of temper, petulance of manners, rudeness of language, a want of civil attention, even occasional sallies of passion."[50] Almost twenty years later, Eliza Waskam got a similar response when she charged that her husband James was "an habitual drunkard." His conduct toward their small children was "vicious, inde-cent, and demoralizing," she said, while his treatment of her was "violent, abusive, and cruel." The unsympathetic Chancery Court judge lectured that "mere intemperance in a man's habits, harshness of manner, and . . . indecency of conduct" might injure Eliza's "sense of delicacy," but were of no concern to the court.[51] With regard to marital relations, the concern of the court was to uphold an institution based not on affection or even civility but on patriarchal authority and household production and to underscore the subordinate role of women within it.

In 1860, nearly all Mississippians lived spread out across the countryside among fields of corn or cotton and freely ranging livestock. At that time, only twenty-one thousand people—less than three percent of the state's population—lived in towns. Twenty years later, while the country at large was in the midst of a post-Civil War industrial boom and northern cities were growing exponentially, the proportion of Mississippians living off of farms had altered very little. After 1880, however, the landscape began to change rather drastically. Between 1880 and 1890, the town population of the state more than doubled. By the next decade it increased by another 72 percent. Although one still could not consider Mississippi significantly urbanized in 1910, the number of people in the state who lived removed from the cycles of production and reproduction had increased ten fold since 1860.[52]

The decline of household self-sufficiency around the turn of the twentieth century was also evident in the barnyard. Whereas there had once been over a million and a half pigs in the state among a population of less than 800,000 people, by 1900 humans outnumbered swine by 85 percent.[53] This precipitous decline in pork production may indicate a more diversified diet, or a growing preference for chicken or beef. But it also suggests the decreasing likelihood of individual acquaintance with livestock reproduction and a corresponding decline in concern for and observability of procreation around and in the household.

In 1892, the same year that Mississippi legislators denounced stallions as obscene, the state issued an elaborate set of new fencing laws designed to sunder the traditional yeoman practice of allowing livestock to range freely across the landscape. The law required all owners of horses, mules, jacks, jennets, cattle, hogs, sheep, or goats to enclose their animals within fences at least five feet high made of rails, planks, pickets, hedges, wires "or other substantial material."[54] Animals that strayed onto the property of law-abiding citizens could be confiscated. Although the primary intent of fencing laws was to reduce the self-sufficiency of rural African Americans, thus assuring a more subservient labor force, they had a similarly stultifying effect on the independence of poor and middling white farmers.[55]

In addition to losing their livestock, fines, and other penalties, farmers who refused to pen up their animals faced the condemnation of their communities. The fencing statute empowered an *ad hoc* committee of three neighbors of the offending farmer to dictate the punishment they deemed "reasonable and just." This clause gave judgmental evangelicals a substantial bludgeon that they could use to subdue locals who chose to live outside the bounds of increasingly strict community norms. It stands to reason that, in addition to blacks and poor whites, those yeomen who engaged in domestic violence or maintained a profane or sexually uninhibited lifestyle would receive harsher penalties than would large landowners, churchgoers, and other more upstanding citizens. Further, fence laws assured that animal reproduction would take place largely out of public view.

Perhaps the most telling evidence of the declining centrality of the ovarian economy in turn-of-the-century Mississippi involves changes in household size and composition and the division of household space. In 1900, the average household in the state had 4.8 members, a full person less than forty years earlier and only slightly above that of the non-southern middle class. In counties that had been dominated by yeoman farmers in the antebellum era, households continued to be slightly larger than in the state as a whole, averaging 5.1 members in 1900. Still, the fact that these households too were shrinking indicates the decreasing importance of the ovarian economy, as the number of one's children was no longer tethered to one's level of prosperity. In addition to having fewer children, by 1900 Mississippi households contained fewer extended family members and non-related individuals, tending instead toward nuclear families.[56]

While the average turn-of-the-century Mississippi family, consisting of two parents and three to five children, was becoming smaller than the previous generation, its houses were growing larger. Beginning in the last quarter of the nineteenth century, the owners of traditional two-room houses in rural Mississippi began to—in the words of their inhabitants— "box in" their back porches to create private bedrooms.[57] Using the existing exterior wall of the house and the porch roof and floor, they needed only three more walls to achieve a new, more private, space. At the same time, the builders of new farm houses opted to forego the back porch all

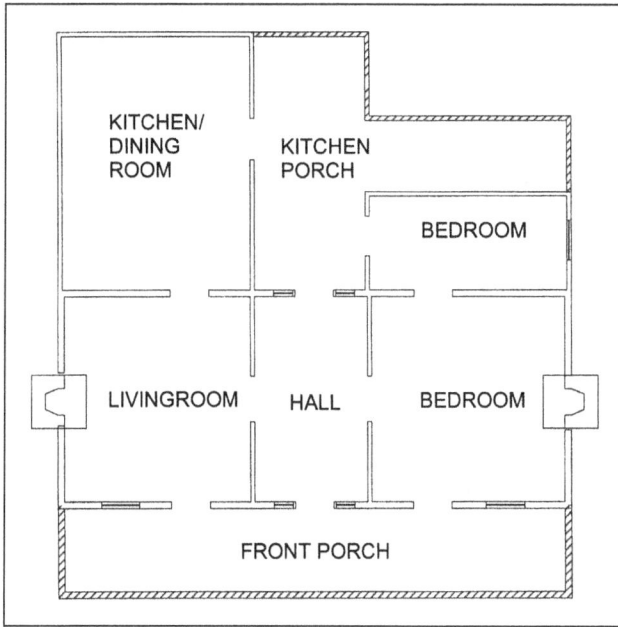

Figure 2: Typical Mississippi Farmhouse 1880–1910

together and construct one or more rear shed rooms from the outset. By 1910, 93 percent of the vernacular houses in counties that had once been predominantly yeoman consisted of three to five rooms, an average growth of 1.26 rooms per home. Their owners designated most of these new rooms as private or semi-private bedrooms.[58]

These larger homes also contained more beds than ever, averaging between four and five beds per household.[59] By the early 1900s, if beds were apportioned equally, and assuming that all married couples shared a bed, every child of a middling household in traditionally yeoman areas of Mississippi could have had a bed of his or her own. Although few of the region's children had an entire room to him or her self, parents almost always earmarked the first private bedrooms in their homes exclusively for children of the same sex.

When first built in the 1890s, the Tishomingo County home of Tobe and Nancy Eaton consisted of four rooms. One of the two front rooms served as a bedroom for the couple's two sons, Lee and Fletcher. Tobe, Nancy, and their youngest child Mattie slept in the adjacent front room, which doubled as the family's living room. Behind this multipurpose room was a bedroom for Tobe and Nancy's older daughters, Liddy and Eller. The other rear room held a combination kitchen and dining area.[60] Like their relatives and neighbors, Tobe and Nancy Eaton chose the gender segregation of their children over a private bedroom for themselves.

The nearby home belonging to Tobe's brother and sister-in-law, John and Fannie Eaton, followed a similar pattern. In the 1890s, John and Fannie and their children, who included two boys and three girls, divvied up sleeping space in the home's two main rooms. Around 1900 they added a rear bedroom for their two oldest boys, John Elliott and Oscar, leaving the boys' sisters Mattie, Emma, and Carrie to share one of the two larger rooms. The elder Eatons continued the traditional yeoman practice of sleeping in the multipurpose hearthroom for the next fourteen years.[61]

Around the turn of the twentieth century, John Eaton built a one-room house across the road for the couple's son Oscar and his new wife. The construction of single-pen dwellings had declined significantly in the last decades of the nineteenth century, comprising only 5 percent of the vernacular houses built in Mississippi after 1880.[62] The younger Eatons' acceptance of a one-room plan suggests the continued ability of rural Mississippians to perceive a single room as a multi-functional space into the twentieth century, but Oscar Eaton's home ultimately came to symbolize the decline of that worldview.

By 1914, Oscar Eaton and his family no longer lived across the road from his parents. Oscar's father John, with the help of some male family members and friends, pushed the one-room house onto a bed of logs and rolled it across the road, aligning it at a right angle to John and Fannie's home. They then "tied" the newer building to the front of the older home by lining up the rear porch of the addition with the front porch of the main house. Thus the Eatons created an L-shaped plan consisting of a sitting room, a kitchen/dining room, and two bedrooms, plus a private bedroom in the new wing. Finally, after two decades of marriage and six children, John and Fannie Eaton had a bedroom of their own.

The well-known influence of religion on southern culture is of more than passing consequence to changing views toward sex and privacy. Evangelical momentum generated during the Civil War steamed into the post-war period, forming the basis of what one historian characterized as a "widespread institutional commitment to a religious vision of reality" between 1870 and 1930.[63] Shell-shocked by the defeated image of Confederate manhood, white clergymen in the post-bellum South elevated the sexual virtue of white women to a "holy idea" symbolizing war-time heroics, the comfort of home, and the innocence of sexual purity.[64]

Lost Cause mythology, created by a post-war imagination that yearned for a glorious past it had never possessed, erased the productive, sensual, self-working woman of the antebellum southern yeomanry and replaced her with the image of the physically weak, emotionally fragile, and frigidly chaste southern belle type. Much of the southern social and political discourse of the late nineteenth century served to elevate and preserve this new southern icon, white womanhood. As white women became the primary vessels of public morality, the home became the moral hub from which all efforts to redeem southern society radiated. The rearing of Christian children and the keeping of a Christian home replaced participation in the ovarian economy as the most vital contribution white southern women could make to their households.

By the turn of the twentieth century, Mississippi jurists no longer viewed white women as sexual beings, and patriarchs no longer looked upon youthful sexual experimentation with permissiveness or amusement. In court cases involving seduction and other crimes against women and girls, there evolved, in the words of one appellate court judge, a "legal presumption [that] need be neither charged nor proved" that "in the multitudinous and varying conditions and ranks of womanhood, personal chastity is the rule; a lapse from virtue is the rare and painful exception."[65]

When, in 1892, the state of Mississippi banned stallions from the sight of church congregants, legislators bolstered the popular perception that the virtue of white women and children needed and deserved protection from unbridled sexuality. In attempting to make virile beasts less visible, lawmakers were heeding demands of evangelical moralists for a more sterile environment, forcing sex and other vices out of public places. They were also giving legal voice to deep-seated tensions involving the explosive combination of sex, race, and power.

The violently masculine image of the unrestrained stallion called to mind a far more sinister threat to white womanhood and girlhood than that posed by a mere glimpse of equine anatomy—the burgeoning fear of rape. Although the part of the Mississippi Code of 1904 regarding rape still defined the act as "carnal knowledge of a female under ten years of age, or, being over ten, against her will," the new penalty for rape was death "as in the case of murder."[66] Further, the 1904 act stated:

> In all cases where the female is under ten years of age, it shall not be necessary to prove penetration of the female's private parts where it is shown that the private parts of the female have been lacerated or torn in the attempt to have carnal knowledge of her.[67]

Hence, in turn-of-the-century Mississippi, even attempted rape could be a capital crime, and violation of the female body was tantamount to homicide.

Concerns about the virtue of white women combined with growing distrust of black men to create the hysteria W. J. Cash called the southern rape complex. Relying on traditional concerns about patriarchal control over their offspring and deeply-rooted racism which equated blackness with sin, white people throughout the South traditionally viewed sex between white women and black men as taboo. By the 1890s, this social proscription against interracial sex had been elevated to dogma in the new civil religion. The ritualistic castration of black male lynching victims throughout the late nineteenth and early twentieth centuries reveals the ferocity with which white men reacted to the perceived threat of African American autonomy (not to mention anatomy). Lynch mobs, like those who scorned well-endowed horses, acted out with surgical precision the desires of a growing number of white Mississippians to excise uncontrolled sexuality from their midst and reassert a sense of mastery over their environment.[68]

Although mob violence had been something of a tradition in Mississippi since the earliest incursions of Euro-Americans into the territory, emotive exhortations of white southerners regarding supposed threats to the purity of white womanhood and the ritualistic lynching of black men both reached a climax in the South between 1889 and 1918. In the 1890s, lynchings were most common in areas like the cotton uplands of Mississippi, which had once contained a majority of yeoman farmers and few slaves. An influx of itinerant African Americans in search of alternatives to plantation labor caused some whites to feel surrounded by "strange niggers" who had no ties to white neighbors or employers, no long-standing local relationships, nor any support network within an existing black community.[69] The resulting air of paranoia and uncertainty proved fatal for many. In historically yeoman areas of Mississippi, the number of African American lynchings per capita was among the highest in the South.[70] The fear and insecurity that motivated this horrific recourse to violence seems inextricable from the simultaneous rise of conviction among common white Mississippians that it was time to shelter their wives and daughters inside boxed-in private bedrooms.

In yeoman farming households in the rural South, sexuality was a ubiquitous and eagerly anticipated part of every day life. As Mississippians neared the turn of the twentieth century, new values like virtue and chastity emerged to dominate sexual discourse. Laws governing women and children began to treat them like objects requiring kindness and protection instead of like servile dependents. Common white families became guardians of a righteous society instead of miniature productive enterprises. Hence, the position of the household in the cultural landscape underwent a concurrent evolution.

The wave of bedroom building among white householders in Mississippi after 1880 is evidence that the often-voiced concern for the sexual purity of white women and girls around the turn of the twentieth century was not *merely* rhetorical. Just as the multi-functional hearthrooms of the mid-nineteenth-century were symptomatic of the ovarian economy in which they were born, the widespread effort to add segregated bedrooms to the two-room houses once occupied by yeoman farmers reflected a more insular, less sexually permissive culture that no longer valued self-sufficiency. After 1880, white females found themselves enveloped in an expanding civil churchyard that held substantially different views about their value to society than those common a half-century before, protected and confined within an ideological landscape as narrow as a fenced-in pasture. The champions of public virtue and social control similarly swept stallions and other reminders of the yeoman way of life out of sight, behind barriers that both literally and figuratively divided an old world of production and reproduction from a new one of apprehension and isolation.

.

Part II

SLAVERY

RELATIONS WHICH MIGHT BE DISASTROUS

Natchez Indians and African Slaves
in French Louisiana

DAVID J. LIBBY

For generations prior to European contact, the main Natchez village stood on a bluff overlooking the Mississippi River. A temple atop a ceremonial mound served as the center of Natchez religious and political life. The village chief and high priest, called the Great Sun, recited incantations morning and evening to ensure the rising and the setting of the sun. The Natchez believed their aristocracy was descended from the sun, and thus called this class the Suns. Beneath the Suns in the Natchez hierarchy were the Nobles, followed by the "honored ones." At the bottom of Natchez society were the "stinkards." The stratification of Natchez society appeared permanent to European explorers.

The Natchez were among the most powerful groups in the Mississippi valley and unreceptive to overtures from European explorers. The Spaniard Hernando de Soto was refused an audience with the Great Sun in 1541.[1] Over a century later, Rene Robert, Cavalier, Sieur de La Salle, arrived, hoping to establish a colony under the French standard.[2] The Natchez were by this time weakened as a result of diseases introduced by European contact. They still remained less than friendly, but the French arrived with plans to stay.[3]

French plans to colonize the Mississippi Valley were based on a number of assumptions. They believed that Natchez and nearby Choctaw Indians would be friendly, and respect France as an ally and protector. The French also assumed that African and Indian slaves would provide labor to make the land profitable. However well the French planned their colonial efforts, they never considered the possibility that Africans and Indians might band together against the colonial presence. The French experience at Natchez illustrates a moment of possibility, where Senegambian slaves, Natchez Indians, and Choctaw Indians variously formed alliances and animosities that destabilized the colonial presence to the point that French plans to establish a colony at Natchez were abandoned.

French colonizers found the Natchez region attractive for many reasons. "The Natchez," as the French called it, was the first well-drained piece of land on the Mississippi River north of New Orleans. The region was not densely populated, the result of epidemics that followed De Soto's visit. European disease forced the consolidation of many Indian tribes. The weakened Natchez absorbed the remnants of several other local groups and became one of these amalgam peoples.[4] Adjacent farmlands boasted some of the world's richest topsoil, producing substantial crops with minimal effort. The hardwood forests around Natchez were parklike in comparison to the surrounding swampy lowlands of the Mississippi valley. An early French visitor wrote that the Natchez region was "even more beautiful than I had realized. There are peach, plum, walnut, and fig trees everywhere."[5] Another described "flower-adorned prairies, broken by little hills upon which there are thickets of all kinds of fragrant trees."[6] All of these features made the region attractive to the French.

Initially, French settlement near the Natchez was part of the French effort to compete with other European powers by staking out New World empires. French explorers attempted to establish outposts on both sides of the Mississippi River, especially near Indian settlements, for the purposes of trade and defense. The first French settlement at the Natchez consisted of a small trading post, along with a military installation to protect the settlers. The French hoped for friendly relations with the Natchez, while profiting in the deerskin trade.[7]

Nearby lived the Choctaw, more populous but less centralized than the Natchez. The Choctaw lived in villages spread throughout modern-day southern Mississippi. The Choctaw organized their society into matrilineal clans, and did not have the rigid class distinctions that the Natchez did. Their power structure was divided among male war chiefs and peace chiefs, who achieved their status by merit—either brave acts in war, or displays of wisdom in peace. Chiefs, or Mingos, had little real power in the modern sense, for tribal decisions were made by consensus. The Chiefs' opinions carried weight, but they could not force or prevent anyone's actions.[8] As a result, the Choctaw society had no central authority, and was united more by familial bond than political organization.

Choctaw relations with the French were friendlier than Franco-Natchez relations. While the French had little affinity for the Choctaw social structure, they found the Choctaw to be both generous, and quite ready to trade.[9] Conflicts occasionally arose between the two societies, but the Choctaw proved themselves to be dependable as guides and military allies.[10] The French viewed the Choctaw as a natural ally, perhaps because of English relations with the traditional adversary of the Choctaw, the Chickasaw.[11] In the early decades of the eighteenth century, as the Choctaw fought off the slaving raids of the English and Chickasaw, they found French guns and bullets to be quite helpful. At the same time, the French gladly purchased and enslaved prisoners captured by the Choctaw.[12]

Concepts of slavery among the southeastern Indians differed significantly from European concepts of slavery. Indians defined slavery in terms of membership in a society. Choctaw society extended a series of familial protections to its members through its clan structure. Outsiders—including slaves—had no such protection. A captured stranger might face torture, maiming, or even death, in addition to enslavement. Those enslaved held no status, and had no guarantee of security. Slaves in southeastern Indian societies remained captives, with no social protection. Slavery was a way of defining social otherness rather than an economic activity. Few Indians kept slaves. A slave was something of a luxury and a sign of affluence. The Natchez also had concepts of slavery, but in the thorough, albeit confused, descriptions of their social structure written by French visitors, little mention of slavery is made. Thus Natchez slavery was probably quite rare.[13]

While the southeastern Indians had well-developed notions of slavery, it was not a widespread practice. Indian societies had no place for large-scale slavery. A household might own a single slave, but probably no more. Slaves generally worked alongside their masters. Socially they were scorned and denied the protections of clan membership.[14] The Indians practiced a brand of slavery that ostracized its subjects, and at the same time created opportunities for their assimilation.

As both Choctaw and Natchez Indians viewed the French developing their own form of slavery in the Natchez region, they probably were only half-aware of the kind of social structure that was developing. They were familiar with the concept of slavery, and must have recognized that the slaves the French brought were forced labor. The economic or racial under-pinnings of the French slave system were foreign. Initially Indians made little distinction between the French and the African slaves who accompanied them. The French settlers and their African slaves arrived in Natchez together, and they were both outsiders.

Early plans to develop Louisiana with slaves involved the trading of Indians for Afro-Caribbean slaves. The King initially resisted such designs as they promised to build resentment among the Indians. But Louisiana's governor, Jean Baptiste Le Moyne, Sieur de Bienville, suggested as early as 1706 that, owing to the "facility" that Indian slaves "have in deserting," colonists could not control them well. He hoped to "sell these slaves to the American islands [i.e. the West Indies] in order to get negroes in exchange, since the English follow the same practice," adding that "this commerce is quite necessary."[15] Because of this request, Louis XIV of France reluctantly authorized the colonists to sell "those slaves to the American islands in order to obtain negroes in exchange."[16] Such plans, while discussed and authorized, never went into operation. Ultimately French Louisiana would get its slaves directly from the Atlantic trade.

In 1717, France ceded the Louisiana colony to the Company of the Indies, a private concern that promised to develop and populate the colony, in similar fashion to English colonies in British North America.[17] Modeled on the success that the British had achieved in plantation agriculture, the Company of the Indies planned a plantation economy for Louisiana. The French constantly observed the British colonial efforts in Virginia and South Carolina, and either tried the same or attempted to learn from their mistakes. The Company began its plans to establish a plantation society during the 1720s.

In Natchez, a small French trading post and military complement lived alongside the Indians. As reparation for their loss in the First Natchez War, the Natchez constructed a fort for the French in 1716. The French named it Fort Rosalie, after the wife of the French Naval Minister, Compte de Ponchartrain.[18] The Company of the Indies made concessions, or grants of land, to virtually any Frenchman who would settle. Three hundred colonists requested farm-sized concessions, although the actual number in residence was much smaller. Two large concessions went to Marc-Antoine Hubert and the company itself.[19]

Because the goal of these concessions was to grow staple crops, Natchez faced a labor shortage. The French faced a challenge in recruiting laborers for their colonies, let alone settlers in general. Their difficulty extended from the absence of major population pressures at home, a factor which had helped the British to populate their own colonies. In addition, the popular descriptions of Louisiana in France portrayed an exciting, but dangerous land populated by terrifying beasts, bloodthirsty infidels, and lascivious women. Narratives of Louisiana were entertaining, but they hardly convinced prospective colonists to migrate; indeed they probably scared people off. While it was good to have the colonies, for they brought glory to France, they were no place for French people to settle.[20] Those French who came to the colonies in the early eighteenth century were either convicts, outcasts, or from especially impoverished regions.[21] The French resorted to recruiting Germans to populate settlements on the Louisiana coast.[22] Natchez, on the fringe of the colony attracted even fewer colonists. Seeking a labor force for the Louisiana colony, the company of the Indies turned to slavery. In keeping with a colonizing tradition established in the sugar islands, the French turned to African slavery.

Virtually all the Africans brought to French Louisiana came from the Senegambia region of West Africa.[23] Much like the Indians and the French, West Africans were no strangers to slavery. They, too, had their own social construction of slavery. Senegambians defined slavery in terms of membership in society. In Senegambia, slavery took three forms. The first was "trade slavery." Trade slaves were those just recently captured and enslaved through war or slave raiding expeditions. The children of trade slaves formed a second group that was one step closer to full membership in society. This brand of captivity is best described as "subordinate membership" in society. These two types of slavery were closer in fact to a process of assimilation than to chattel slavery. Indeed, Senegambian slaveowners held no property rights in their slaves, and thus slavery was essentially a social rather than an economic relationship.[24]

A third form of slavery in Senegambia was royal slavery. Royal slaves served regional kings as administrators and bureaucrats, a sort of power conservatory. Their work prevented aristocrats or others from seizing a power base and undermining the king's rule. Other royal slaves served in the military, and in times of peace they constituted the only standing army in a kingdom. One ethnicity particularly prized by both Senegambian kings and the Company of the Indies was the Bambarra. They had a reputation for loyalty in administrative and military slavery. Bambarra loyalty stemmed from their lack of personal interests in regional politics, because they came from the distant interior.[25]

As the French ships carried slaves away from the African coast toward North America, the captives saw dim prospects for their future. African slave traders terrorized the slaves with tales of cannibalistic Europeans who bought them for food.[26] As they waited in the stockade at Fort St. Louis on the Senegal coast for the arrival of the slave ship, their health deteriorated. The infamous journey across the Atlantic added to their misery.[27] Quite often the slaves in transit rebelled.[28] More frequently, they fell sick owing to malnutrition. By the time of their arrival, weakened by sickness and malnutrition, the slaves were in no condition to be forced into labor. Already enslaved when leaving Africa, they still knew little of the form of slavery practiced by the French. The disjunction between the more assimilative west African slavery and the exploitative bondage of the New World would strike its victims only after they resigned themselves to their fate.[29]

French slavery had little in common with the enslavement practices of southeastern Indians or Senegambians. Three aspects in particular are most notable about French slavery in distinction to Indian and African slavery. First, French slavery was racial slavery. The French never enslaved Europeans, but readily enslaved Indians and Africans. Second, the French practiced a form of slavery based on property rights, known as chattel slavery. The possibility of manumission was much less than in African or Indian societies, for the master-slave relationship was economic more than social. Finally, French slavery was plantation slavery. The chief reason that the French brought slaves to the sugar islands and to Louisiana was to cultivate export crops for the market economy. From its beginnings, the French system of slavery in the New World was intimately related to the mercantilist economy of the French Empire, in sharp contrast to the traditional assimilative slavery of both Senegambians and Southeastern Indians. The social and legal distinctions were not immediately apparent to Senegambian slaves upon their arrival. As a result, the slaves could accommodate French slavery, for initially it resembled the slavery that they had seen and experienced in West Africa.[30]

Soon after their arrival in Natchez, African slaves fell victim to tensions between the French and the Natchez. In 1722, following a trade dispute, the Natchez attempted to drive the French and their slaves out of their territory. On October 22, Natchez warriors attacked several slaves who were cutting wood near their settlement, beginning what the French called the Second Natchez War. This attack resulted in the death of one slave and the injury of another. Until the French counterattacked, the Natchez fired on anyone who left the safety of Fort Rosalie, and settlers and slaves alike were unable to tend to the crops.[31] The French responded by forging an alliance with neighboring Indian groups, including the Choctaw, and counterattacking.[32] The French-Indian alliance made victory quick and decisive. It weakened the Natchez considerably.

In such moments of instability some African slaves took advantage of the chaos to secure their freedom. For example in the final settlement of this conflict, the French insisted upon, and received, the return of a slave who had "taken refuge among them [the Natchez] for a long time and makes them seditious speeches against the French nation."[33] The resolution of this conflict, and the French show of force in punishment of the Natchez, prevented the Natchez from challenging the French presence. The Natchez allowed the French to continue residing alongside them.

Although the first slaves to arrive in Natchez came in the early 1720s, large-scale development began several years later. In the meantime, Natchez languished as an agriculturally unproductive colony. French settlers proved themselves a poor workforce. Illustrative of their work ethic is the case of the settler, Fazende, who registered a complaint with Louisiana's Superior Council concerning the confiscation of his house slave. He based his demand for a new slave on "the fact that it is impossible to use white men or women both because of their laziness and because of their bad character. . . ." The council granted his request.[34] The failure of the white settlers in Natchez to grow sufficient tobacco led the Company of the Indies to replace them with a Carolina-trained tobacco grower and a workforce of African slaves.[35]

The influx of slaves achieved significant returns almost immediately. A 1725 evaluation of Louisiana's Governor Bienville reported that, from 1721 to 1723, "as there are only eight hundred negroes in the colony . . . it has been impossible for the colony to produce returns for France. . . ." Only "when the Company is willing to send negroes" would a return be likely.[36]

In Natchez, tobacco grew especially well and the crop became the dominant staple during the French era. Bienville suggested the possibility of employing slaves in the winter to "make timber of every sort" if the Company saw the need. Of the fifteen major slaveowners who held more than twenty slaves in Louisiana, two lived in Natchez.[37]

The first major slaveowner in Natchez was the Company of the Indies. The directors of the Company built its plantation "to give an example first and to convince the inhabitants that the Company will not change its determination" to settle Natchez.[38] To achieve this end, the company employed thirty slaves on its tobacco fields. Because of the large number of slaves, the company's local manager recommended that a foreman or overseer be retained to supervise their labor.[39]

Although virtually every French settler in Natchez wanted slaves, the Company soon found that only a few had lands sufficiently prepared for intensive cultivation. Nineteen settlers were named to the Superior Council of Louisiana as "those whom negroes could be given with safety." The scarcity of slaves in comparison to the demand led the company's agent to recommend that "it would be well to oblige them [the settlers] to become partners, three or four together, in order that they may be in a position to form an indigo manufactory."[40] Such assessments suggested that Natchez would soon be a prosperous settlement for the French.

A year after the arrival of the slaves, Natchez again seemed to be in chaos. The Superior Council wrote the Directors of the Company, complaining that "the plantation of the Company would succeed well if these were good negroes." Further, fewer than expected arrived, "disgusting the inhabitants who are all asking to return to France." At the same time, "the inhabitants cannot keep their negroes occupied during four to five months of the year" and therefore they needed to be employed "in cutting and dressing timber."[41] The mismanagement of the Natchez settlement continued following the departure of Governor Bienville, as a series of poorly qualified commanders were assigned to Natchez.[42] In the jockeying for control of the colony that followed the departure of Governor Bienville, the Superior Council replaced the commander, Desliettes, with Sieur Du Tisné, a man immediately characterized as "not at all suited to command." In contrast, Desleittes had "brought the Indians under subjection and established tranquility between the French and them."[43] Within months, the Natchez colonists began expressing their dissatisfaction with the slaves so recently arrived.

Owing to the Company's continued investment in its own plantation, Natchez was not abandoned. In 1728, the Company began construction of a tobacco shed to warehouse the crop as it awaited shipment from the Natchez. The plans were slowed, owing to natural obstacles. After cutting timber for the shed, the slaves, upriver from Natchez, floated it down the river on a raft. Company agents reported that "their raft went past that post without their having been able to stop it because of the currents which are violent. This timber . . . even went past New Orleans." The slaves had to start cutting timber again for the tobacco shed.[44]

In time, the Natchez settlement began to exhibit potential as a prosperous colony. Notwithstanding the yearly springtime ritual of local company agents predicting that Natchez would finally turn a profit, that potential was never realized. The Company's less than constant attention, coupled with poor local leadership, prevented the colony from achieving any financual success. At the same time the French had worn out any welcome the Natchez extended and were now unwanted neighbors. Misunderstandings, colonial arrogance, and general discontent eventually boiled over into conflict with the Natchez.

Conflict with the Natchez came as a major surprise to the French. The Company considered its treatment of the Indians to be very considerate. For instance, the Company abandoned Indian slavery. Etienne Boucher de Périer, the Governor of Louisiana, reasoned that Indian slavery was "the reason that the nations are most often at war." Abandoning Indian slavery bore certain benefits for the French as well. Governor Périer feared that "Indian slaves being mixed with our negroes may induce them to desert with them . . . , as they may maintain relations with them which might be disastrous to the colony when there are more blacks."[45]

The Natchez uprising of 1729 and its aftermath illustrated that the relations between the Indians and the Africans were disastrous indeed. The uprising began when Sieur de Chepart, newly appointed commander of Fort Rosalie, granted himself a concession for "one of the most eminent settlements of the whole colony." The existence of the Natchez village of White Apple on the land in question seemed a minor obstacle. He invited the Sun of the White Apple village to his fort and bluntly told him to "look out for another ground to build his village on."[46] The Natchez bought time by telling Chepart they would leave after the harvest. While offering

Chepart as tribute a bushel of corn and a fowl each week to appear coop-
erative, Natchez elders planned an uprising.

On November 28, 1729, an armed group of Natchez visited the commandant under the pretense of offering tribute. Exhausted from a night
of carousing, Chepart neither suspected an attack (despite having been
warned), nor was he prepared to fend one off. The Indian visitors disarmed
the French soldiers by simply borrowing their guns, under the guise of
needing the weapons for hunting. The French suspected little, for they
readily disarmed. The Natchez slaughtered all the men in the French village, taking the women, children, and slaves hostage.

As the Natchez seized power, it might have seemed that the African
slaves would again have no control over their destiny. In the Second
Natchez War, the slaves were little more than targets of the Natchez raids.
The sole slave defector, whom the French demanded be returned, seemed
to prove a general rule that few slaves took advantage of political instability. The Natchez uprising followed six years of enslavement, accompanied
by annual shortages of food, and it increased the slaves' discontent.
Africans in the Natchez district seized their opportunity: some slaves sided
with the French and some with the Natchez.

How the Natchez viewed Africans matters, because even those slaves not
allied to the Indians survived the uprising. The Natchez promised slaves
"that they would be free with the Indians, which was in fact the case during
the time that they remained with them."[47] Kind treatment of the slaves by
the Natchez surprised the French, for experience taught them not to expect
it. Governor Périer commented that "the preservation of the negroes is not
at all characteristic of the Indians," and speculated that perhaps there were
"some Englishmen in disguise with them."[48] But the Natchez accepted the
slaves as allies, to weaken French influence in the region.

Those Africans siding with the Natchez were almost all Bambarra,
according to the French. Bambarra ethnicity very well may have been a
French designation to identify rebellious slaves. This definition seems to
have been peculiar to colonial Louisiana. In Senegambia, French slave
traders as well as local peoples considered the Bambarra to be singularly
loyal, and prized them as military slaves. The Bambarra designation in
Natchez is problematic, and it is likely that most slaves in Natchez were
not Bambarra. Nonetheless, those slaves whom the French identified as
Bambarra had been particularly rebellious in Louisiana.[49] In fact, two years

after this uprising, slaves the French called Bambarra would plot a revolt in New Orleans in which they intended to kill all the French, and then enslave the surviving Africans and Indians.[50] Despite their ethnicity, some slaves supported the Natchez when they planned the attack on the French. In this vein, the Natchez war of 1729 was both a native insurgency and a slave rebellion.

Such organized collective action between the slaves and the Indians was the result of a degree of communication not recorded in the French documents. Although the French quickly established that Chepart had been warned of the attack in advance, the slaves' knowledge of the uprising seemed more detailed, for they expressed no surprise, and most knew which side to take. The Natchez war was a moment when the dialogue between the Indians and the slaves became visible, despite efforts by the French to present the opposite as the case. Yet the decision by some slaves to remain with the French suggests that, as a whole, the slaves would be obligated to no one. They would not simply choose the Natchez out of opposition to the French.

Very quickly, three of the slaves escaped to the French. The escapees reported that the Natchez intended to free the slaves, and to use the temporary disorder of the uprising as a starting point for driving out French colonists. The escapees said that the Natchez offered freedom to slaves who backed their cause and threatened "to take the negroes who were not of their party to the Chickasaw with the French women and children."[51] In short, the Natchez offered slaves who accepted their protection an end to their bondage.

The actions of the slaves among the Natchez illustrate their accurate reading of the crumbling colonial power structure. Most of the captured slaves neither defended the French, nor trusted the Natchez. Instead, Africans awaited the French counterattack. This decision indicates slaves either preferred slavery to freedom—an unlikely conclusion—or else they had little faith in the Natchez and expected the French to return.

The slaves who did not take up arms with the Natchez also did not take up arms against them. By refusing to take one side or another, the slaves began to negotiate for their future. Such a process of negotiation would not have been acceptable to members within either Natchez or French society, yet the slaves seized on this opportunity to assert their identities. They were not French, they would not become Natchez, but they would negotiate with either side for the best outcome. Ethnic differences among them may have led the slaves to respond in a variety of ways to the tumult. Various antipathies rooted in their African past led some to oppose the Natchez simply because traditional enemies sided with them. The captured slaves accepted the outsider status that slavery assigned them. This acceptance played on the weaknesses of both the French and the Natchez, for both would then make offers to them in exchange for their loyalty.

Reports that the Natchez uprising was part of a broad, intertribal conspiracy to overthrow the French seem unlikely.[52] Only the Natchez had an immediate quarrel with the French, namely the unreasonable French demand for the White Apple village. Further, only Franco-Natchez relations had a long history of tumult. Their difficulties went as far back as first contact. On the other hand, the French had a history of Choctaw alliance dating back to 1700.[53] Indeed, shortly after the uprising, a large group of Choctaw exacted revenge on behalf of the French, indicating that the Choctaw at least sided with the French and may not have even been aware of the planned uprising.

Acting on behalf of the French, an army of five hundred Choctaw attacked the Natchez on January 27, 1730. The Natchez suffered 150 casualties, and the Choctaw recovered 54 French women and children, and between 50 and 150 slaves.[54] In the middle of this battle, the Choctaw were surprised by a group of Africans who "prevented the Choctaw from carrying off the powder and who by their resistance had given the Natchez time to enter the two forts." Indeed, the Choctaw reported that, had it not been for the unexpected interference of these Africans, the "defeat [of the Natchez] would have been complete."[55]

The Choctaw-Natchez-French-African battle and its aftermath offer further texture to the effect that the Africans had on the course of events in Natchez. During the fighting, as the Choctaw attempted to "liberate" the hostages (only to return them to their French masters), a contingent of former French slaves defended the Natchez' gunpowder stores, allowing the Natchez to return to safety. This unexpected support from apparent hostages illustrates how Africans could influence the outcome of the confrontation. In contrast to the previous Natchez conflict, this time the slaves offered assistance to the Indians.

While the Choctaw may have been taken aback by the support that the Natchez received from the slaves, the French must have been even more surprised. As a show of colonial strength intended to impress Indians and French colonists alike, Governor Périer sent a band of company-owned slaves to slaughter the Chaouachas. The intent was to demonstrate that the French were in the region to stay, but this decision also displayed his trust in company slaves. While these slaves were not strangers to the idea of acting as a Janissary force, it seems that the governor was a bit less comfortable in using slaves this way. He reported his concern that such actions "might on the contrary cause our negroes to revolt as we see by the example of the Natchez," and thus limited the military use of slaves to this one raid.[56]

The Choctaw inflicted severe damage on the Natchez. In the months that followed, the Natchez abandoned their settlement, as French and Choctaw raids hunted them down and enslaved them.[57] The outcome of the Natchez war turned, in good part, on the participation of Africans, whose assistance prevented the immediate defeat of the Natchez. These Africans acted on their own agendas and in their own interests. African slaves did not simply follow the French out of loyalty or the Indians out of a sense of common cause. Indeed the diversity of their African origins rendered the possibility of any collective action unlikely.

In resolving the issue of the recovered slaves, the Choctaw and the French both acted in ways that they normally would not have, in order to achieve their objectives. Since the French defined their slaves as property, the Choctaw, in their negotiations, also defined slaves as property, despite their somewhat different understanding of what slavery was. While the slaves were the basis for much of the material negotiations between the Choctaw and the French, they never were a party to them. Even so, the slaves had begun their process of mediating their situation. Given these circumstances, the African slaves acted in ways that frustrated negotiations during several months in 1730. In the negotiations, French concerns over the return of the hostages were matched by Choctaw demands that they be paid for their attack.[58]

The Choctaw shocked the French after recovering the hostages by thinking "only of asking for goods" in exchange for their recovery. These demands "maddened" the French, especially because the Choctaw were "unwilling to send back our women or our negroes before they obtained some."[59] But for reasons that remain unclear, the French did not offer the Choctaw their normal peace offering, a decision which seems at the least misguided considering that the Choctaw were emerging as the only native power in the region and French influence was waning.[60]

The continuing negotiations illustrate the relative weakness of the French bargaining position. The weakness came from the French shortage of supplies for trade. They "had been promised that two big pirogues loaded with merchandise would come up to the Natchez for them and there had come only a miserable little one inside of which there was nothing."[61] Apparently the French wanted their slaves back first, a difficult proposition for the Choctaw to consider. Compounding the French weakness was their cultural inability to conceive of the matrilineal Choctaw authority structures, which placed little power in the father figure. The French continually asserted a patriarchal authority over the Choctaw. The Choctaw did not object, for in their matrilineal culture, male authority rested in the brother of one's mother.[62] After some Choctaw refused to return African hostages, the French began to make exaggerated demands for their return, at one point asserting that detaining these slaves "was as if they were detaining Frenchmen."[63] Although some Indians traded the slaves back to the French, others traded them to the Chickasaw, who no doubt traded them to the English in South Carolina. As the affair drew longer, the Choctaw began to demand "the goods at English prices," for, as one chief reasoned, "since the French needed him it was just that he should have himself well paid" for the slaves.[64] The Choctaw understood the French well enough to know that the French would not risk the alliance over a few slaves. They made specific demands that French debts be paid before the return of any slaves.[65]

The actions of the slaves recovered by the Choctaw undermined negotiations for their return. This behavior stemmed from the harsh treatment the slaves received from the Choctaw, which indicated the regard in which the Choctaw held the Africans. Runaway slaves quickly found the French and asked for protection. Some ran away even as they were being returned to the French, as demonstrated by two of five slaves whom Alabamon Mingo was returning to Regis du Roullet. The remaining three asked Du Roullet to be returned to the outpost at Mobile, "but they did not want to be taken by the Indians." When Du Roullet asked why, they told him that "the Indians make us carry some packages, which exhausts us, mistreat us much, and [have] taken from us our clothing down to a skin shirt that we each had." One of these slaves had a tomahawk wound in his head that exposed his skull, which, Du Roullet wrote, "made me think."[66] Harsh treatment of the slaves suggests that, whatever economic value slaves had, the Choctaw still viewed slaves as complete outsiders, and extended them no social protections.

Another slave ran to the French and told Du Roullet that "the Indians do nothing but tell the negroes continually that all those that you trade for are burned on arrival at New Orleans, and the fear that the negroes have causes them to run away when they learn that they are going to be traded for, but when you go to the Choctaws you have only to bring with you a negro from those for whom you have traded to bring you all those who are among the Indians, who would already have come to find you if it were not for the fear that they have of being burned." Du Roullet began keeping a returned slave to explain that the French would not torture them upon their return.[67] Returning to their French enslavers was an act of desperation, as the slaves found the Choctaw unwilling to grant them their freedom. The strength of Choctaw society here is illustrated by their unwillingness to let outsiders—be they French or African—to impose the terms of their presence. As a result of the Choctaw unwillingness to compromise, the Africans' position suffered.

In some extreme cases, slaves killed themselves while in Choctaw custody. When discussing the return of some slaves, a council of Choctaw chiefs informed Périer that several of the slaves committed suicide before they could be returned.[68] This act reflected the desperation of these slaves' circumstances. Committing suicide indicates that the treatment they received from the Choctaw must have been incredibly harsh. Although the French and the Choctaw left little record of remorse for the suicides, they stand as evidence that the slaves' efforts to influence the Choctaw-French negotiations were not always successful.

While negotiating with the French, the Choctaw treated the slaves as a valuable commodity; but in their own society the African had no place. The Choctaw seemed to have little use for them, except as hostages for French goods. In circumstances where Africans spent prolonged periods with the Choctaw, their chances for safe return to the French diminished. Only those slaves whom the Choctaw adopted as their own—and who effectively became Choctaw—had a chance of improved treatment, for

82   David J. Libby

they would soon become accepted as Choctaw and were not to be traded. Others received better treatment when they had value, and their value bore a direct relation to the esteem in which the Choctaw held the French. When Lusser invoked the Choctaw history of friendly relations with the French, he did so by pointing out the English practice of trading in Choctaw slaves. "If it had not been for our powder and our bullets," Lusser claimed, the warriors who fired them "would be slaves of the English," like many of their relatives. Adaptive to the times, the Indian "captain" replied that "long ago the English had ceased taking their people as slaves," and expressed his chief's dissatisfaction with the French failure to honor their promises.[69]

Choctaw dissatisfaction undermined French efforts to recover their slaves. Besides those who absconded to the French, the Choctaw returned only a few. In March 1731, a slave who had escaped to the French told Du Roullet "that there were still thirty-two negroes of the Choctaw, including six negresses belonging to the Company and eighteen belonging to private persons; [and] that seven . . . had died."[70] Before their return to the French, some Indians gave the slaves the opportunity to be traded to the Chickasaw and eventually the English. Sale to the Chickasaw may have brought a better price, and may also have served some diplomatic function, but there was little benefit for the slave. By May 1731, the Choctaw returned fifteen slaves who had been scattered throughout the villages in the area.[71] The transfer of Louisiana's administration back to the crown, and the impending war with the Chickasaw Indians, made the return of the remaining slaves less important to the French.[72]

Those slaves who were not returned to the French had few options. Had it not occurred already, assimilation with the Choctaw was unlikely, for Choctaw assimilation usually occurred relatively quickly. Unless the refugee had some sort of protection from a clan, survival in Choctaw society would have been unlikely. Without protection, a newcomer would within a few months be either dead, abandoned, or traded as a slave.[73] It was more likely that they would be sold to neighboring Indian groups. The Choctaw already threatened to sell the slaves to the Chickasaw. Chickasaw slave traders could easily sell the slaves to the British in Carolina. The demand for slaves in Carolina was great during the early 1730s, and the British were unlikely to question the origins of a French-speaking slave at a good price.

With their options limited, the slaves still found ways to navigate their circumstances. They sided with local Indian groups. When treated brutally, they ran away to the French. Some established maroon societies.[74] Most importantly, in circumstances that often seemed desperate, the Africans on the French colonial frontier played a role that had a significant impact on the course of events which would effectively end French settlement in the Natchez district.

CHRIST IN CHAINS

Slavery's Negative Impact on the Conversion of African American Slaves

Daniel L. Fountain

Slaves, obey your earthly masters with respect and fear, and with sincerity of heart, just as you would obey Christ. (Ephesians 6:5)

Church was what they called it but all that preacher talked about was for us slaves to obey our masters and not to lie and steal. Nothing about Jesus was ever said and the overseer stood there to see the preacher talked as he wanted him to talk. (Charlie Van Dyke, North Carolina slave)

Slave Christianity is frequently described as "a source of strength and endurance that enabled [African Americans] to triumph over the collective tragedy of enslavement."[1] Such words are typical of the way that most historians use Afro-Christianity to counter the argument that slavery stripped Africans of their culture and reduced them to an infantile state of existence. However, in their worthy attempts to refute racist or inaccurate interpretations of the past, historians have created an illusion of widespread slave Christianity by attributing the behavior of a few slaves to the many. While Afro-Christianity as described in current historical literature was an important and influential cultural force created within the slave community, its overall impact has been overstated. In fact, the strident defense of African American spiritual vitality even suggests that no master-imposed boundary was too great for the slaves to overcome.[2] Nevertheless, despite the slaves' numerous heroic achievements within slavery, real institutional boundaries and obstacles restricted and shaped the African American experience in profound ways. Too often historians overlook or downplay these boundaries for fear of conjuring older images of African Americans as helpless, dehumanized drones. This is an unnecessary precaution because historians have demonstrated repeatedly the individual and collective strength of African American slaves. Therefore, focusing on barriers within slavery does not mean questioning the value of African American achievements, but simply provides evidence for just how deplorable the peculiar institution actually was. One of the ways the institution of slavery shaped the African American experience from 1830 until emancipation was by significantly limiting the number of slaves converting to Christianity.

The visible signs of slavery's restricting influence over slave conversion fit within three general categories: slave access to religious instruction, the Christian message offered to slaves, and slave religious identity. First of all, slavery helped create regional settlement patterns that made regular contact with religious instruction the exception rather than the rule for most slaves. Furthermore, the religious and ideological debates surrounding slavery only exacerbated this situation by limiting the already small number of ministers available to preach in the South. Secondly, African American access to religious instruction depended upon the attitude and actions of the slaveowners. Non-Christian masters or those with only a slight interest in religion were often less than enthusiastic about or openly hostile to the idea of evangelizing their slaves. Such apathy or hostility meant that many slaves could not attend Christian services even if they were available. Finally, institutional safeguards like the prohibition of literacy, the monitoring of services, and a limited Gospel message made the transmission of religious ideas more difficult and less compelling. Despite the various denominations' differing approaches and levels of enthusiasm for African American evangelization, countless slaves found the messages offered to them grounded in hypocrisy or unappealing. As a result, most slaves simply did not become Christians.

Leaders of the two largest Protestant denominations in the antebellum South routinely described vast areas of their region as being religiously destitute. In 1850, the *Alabama Baptist Advocate* lamented this fact in the article "Destitution of Religious Knowledge": "That there is a great destitution of religious knowledge—"a famine of the word of the Lord "—in many portions of our country, South and West cannot be denied. Our ministry are too few to supply the wants of our extended and increasing territory. Comparatively few of our churches are supplied with more than monthly preaching, while vast numbers of them have not even that—to say nothing of the wide fields wherein as yet no churches have been planted. In this state of things, it can be imagined that a most lamentable want of instruction . . . prevails in many parts of the country." Eight years later in an address on domestic missions, the Methodist Episcopal Church, South, would offer a very similar assessment of the southern population's access to religious instruction: "It is found, upon close examination, that in all the Conferences there are numerous tracts of country, sparsely settled, which are without the regular ministrations of the gospel: there are few, if any houses of worship, and the people are either too poor to pay for the gospel of Christ, or have never learned to value the instructions of Christianity. It is a lamentable fact that many of these communities are to be found in our oldest States and within the geographical limits of long-established and numerically strong Conferences." An 1849 report by Baptist missionary James E. Sharp gives specific mention of his embryonic efforts in a region fitting this description. Rev. Sharp identified the region, dubbed Africa, as a place in the interior of Georgia where "[n]ot more than one half the inhabitants hear preaching once in the year." It was locations such as "Africa" that led the Alabama Baptist State Convention of 1850 to estimate that in the South "[o]nly about one-tenth of our population, according to a most liberal charity, can be regarded as pious."[3] Obviously, many mid-nineteenth century southerners of all races had little to no access to Christian instruction.

This absence of religious instruction is a principal reason for the low percentage of Christians within the slave community. Many southerners of all races simply had little exposure to the Gospel.[4] There is no doubt that the institution of slavery exacerbated this situation, since the regional emphasis on staple crop agriculture created a highly mobile and widely dispersed slaveowning population. The ongoing chase during the early to mid-nineteenth century for the Old Southwest's more productive cotton lands only increased the difficulties facing antebellum evangelists by greatly enlarging their field of labor. The Southern Baptists pointed to these difficulties during their biennial convention of 1853. Domestic missionaries complained that they faced great burdens on account of "the great extent of country over which our labors extend . . . the sparseness of population, the want of facilities of communication and [the difficulty of] receiving intelligence, and the inaccessibility of many of these communities which need aid."[5]

Six years later the Domestic and Indian Mission Board continued to lament the difficulties of reaching many slaves: "there are many districts of country, rich planting districts, where the white population is too sparse to demand such gospel provisions. Unless special missions are made to these blacks they must live and die without the gospel."[6] Indeed, a quick perusal of a few antebellum descriptions of religious life produces a variety of obstacles that limited an individual's access to worship. Illness, great distances to meeting places, rain, high water, absent plantation owners, and sea island hopping in small craft are but a few of the obstacles and dangers many southerners faced in seeking to deliver or hear the Gospel.[7] Where missionaries did make an appearance, many found circumstances similar to that described by an Alabama minister: "The people are generally very poor, and have but little opportunity of going out of the neighborhood to hear preaching; and those desiring to hear the word of God are deprived of that blessing for months. There are many who seldom appear at a place of worship. Not a few spend the Sabbath in hunting, fishing, shooting at a mark, & c. There are many families in which there is not a religious person; and many which, until I came here had no Bible, no religious book, and scarcely any kind of books at all. Children, not a few from 10 to 15 years old there are who have seldom or never entered a place of worship."[8] Mother Hyacinth LeConnait, a Catholic missionary to northern Louisiana, offered a similar assessment of her mission field: "These people need much good example, counsel, to redeem themselves to live in a much more edifying way. To my knowledge, the American farmer is as far away from the good Lord as the savage indian is."[9]

Further complicating the issue of southern religious destitution was the ever-present shortage of missionaries and preachers. Pleas about the need for more Christian ministers working in the South litter the antebellum publications of nearly all denominations.[10] For example, the Alabama Baptist convention noted that only 14 of 114 state missionary positions were filled for the year 1846.[11] Likewise, in 1853, the Synod of Tennessee bluntly stated, "We need means to support the ministers we have, and we are in great want of more."[12] Exacerbating this shortage was the disproportionate emphasis that evangelicals gave to the South's urban population. Many evangelicals recognized that cities had greater numbers of white and black conversions and directed their "greatest energies" to these "large multitude[s] of immortal beings." Perhaps many evangelicals even felt that the larger number of converts had divine sanction. For instance, in 1855 the Baptist *Home and Foreign Journal* pointed out that, "Our Lord and his apostles directed their labors toward towns and cities; and it is a fact, which a trial of the past two years has abundantly verified, that missionary labor in those places succeed better, and yields larger results, than the same amount of labor does in the country. While therefore we should not neglect the country, we should provide promptly for towns and cities." As a result of this urban focus, in 1860 nearly half of the denomination's 69 domestic missionaries held assignments in cities. This is a surprisingly large proportion given the South's overwhelmingly rural population and it meant that rural and frontier areas bore the brunt of the shortage of ministers. Since most slaves lived in areas fitting this description, they were among the population least well-served by the clergy, even when considering the missions established upon their behalf. In describing the religious conditions of Louisiana, historian Joe Gray Taylor wrote that "Not enough priests were stationed in Louisiana to supply the needs of white communicants; neglect of the blacks was almost inevitable."[13]

The Episcopal Church blamed some of its ministerial limitations in the South on a "lack of the missionary spirit."[14] Although their analysis of the shortage mirrors the complaint of many southern denominations, slavery was also a central cause for the lack of ministers and missionaries in the South. In particular, slavery greatly limited the number of ministers who were available to serve southern religious needs. The mere presence of slavery kept many northern Christians from entering the South as a ministerial field of labor. Philadelphia's Christian Observer plainly argued that slavery prevented ministers from going South because it was "unfavorable to religion, and naturally offensive to ministerial laborers from the North."[15] After 1845, the North-South split of Methodists and Baptists over slavery further limited the pool of available ministers by creating region-specific denominations. Another factor complicating the South's minister shortage was the fact that slaveowners were not enthusiastic about allowing unknown individuals to preach to their slaves. This was particularly true after Nat Turner used religious imagery to motivate his Southampton compatriots. Several decades after these bloody events, the Richmond *Christian Advocate* still proclaimed that preaching to slaves "cannot be performed by strangers" and that religious instruction must be "taught by those who have the confidence of the community."[16] Likewise, Bishop Augustin Verot of

St. Augustine, Florida noted in 1860 that "many masters do not like for us to preach to these Negroes for fear that they will be given ideas which are now far from their heads."[17] Thus, the constant fear of further slave uprisings meant that many ministers entering a new region found themselves the objects of suspicion or isolation until they could prove their loyalty with regard to the slavery issue.[18]

The shortage of preachers and rural isolation meant that most southerners had limited and irregular access to religious instruction. In most cases, those with regular access to services met only once or twice a month.[19] Slave testimony suggests that religious exercises could be even more infrequent than that. Virginia slave Fleming Clark recalled that "We had no school or church. We were too far away for church."[20] Likewise, Josephine Bristow of South Carolina stated that "us didn't go to no church neither cause we was way off dere on de plantation en wasn' any church nowhe' 'bout dere."[21] Both Hattie Sugg of Mississippi and Louisa Adams of North Carolina indicated that they attended church only one time during slavery.[22] Similarly, by the age of twenty-one, James Pennington of Maryland had heard only two sermons and seen one copy of the New Testament.[23] Finally, Arkansas slave Betty Brown remembered that church services came only once a year in the form of a camp meeting: "We diden' know what church wuz . . . an' the whites nevuh neither. Dey wuz a couple o' men us' ta come by an' hole a camp-meetin'. . . . [D]ey'd come aftuh crops wuz laid by an' preach 'til cotton wuz openin'."[24]

Of course, the irregularity of worship services only affected those slaves who were allowed to attend church at all. Not all masters were Christians, and even some who claimed allegiance to Jesus Christ did not allow their slaves to attend worship.[25] A survey of slave religious experiences conducted for this study demonstrated that 18.1 percent of all slaves could not attend any form of Christian worship. However, the recollections of unconverted slaves in the survey indicated that masters barred slightly over 30 percent from going to church. Therefore, as the survey also revealed that a majority of slaves were unconverted and the survey methodology actually inflated the number of converted slaves, the percentage of slaves barred from worship was undoubtedly higher than 18.1 percent. This is particularly true given the survey's lenient criteria for identifying a master as allowing worship.[26] More likely, at least one out of four slaves was prohibited from attending any form of Christian services.

Having a master who "allowed" slaves access to worship also did not mean that all slaves on a given farm or plantation could attend church services. Numerous slaves described how some masters only permitted a select few to attend church with them. Callie Bracey of Mississippi recalled that "On special occasions, the older slaves were allowed to go to the church of their master. . . ."[27] On the Georgia plantation where Emma Jones lived, only house slaves could join the family in nightly scripture readings.[28] "[S]laves that could be trusted" went to church where David Hall lived in North Carolina, while John Becton recalled that only "coach drivers" were permitted to attend church with their masters.[29]

John Becton's recollections identify a very special segment of the slaves who attended worship along with their masters: those who went in order to serve their owners' needs. Sylvia Cannon had to care for the masters' baby while she attended their South Carolina brush arbor church.[30] When accompanying her mistress to the Episcopal church in Alabama, Sally Murphy "sot in de foot of her carriage . . ." in order to "open gates and hold de horses."[31] Manda Boggan provided a wide number of services for her masters who attended church. "Us waited on 'em, toted in water an' 'tended ter de chilluns. When de meetin' wuz ober us kotched de horses an' led 'em to deir blocks an' brung de carriages 'round fer 'em."[32] For many slaves, these Sunday duties gutted the church services of any special meaning. One slave who had to tend to the children outside the church while her masters worshipped inside bitterly recalled that as a result of her duties "I was almost grown before I had ever heard the Bible read and the word of God explained."[33] Others, however, managed to extract some value out of their unique form of Sunday "services." The coachman on the plantation where Silas Jackson lived would listen to the services while waiting to drive his owners home. As a result of his greater familiarity with the Gospel message preached in the masters' church, the coachman, Sandy Jaspar served as the slaves' preacher.[34]

Even if a master allowed slaves to attend worship with them or hold their own services, very few did so without imposing restrictions or special conditions on slave participation. Masters often gave overseers the discretion to determine who could attend church or required them to monitor any services where their slaves were present. Overseer discretion was then a common barrier for many slaves who wanted to attend church. Both Susan Bledsoe of Tennessee and Ella Grandberry of Alabama noted that slaves could not go to church unless a white person or overseer went with them.[35] If no whites were willing to go, then neither could the slaves. Overseers could also use church attendance to influence slave behavior. The overseer in charge of Mrs. Lou Griffin exemplifies this practice, for he allowed only those slaves who "suited" him to attend Sunday services.[36] Where an overseer determined that church services undermined his authority, he could oppose religious instruction in all cases. For instance, Mississippi slave Henry Cheatam accused his overseer of attempting to keep all slaves from going to church or holding any meetings of their own.[37] Huckstep, the overseer in charge of James Williams, went even further in opposing Christianity among the slaves. According to Williams, "Huckstep was himself an open infidel as well as blasphemer. He used to tell the hands that there was no hell hereafter for white people, but that they had their punishment on earth in being obliged to take care of the negroes. As for the blacks, he was sure there was a hell for them. He used frequently to sit with his bottle by his side, and his Bible in his hand, and read passages and comment on them, and pronounce them lies."[38] Given the behavior of some overseers like Huckstep, it is not surprising to find slaves like Joseph Farley and Green Willbanks who believed it was easier for slaves to obtain passes for visiting, dancing, and playing music than it was for attending religious services.[39]

Masters also shaped the slaves' religious exercises in other ways. Perhaps because of space limitations, work requirements, or fear of large slave gatherings, Spencer Barnett's master made the slaves take turns rather than allow them all to attend church on the same day.[40] Randall Lee's Virginia master allowed his slaves to hold as many prayer meetings as they wished but "did not allow much preaching in the church."[41] Conversely, the master of Millie Simpkins found slave prayer objectionable.[42] "Shouting" slaves had their hands burned where O. W. Green lived, but the master of Siney Bonner only required religious enthusiasts to use an overturned kettle to keep the volume down.[43] Other masters entirely forbade their slaves from participating in any aspect of the church services they attended. According to Anna Scott, "The slaves were forbidden to sing, talk, or make any sound" at church "under penalty of severe beatings."[44] In addition to receiving beatings, slaves who did not worship in accordance with the masters' desire might lose their religious privileges altogether. For instance, the Baptist Church in Elkton, Kentucky, unanimously adopted the following resolution in 1846: "Resolved that it is the opinion of this church that the meetings of the colored people conducted as they are, are of no benefit to them either in a religious or cival point of view and that the secston of this church be instructed not to allow them the use of this house any more for that purpose."[45] The message of the resolution is as clear today as it undoubtedly was for the slave members of the Elkton Baptist Church. While salvation was an individual choice free from external interference, how, when, and where the slaves celebrated that heavenly gift was subject to white approval and control.

While these religious restrictions had the consequence of easing the masters' fear of religion-induced rebellion, the white micro-management of the slaves' religious life also limited the communal spirit and satisfaction that some slaves drew from Christianity. The words of Mingo White testify to the destructive effect that such precautionary measures had on slave conversion: "Us didn' have nowhar to go 'cep' church an' we didn' git no pleasure outten it 'case we warn't 'lowed to talk from de time we lef' home 'twell we got back."[46] Ella Grandberry echoed White's remarks and demonstrated how masters' religious restrictions impacted the slaves' church attendance. "On Sundays us jes' laid 'roun' mos' all day. Us didn't git no pleasure outten goin' to church, 'caze we warn't 'lowed to say nothin'."[47] Such remarks leave little doubt that white efforts to shape the slaves' religious expressions in effect limited both their access to and interest in Christianity.

Of all the obstacles hampering the slaves' access to Christianity, none was more obvious or greater than the prohibition of teaching bondsmen to read. Clearly, understanding the central tenets of a religion is a vital part of being a believer. Since Christianity's central tenets appear in the Bible as written word, literacy greatly facilitates Christian religious instruction because interested persons can examine the faith on their own rather than having to trust the words of someone perhaps unknown to them. Literacy and being allowed access to religious literature also means that an individual can pursue his or her religious studies without access to clergy, an advantage southern ministers could have desperately used in their efforts to convert the slaves.[48] Southern Baptists readily acknowledged the importance of literacy for slave conversion by declaring, "The reading of his word we consider next in importance to the preaching of it."[49] So important was literacy for conversion that one of the first acts of the Southern Baptist Convention after the Civil War was to establish and encourage schools among the freedmen.[50] However, in spite of the obvious religious advantages literacy afforded, most southern states prohibited teaching slaves to read for fear of triggering insurrection and helping runaways forge passes.[51] In addition, "[b]y 1855 nine of the fifteen slave states had made it illegal to distribute Bibles among the slaves."[52]

By denying slaves access to literacy, slaveowners in effect required that most slaves had to come into contact with persons familiar with the Gospel. While many African Americans did an admirable job of spreading the Christian message within their own community, in most cases, the prohibition of literacy meant that white Christians were the largest source of religious information available to the slaves. As a region desperately short of access to regular preaching, the burden of slave conversion fell largely on the slaveholders themselves. This meant that slaves of non-Christian masters faced the previously discussed possibility of being shut off from any religious instruction. Furthermore, as most slaveowners obeyed the state literacy laws pertaining to slaves, Christian masters typically had to sell the message of salvation to persons who could not verify the validity of the masters' scriptural interpretation.[53] Such a situation requires a great amount of trust between the communicator and his audience. As trust between the races could be a rare commodity on most southern farms, Christian slaveholders faced tremendous institutional obstacles to converting their illiterate slaves.

The testimony of many ministers, slaveowners, and slaves shows that catechizing the slaves orally was a tedious and less efficient means of converting African Americans. Concerned Christians particularly complained that by stripping literacy training from religious education, southern lawmakers removed a key incentive for slave attendance at church services and made instruction more difficult. For example, the Moravian missionaries to slaves in North Carolina blamed a considerable decline in African American attendance at Sunday schools on the fact that they were "no longer permitted to teach them to read. . . ."[54] Plantation mistresses, on whom the task of catechizing slaves usually fell, expressed similar frustrations about the difficulties of teaching an illiterate people the word of God.[55] In 1860, Catherine Edmondston recorded in her diary her feelings about the effectiveness of catechisms for teaching slaves about Christianity and attracting them to the faith: "I heard all that Gatty calls the 'sponsible ones' say their catechism, but I do not hope for much from it. It is uphill

work and ought to be done more regularly than I do it. Bishop Ives catechism I do not like at all; the repetition is tiresome. . . . They learn nothing from me but the mere rudiments of Christianity—who made them,
who Redeemed them, with the certainty of a future of reward or punishment, the Creed, the ten Commandments & exhortations against lying &
stealing—and only the little ones get that. They will not come to church
even when Patrick has it for them."[56] Mary Boykin Chesnut expressed
great admiration for a minister's success in teaching the catechism to slaves
because her own efforts had fallen woefully short. Chesnut admitted to her
diary in 1861 that after failing to teach her slaves the catechism she "let my
Sunday School all drift into singing hymns." Rather than continue her
effort to provide religious instruction other than hymns, she decided it
would be better "to wait until they developed more brains. . . ."[57]

The religious ignorance that Chesnut saw as resulting from a lack of
brains was more properly understood by the slaves to be to a lack of literacy and proper instruction. Minksie Walker complained of such in her
description of the worship services she attended as a slave in Tennessee:
"De meeting was about like it is now 'cept we didn't know half de time
what dey was talking about, we couldn't read and learn."[58] Further complicating this fact was the racist assumption that ministers had to tailor
religious instruction "to the capacity of their minds."[59] This meant that
much of the religious education provided to slaves was overly simplistic. In
fact, many of the catechisms used to instruct the slaves doubled as children's religious literature.[60] South Carolina slave Ervin Smith remembered
his basic catechism lessons of "Who made you?" and "Why ought you to
love God?" well into the twentieth century. However, while Smith easily
remembered his catechism lessons, he blamed its brief questionnaire form
for providing slaves with too little knowledge about Christianity.[61] Perhaps
it was for this reason that Arie Binns described white preaching as being no
more than "long tiresome sermons."[62] Indeed, anyone who has sat through
an exhortation on the doctrinal differences between various denominations can imagine the frustration that an illiterate slave might feel while
taking in a Sunday sermon on transubstantiation or predestination. That
many ministers did preach about subjects that were beyond the slaves'
knowledge base is clear. As late as 1861, Charles Colcock Jones, an experienced and concerned missionary to the slaves, continued to admonish
many of his fellow ministers for preaching above the understanding of

their congregations. Jones openly lamented that despite decades of advice from missionaries involved among the slaves, "Much of our preaching does not reach our congregations."[63]

Ironically, most African Americans found the messages that did reach their congregations lacking in value. To begin with, the Christian New Testament suggests that only a small percentage of people hearing the message of Jesus Christ will respond to the Nazarene's teachings. In the Gospel of Matthew, Jesus commands his followers to symbolically "Enter through the narrow gate. For wide is the gate and broad is the road that leads to destruction, and many enter through it. But small is the gate and narrow the road that leads to life, and only a few find it."[64] In other words, many people simply do not find the message of Christianity appealing no matter how clearly or enthusiastically it is preached. However, if Christian theology suggests that only a few follow the path to salvation under normal circumstances, African Americans living under the institution of slavery often found the path blocked by man-made obstacles.

Numerous slaves testified that the Christian message presented to them during slavery was of little appeal for them. The two principal causes for this lack of appeal were the content of the sermons preached to slaves and the hypocritical actions of many white southern Christians. These two factors together created such negative feelings about Christianity that a majority of the slaves ultimately rejected the faith offered them.

African American slaves lived in an extremely restrictive environment. While it was not a totally closed system, the institution of slavery did limit free expression, movement, familial and personal relationships, as well as control over the slaves' bodies.[65] Because whites dictated so much of their lives, slaves rejoiced in the liberties they were allowed, bargained for, or took covertly. Music and dance were two of the principal areas of African American independence and creativity.[66] Frolics and corn shuckings provided slaves with important opportunities for allowing individual expression and strengthening communal ties. However, the evangelical Christianity of the slaves prohibited dancing and secular music, thus reducing the slaves' already limited social space even further. In addition to these restrictions, Christianity teaches that lying, stealing, and physical resistance to worldly authorities are also inappropriate behavior. Trapped in an environment where honesty and obedience could mean hunger, exile, physical abuse, and death, slaves understandably found that such injunctions only complicated an already difficult situation. Faced with such a scenario, it is no surprise that most slaves did not convert to Christianity. This is not to suggest that slaves were libertines devoid of morality. Slaves of many religious backgrounds struggled admirably to forge their own moral order within an immoral institution. But the slaves were human, and adding new restrictions to an already fettered world could only prove irksome. This is especially true since the heavenly master's word usually came out of the mouths of men demanding earthly obedience to themselves.

Indeed, the slaves' most consistent complaint against the teachings of the various Christian denominations was the nearly omnipresent focus on the theme of "Servants, be obedient to your masters."[67] Plagued by nightmarish visions of slaves using biblical inspiration to rise and destroy the South's peculiar institution, southern slaveholders typically demanded that Christians present African Americans with a limited version of their Gospel message. Rather than lose access to the slaves or threaten the social structure they embraced, southern Christians willingly constructed a slave-specific version of the Gospel that emphasized otherworldly salvation in exchange for moral behavior and earthly obedience to whites.[68] In fact, southern Christians routinely gained access to the slaves by touting the Gospel's potential for producing good order on a plantation as a selling point.[69] Some historians argue that this eclectic form of the Christian Gospel provided both slave and master benefits since it identified duties that each party owed to the other.[70] In contrast, the research presented here suggests that most religious messages did not emphasize such reciprocity.[71] Most slaves complained that discussions of Christian duties focused solely on their obligations to the master. Furthermore, while some argue that the slaves saw through the masters' religious duplicity and extracted their own value from Christianity, the findings of this study suggest that most slaves extracted little from the faith offered them and as a result overwhelmingly rejected it.[72]

Charles Ball made a valid observation in explaining why his African grandfather rejected Christianity. Ball's grandfather did see through the version of Christianity that Maryland slaveholders offered to the slaves. But rather than finding the rudiments of a faith that he could shape and call his own, Ball's grandfather only found "the religion of his oppressors to be the invention of designing men." As a result of his discovery, the old African rejected Christianity and "retained his native traditions."[73] Stories like this would occur again and again throughout the antebellum South. In fact, Virginia slave and Baptist minister Peter Randolph argued that the Gospel offered to the slaves "had better be buried in oblivion, for it makes more heathens than Christians."[74] Emma Tidwell elaborated on such criticism by characterizing sermons to the slaves as nothing more than "Mind yo mistress. Don't steal der potatoes; don't lie bout nothin' an don' talk back tuh yo boss; ifn yo does yo'll be tied tuh a tree an stripped necked. When dey tell yuh tuh do somethin' run an do hit."[75] Alice Sewell, like many other slaves, never heard about Jesus or " 'bout a slave dying and going to heaven."[76] Because of such content, Hannah Austin argued that she and her fellow Georgia slaves "seldom heard a true religious sermon."[77] Accordingly, such preaching led to much feigned religion and few conversions. Henry Wright argued as much when he noted that "None of the slaves believed in the sermons but they pretended to do so."[78] Similarly, Tom Hawkins responded to questions about slave Christianity by asking "How could anybody be converted on dat kind of preachin'[?]"[79]

Given the slaves' reaction to most sermons, the axiom "actions speak louder than words" had significant meaning for African Americans belonging to or living among professed Christians. Slaves frequently took note of white behavior in view of the spirit of Christianity and made value judgments about the faith based on white efforts to live up to the ideals of Jesus Christ. Clearly, the inhuman or inconsistent behavior of many professed Christians hindered the effort to convert the slaves. For example, Cureton Milling's master shocked him by selling his own mulatto children despite being a member of the Presbyterian Church.[80] John Smith noted that his master, an unmarried preacher, had several children by his married slave mistress.[81] Mattie Curtis found fault with her master, also a minister, because he beat his slaves badly and gave them minimal food.[82] Finally, Leah Garrett criticized the preacher who owned her for whipping an old cook to death before he left to conduct services one Sunday.[83] The narrative of Frederick Douglass provides an extremely eloquent and detailed summation of the disgust that many slaves felt toward white southern Christianity because of such failings. "I am filled with unutterable loathing when I contemplate the religious pomp and show, together with the horrible inconsistencies, which every where surround me. We have men-stealers for ministers, women-whippers for missionaries, and cradle-plunderers for church members. The man who wields the blood-clotted cowskin during the week fills the pulpit on Sunday, and claims to be a minister of the meek and lowly Jesus."[84]

Many other narratives demonstrate that African American slaves often doubted or rejected Christianity because the white people around them failed to lead a consistent Christian life. Moses Roper identified his master as "a member of a Baptist church" but pointed out that "[h]is slaves, thinking him a very bad sample of what a professing Christian ought to be, would not join the connexion he belonged to, thinking they must be a very bad set of people."[85] Harriett Jacobs refused to join the church because her married Episcopalian master continually hounded her for sexual favors.[86] Charles Ball rejected Christianity because after his sale further South, "I could not pray, for the measure of my woes seemed to be full, and I felt as if there was no mercy in heaven, nor compassion on earth, for a man who was born a slave."[87] Lorendo Goodwin abandoned his Catholic faith after a priest violated the confessional by reporting that his cousin requested prayers in behalf of emancipation.[88] Finally, after his Methodist class leader attempted to kill him, Isaac Mason pondered the validity of Christianity by asking "How could I judge of his religious profession? How could I receive his religious instructions?"[89] Isaac Mason was not alone in his questioning of Christian sincerity among white southerners. Widespread African American doubts about the message and messengers of the church created a spiritual rift between white and black that few were willing to reach across.

American slavery and its emphasis on racial differences created separate identities for white and black members of southern society. The presence of these separate identities complicated and undermined the Christian ideal of unity within the body of Christ. White and black southerners saw each other as being so different that many African Americans simply could not accept the idea of sharing the same beliefs with whites. As with Charles Ball's African grandfather, the religion of their oppressors was not to be believed. While there is evidence that some white and black Christians did enjoy a shared religious experience, most African Americans did not view themselves as a part of white Christianity.[90] Most slaves saw the Gospel offered them as a perversion of the truth or as proof that Christianity was a false religion.[91] In either case, most African Americans placed little faith in what white Christians had to say about religion. Understandably, such a division hindered the conversion of slaves to Christianity and ultimately contributed to the development of segregated churches.

African American slaves clearly articulated their separate religious identities throughout the narratives, interviews, and autobiographies they have
given us. Although many slaves attended integrated services, most did not
feel that they were truly a part of those churches. For instance, Mingo
White and C. B. Burton described their church attendance in the following
manners: According to White, "Us didn't have no church 'cep de white
folks church."[92] Similarly, Burton recalled that "We had no school and no
church: but was made to go to de white folks church and set in de gallery."[93]
In addition to being typical, White and Burton's descriptions both show
that they did not invest their spiritual being in the "white folks church." As
with most African Americans, that institution was not theirs; it belonged
only to the whites. In fact, former slave Georgia Baker even felt great dissatisfaction with the integrated church she joined after the Civil War while
living up North. Baker identified her main objection to the church in saying, "Northern churches ain't lak our southern churches 'cause de black and
white folkses all belong to de same church. . . . On dat account I still didn't
feel lak I had jined de church."[94] To a significant degree, reactions like
Baker's stemmed from the belief that racists, especially slaveholders, could
not be Christians. Therefore, joining a church that was full of heathens was
the spiritual equivalent of not joining a church at all.

Slaves regularly expressed their doubts about the legitimacy of white
Christianity. For instance, Lydia Adams was hardly alone when she said, "I
don't think any slaveholder can get to the kingdom."[95] Henry Bibb noted
that fugitive slaves that had been baptized by slaveholding ministers often
had the ritual redone in the North.[96] Others argued that having a
Christian master was as bad as, if not in fact worse than, having a non-
believing owner. Maryland slave Joseph Smith bluntly stated that "I'd
rather live with a card-player and a drunkard than with a Christian."[97]
Clearly, most slaves did not believe that whites and blacks could share the
same religious experience. Matilda Perry argued as much when she stated
that "White folks can't pray right to the black man's God."[98] Kattie Sutton
elaborated further about this spiritual separation when she stated that
"White folks 'jes naturally different from darkies. . . . We's different in
color, in talk and in 'ligion and beliefs. We's different in every way and can
never be spected to think to live alike."[99] American Missionary Association
(AMA) teachers working with the freedmen found that this perception of
white and black difference hindered some of their efforts to convert

African Americans to Christianity. For example, in the Chesapeake region, AMA teachers had some difficulty in getting the older generation of freedmen to read the Bible. According to the teachers, the freedmen hesitated to read scripture because "their masters and families were Bible Christians, and they did not want to be like them."[100]

Many slaves did not only see whites as different, but viewed them to be oppositional in nature.[101] However, they were not opposites just because they were slave and free or white and black. As exemplified by their approach to religion, whites and blacks held diametrically opposed beliefs and thus viewed the world with greatly different eyes. For example, while whites believed they preached sound doctrine, slaves believed the messages usually amounted to "all lies . . ." and telling "stories 'bout 'ligion."[102] When white southern preachers prayed for Confederate success, slaves like Minnie Davis's mother asked God for northern victory and freedom.[103] Some slaves even believed that contact with whites destroyed African Americans' innate goodness. In Mary Ferguson's eyes, "colored people are naturally religious . . . [but] they learned all their 'devilment' from the whites."[104] Thus, in the eyes of many slaves, white and black southerners were spiritually incompatible and did not benefit from the time they spent together in worship.

Because most slaves drew little comfort from the religious aspects of attending church, African Americans routinely used Sundays to meet their own earthly needs. Many African Americans who were not required to attend church spent Sundays resting from the past week's labor. For example, Wash Hayes of Mississippi recalled that "De slaves mos' an' generally wuz tired out an lay 'round an' rested."[105] Others used the freedom from work to spend time with their families and friends on and, if allowed, off of the farm where they lived. In fact, slaves commonly referred to Sundays as "visitin' day."[106] More energetic slaves might go to town or the woods to play, court, gamble, fight, drink, or go dancing.[107] Still more spent the day in productive family labor such as washing clothes or supplementing their diet with fresh fish.[108]

Unconverted slaves who had to attend worship services also used these events for their own purposes. Slaves often saw worship services as a relaxing break from the routine of work. According to Hannah Davidson of Kentucky, Sunday services were "the only chance we'd get to rest."[109] However, as Sena Moore discovered when her master whipped her for snoring in church, slaves had to be very careful not to become too comfortable during worship services.[110] Nonetheless, Matthew Hume eagerly went to Catholic catechism class, not for sweet dreams, but for the candy or sugar his mistress gave to those attending.[111] Likewise, William Wells Brown enjoyed the sweet taste of secretly imbibed mint juleps during compulsory family prayer meetings.[112] In contrast to Brown, Arthur Colson and George Morrison used chicanery to pursue more innocent pastimes. Colson used the distraction of church services to slip outside and go fishing, while Morrison employed the same scheme to enjoy a game of marbles.[113] Finally, slaves who had no choice but to sit outside of the church during services could use the occasion to entertain themselves at the minister's expense. Horace Tonsler of Virginia described how slaves "would git up outside an' start in to preachin' right along wid preacher Woodson. Softlike, of course, wid a lot of handwavin' an' twistin' of his mouth widdout makin' no noise. We would sit up an' listen to him an laugh when he say just what de preacher say."[114]

As Tonsler's recollection suggests, most African Americans saw church attendance as an opportunity to enjoy the companionship of their fellow slaves. As recalled by North Carolina slave Robert Falls, church was the only place that many slaves were allowed to go to away from their owner's property.[115] Such travel restrictions meant that church provided one of the only sanctioned settings where large numbers of slaves could meet together in relative peace. As church meetings usually occurred only once or twice a month and often required long distance travel, Sunday services could last all day and include a scrumptious dinner on the grounds. Likewise, annual camp meetings lasted a week or more and featured large quantities of food. Isaac Stier, like many slaves, remembered the food more than the worship at these events: "Dey cooked up whole trunks full o' good things an' driv' over to de camp grounds. . . . Whilst dey was worshipin' I'd slip 'roun' and tas' out of dey basket. Ever'day I'd eat till I was ready to bus'."[116] More importantly, these occasions provided slaves opportunities to renew or begin kinship and friendship ties. Families, separated by sale or interplantation marriage, could reunite at these times and lonely souls could seek out new associations or support networks. Since there were few opportunities for off-property romantic encounters, numerous slaves remembered church services as the time when "boys shined up to de gals."[117] Candis Goodwin recalled how she first met her husband Jake in church: "We all was to church one Sunday, an' Jake he kep' cidin' up to me. An' I's lookin' at him outer de coner o' my eye, till finally he come up an' took holt o' my hands."[118] Indeed, dressed in their finest clothing, young African American men and women like Candis and Jake eagerly sought to find potential spouses and lovers from among church and camp meeting congregations.

In addition to food and fellowship, camp meetings, unlike church services, provided slaves with a brief but significant amount of freedom. While whites closely monitored the behavior of slaves sitting in a church balcony, camp meetings took on an almost circus-like atmosphere where one could more easily slip away unnoticed by the master's watchful eye. Minister and former Tennessee slave J. W. Loguen provided an eloquent description of the carnivalesque qualities of an antebellum camp meeting in his mid-nineteenth century autobiography.

> As a general thing, the slaves also were there, as servants of their masters and mistresses, or to enjoy a holiday of personal relaxation and pleasure, or to sell the fruits some of them were allowed to raise on their little patches of ground. The free blacks and poor whites were there also, with meats, fruits, and liquors of various kinds, to sell to the white aristocrats, who from pride, or fashion, or religion, were attracted to the place. The camp was the universal resort of lovers and rowdies, politicians and pleasure seekers of every kind, as well as religionists, who gathered about the preachers, or promenaded in the woods, or refreshed at the booths, where the poor whites and blacks exposed their provisions for sale.[119]

Obviously, camp meetings offered something for everyone, and the slaves relished the memories of the temporary freedom provided by these annual events. For example, John Hill remembered that during the slaves' annual August camp meeting the whites "fixed good dinners for us, 'an let us go off in de woods an' stay all day."[120] Despite not caring much about church, William Byrd described camp meetings as being great "cause you could see every body two or three counties around. . . . They let's the negro do most as he pleased there sos he behaved his self. . . ."[121]

As the preceding evidence suggests, slaves routinely attended church services for a multitude of reasons other than seeking conversion. Again, this evidence underscores the need for scholars to separate antebellum African American church attendance from actual conversion to Christianity. Furthermore, when viewed alongside the barriers hindering slave conversion, this evidence also suggests that slavery was far from a Christianizing institution. In fact, as presented here, slavery was a major hindrance for Christians concerned about the souls of slaves. While slavery brought Africans and African Americans into proximity with Christianity, the institution as established in the United States made conversions unnecessarily difficult and in some cases, virtually impossible.

Nineteenth-century Christians recognized that slavery as it existed in the United States prevented most slaves from converting. In particular, Christians realized that allowing imperfect humans to own their fellow humans placed too many African Americans in a condition of spiritual neglect. In order to call attention to this problem, Christians from many denominations openly criticized their own lack of effort to evangelize the slaves and repeatedly called on masters to live up to their moral duty to their bondsmen. For example, William Wightman, Methodist minister and biographer of William Capers, wrote that despite Rev. Capers's heroic efforts, "it is not claimed that any very extraordinary success in the conversion of the blacks has crowned the exertions of the missionaries. . . ."[122] Methodists blamed their less than extraordinary results on the fact that as of 1858 "we have as yet very imperfectly entered into the work which God has assigned us."[123] Episcopalians described their efforts as "ineffective" and noted that "It has been painfully experienced, heretofore, in the acknowledged fact that our missionary contributions have not been made according to the high standard of the Gospel. . . ."[124] Even C. C. Jones believed that African Americans exhibited a poor moral and religious condition because of "the little, comparatively speaking, that we are doing for them."[125]

Such self-flagellation in part reflects the deep concern that many committed white Christians had about the spiritual state of the slaves. However, it also reflects the fact that heart-felt ideals espoused on a national level did not always affect local circumstances. For example, despite decades of region-wide preaching about the need to increase the slaves' religious privileges, C. C. Jones' highly praised efforts in Liberty County, Georgia, did not even produce similar results throughout his home state. Specifically, in 1860, Liberty County had enough church pews to accommodate over 146 percent of its population. In contrast, a survey of the other nine leading black majority counties in Georgia shows that they averaged enough church pews to seat only 48.8 percent of their residents.[126] Obviously, while many pointed to Liberty County as worthy of emulation, few followed their pioneering example. Likewise, the decentralized organizational structure of the

Southern Baptists meant that local religious bodies did not have to implement policies recommended by the denominational convention. As late as 1859, the Southern Baptist Convention had to stir their churches into action on behalf of the slaves by pleading, "Shall we not—ought we not to feel a deeper interest in this work?"[127] Such pleas reveal the frustration that many missionary agencies felt about the recurrent reports of ministerial destitution that hindered missions to the slaves. For example, in 1857, the Bethel Baptist Association of Alabama awaited "the time . . . when the colored man's spiritual interest will be regarded according to its magnitude, and corresponding efforts be put forth for its promotion."[128] Six years later, Alabama Baptists still waited for their season of awakening as they openly acknowledged that the slaves' "moral and spiritual culture have been sadly neglected."[129] However, Alabamians were not alone in admitting their neglect of African American spiritual needs. In the wake of Confederate defeat, white Christians throughout the South openly acknowledged that they had not lived up to their moral obligations to the slaves and interpreted the Civil War and emancipation as God's punishment for their negligence.[130]

Given the numerous barriers to conversion and the inadequacy of the South's missionary efforts, it is a wonder that as many African Americans converted as did. C. C. Jones attributed many of these conversions to the fact that African Americans "preach[ed] the Gospel to each other. . . ."[131] Indeed, the religious fervor and faithfulness to Christianity of the small core of African American Christians made them a dynamic force for conversion within the slave community. As slaves, they regularly but quietly prophesied and prayed about the day when God would break the shackles of bondage and set his righteous people free. When that anticipated deliverance arrived, slave Christians stood as a people justified in their faith and served as the greatest testament of their God's power.[132] The Christian core's faithfulness and accuracy in anticipating emancipation thereby attracted ever greater numbers of African American freedmen to Christianity. Freedom, rather than slavery, proved the greatest force for conversion among African Americans in the South.

Part III

RACE

WHAT'S CRITICAL ABOUT WHITE STUDIES

Paul Spickard

In the spring of 1966, many black and some white and Asian students at Seattle's inner-city Garfield High School went on strike, asking the school board to devote more resources to educating minority children, hire more minority teachers, and install an antiracist curriculum. One of the speakers at a rally and workshop at Mt. Zion Baptist Church was James Bevel, an organizer for the Southern Christian Leadership Conference and intimate of Dr. Martin Luther King. One of the white participants asked Bevel, "What is the place of white people in the Negro revolution?" (Remember, this was 1966 and the terminological turn to Black Power would not hit the streets of African American neighborhoods for another year). He apparently regarded himself a member of the liberal vanguard, was excited to be at this revolutionary gathering, and wanted specific direction as to how to be helpful. He may also have wanted to be told what a fine thing it was for a white person such as himself to do something on behalf of blacks.

So it was with some dismay that he received Bevel's reply: "There is no place for white people in the Negro revolution. We are trying to organize ourselves to take control of our lives. White people are the problem. You need to go back to white people and teach them not to be racists." It was not what that white person wanted to hear, for he was looking for a way to be at the center of the action, where black people were making a social revolution. Now he was being told not to sap the energy of the black people around him, to go home and attend to a less glamorous chore, the subtle and difficult task of addressing white racism from within the white community. To his credit, he did just that, and spent much of the next decade talking to white people about their problems with racism.

The sentiment in Bevel's injunction to go back to white people and teach them not to do bad stuff about race seems to be at the base of the recent vogue in white studies. There has been an extraordinary outpouring of literature examining whiteness. If one typed the word "whiteness" into a library catalogue in 1995, one might pull up a half-dozen references. Typing the same word in 2000 yields hundreds. This essay surveys that literature, its premises, preoccupations, and themes. Further, it attempts to sort out what parts of the white studies literature are helpful in challenging the system of racial hierarchy that governs American social relations, versus those parts that tend toward other effects—to determine, in short, what is critical about white studies.

Jonathan Rutherford, a British critic, writes about his motivation to study whiteness:

> *I was prompted to start thinking about my own ethnic identity by the contemporary generation of black and Asian English intellectuals—Paul Gilroy, Stuart Hall, Kobena Mercer, Isaac Julien, Lola Young, Pratibha Parmar—who were thinking reflexively and historically about race, gender and ethnicity. My involvement in radical politics on the left had taught me to disavow the racial exclusivity of white ethnicity, but never to analyse or try and understand it. Being white was a vague, amorphous concept to get hold of; it wasn't a colour, it was invisible. And who wanted the risible, sometimes ugly, baggage of Englishness? Everything which signified Englishness—the embarrassing legacy of racial supremacy and empire, the union jack waving crowds, the royalty, the rhetoric about Britain's standing in the world—suggested a conservative deference to nostalgia. The problem with intellectually disowning white English ethnicity was that the left never got around to working out what it was, and what our own emotional connections to it were.[1]*

Noel Ignatiev and John Garvey pride themselves on being "race traitors." Like Rutherford, they are white but would disavow whiteness. They begin with an insight with which this writer would not disagree: "the key to fundamental social change in the U.S. is the challenge to the system of race privilege that embraces all whites." Their definition of whiteness is perhaps a bit idiosyncratic: "The white race consists of those who partake of the privileges of white skin. . . . people were not favored socially because they were white; rather they were defined as 'white' because they were favored." Then, invoking the memory of John Brown, they issue a call to "focus on whiteness and the struggle to abolish the white race from within," by disavowing the privileges of white skin.

This, they say, is the "key to solving the social problems of our age. . . . the majority of so-called whites in this country are neither deeply nor consciously committed to white supremacy; like most human beings in most times and places, they would do the right thing if it were convenient. . . . By engaging these dissidents in a journey of discovery into whiteness and its discontents, we hope to take part . . . in the process of defining a new human community." They conclude: "The existence of the white race depends on the willingness of those assigned to it to place their racial interests above class, gender, or any other interests they hold. The defection of enough of its members to make it unreliable as a determinant of behavior will set off tremors that will lead to its collapse." What is not clear in this formulation is just how that "defection" from the white race is to be accomplished, nor how one can disavow one's whiteness and make it stick.[2]

Garvey, Ignatiev, and Rutherford would study whiteness in order to dethrone it. This is a different business than older studies of white people.[3] Those took several perspectives. First were the rantings of early-twentieth-century pseudoscientific racialists. Their name was legion, but among the most memorable of such writers were Madison Grant and Lothrop Stoddard. Grant's masterwork was *The Passing of the Great Race, or The Racial Basis of European History*, in which he divided all of humankind into "races" on supposedly scientific principles and told why it was that vigor and virtue emerged out of competition among races as the distinctive qualities of Nordic peoples who drew their origins from Aryan ancestors. Grant argued that "conservation of [the white] race" was "the true spirit of Americanism." Hitler apparently read Grant, and thought it the true spirit of the Third Reich as well. Stoddard followed shortly with *The Rising Tide of Color Against White World-Supremacy*, which made dire predictions of white people in Europe and North America being outbred and eventually overrun by fecund hordes of "inferior stocks"—Asians, Africans, and Latin Americans. Stoddard's writing and Grant's played a part in the racially-inflected quotas and exclusions that distinguished the Immigration Act of 1924.[4]

Grant and Stoddard were crude, white-supremacist race-baiters. Yet their racial assumptions have found marginally more genteel echoes in our own time, covered by a thin veneer of pseudoscience and policy concern. None is more prominent than Richard Herrnstein and Charles Murray's

The Bell Curve, an attack on affirmative action hidden in a welter of bad science and bogus statistics. Almost as widely read and no less pernicious was Peter Brimelow's *Alien Nation*. Here, an Anglo-Saxon immigrant attempted to pull up the ladder behind him, charging that brown and yellow immigrants were "making America . . . a freak among the world's nations because of the unprecedented demographic mutation it is inflicting on itself." These were relatively explicit celebrations of what the authors regarded as white superiority, a kind of literary Klanism.[5]

There has been a less overtly malevolent but still insidious literature—studies that focused on the experiences of white ethnic groups in such a way as to tend to ignore the fundamental differences between the experiences of white people and those of people of color in the United States. Books like Thomas Sowell's *Ethnic America*, Nathan Glazer's *Ethnic Dilemmas*, and Michael Novak's *The Rise of the Unmeltable Ethnics* all wrote about African Americans and other peoples of color as if they were ethnic groups just like Greeks and Swedes. The tendency of such works was to focus on the hardships faced by some white immigrant groups, to bare their grievances, and to shade into justification of white privilege by denying its distinctive existence.[6]

Then there was quite another vector in whiteness studies after mid-century: a large number of studies of white attitudes about race and of white immigrant groups, which had none of the racist political agenda of the books described above. The list of such books includes many distinguished titles, for example: *The Nature of Prejudice* by Gordon W. Allport; *White Over Black* by Winthrop D. Jordan; *American Slavery—American Freedom* by Edmund Morgan; *The Transplanted* by John Bodnar; *Voyagers to the West* by Bernard Bailyn; *Albion's Seed* by David Hackett Fischer; and *Ethnic Identity* by Richard D. Alba.[7] These were varieties of whiteness studies, too, although of a very different sort than the racist whiteness studies of Grant, Brimelow, and their ilk.

Most older strands of whiteness studies (not the last) had origins or at least ties on the political right. The new whiteness studies of the 1990s and the twenty-first century, by contrast, stem from the political left. The founding parents of this movement were Alexander Saxton, David Roediger, and Toni Morrison. Saxton's book, *The Rise and Fall of the White Republic*, started the trend in 1990. It is an analysis of the role of racial thinking in the shifting class bases of political parties in the United States over the course of the nineteenth century. Saxton begins with the assumption that racial ideas began in North America as an attempt by Europeans to justify enslavement of Africans and expropriation and expulsion of Native Americans.[8] He then traces changes in racial thinking by various groups of Americans, the vehicle by which he explains the changing alignments of white class groupings in the major political parties. In short, Saxton treats "the generation and regeneration of white racism 'as part of the process of class conflict and compromise'."[9]

Saxton, then, is interested in the history of the creation and transformation of concepts about racial inequality. Behind that, he is interested in the course of class conflict. He sees racial thinking primarily as a tool created and used by white people to pursue class-based political alliances among white people. This is not quite crude Marxism—race as mere false consciousness, a gloss on class. It nonetheless amounts to an admittedly sophisticated and informed attempt to reduce racial oppression to an expression of class conflict.[10] *The Rise and Fall of the White Republic* is a serious attempt to understand the ways that racial ideas and racial marking on the part of whites shaped United States politics in the nineteenth century.

David Roediger's much-acclaimed *Wages of Whiteness* is a book about class formation among whites, too. Bearing the subtitle, *Race and the Making of the American Working Class*, it argues that white workers in the mid-nineteenth century gathered themselves into a self-conscious, activist working class, not only on the basis of class interests but also on the basis of a racist intention to distance themselves from that other great part of the working class, black workers. Roediger starts from an elaboration of W. E. B. Du Bois's notion of a psychic wage that accrued to whites from their very whiteness: "[T]he pleasures of whiteness could function as a 'wage' for white workers. That is, status and privileges conferred by race could be used to make up for alienating and exploitative class relationships, North and South. White workers could, and did, define and accept their class positions by fashioning identities as 'not slaves' and as 'not blacks'." Thus, "working class formation and the systematic development of a sense of whiteness went hand in hand for the US white working class."[11]

The power of Roediger's book is enhanced by the subtlety of his argument and the variety of his methods and areas of inquiry. He examines political speech, crowd behavior, folklore, humor, and audience responses to minstrel shows, among other things. His argument is, in the end, equal parts psychological and class analysis:

> *"[W]hiteness was a way in which workers responded to a fear of dependency on wage labor and to the necessities of capitalist work discipline. As the U.S. working class matured, principally in the North, within a slaveholding republic, the heritage of the Revolution made independence a powerful masculine personal ideal. But slave labor and 'hireling' wage labor proliferated in the new nation. One way to make peace with the latter was to differentiate it sharply from the former. . . . [T]he white working class, disciplined and made anxious by fear of dependency, began during its formation to construct an image of the black population as 'other'—as embodying the preindustrial, erotic, careless style of life the white worker hated and longed for."[12]*

Roediger starts from the conviction, adopted from Coco Fusco, that "To ignore white ethnicity is to redouble its hegemony by naturalizing it."[13] This conviction stands at the ideological base of whiteness studies. Yet if there is a criticism to be made of *The Wages of Whiteness*, it is that in it Roediger, like most of the whiteness studies writers, expresses a rhetoric of normative whiteness. "Workers" are assumed to be white unless they are racially marked as "blacks," and the most important thing about black workers is their blackness, not their participation in the working class.[14] Roediger recognized the dangers in this posture and worked to undercut it in two later works. A volume of essays, *Towards the Abolition of Whiteness*, took up several themes tangential to *The Wages of Whiteness*. More consistently than in the first book he treated blacks and other people of color as actors in their own rights, not merely as foils for white workers. In *Black on White: Black Writers on What It Means to Be White*, Roediger reproduced the writings of four dozen African American writers from Anna Julia Cooper to Lewis Gordon. Here was a book about whiteness, but it was not fixed on the ideas of white people. Rather, it sought to dethrone white privilege by putting the analysis of whiteness in the hands of blacks.[15]

Toni Morrison completed the foundation of the white studies movement in 1992 with *Playing in the Dark: Whiteness and the Literary Imagination*. Roediger and Saxton are interested in the white working class and its relationship to racial identity politics. Morrison's interest is American literature. Not only, Morrison said, has American literature been dominated by white male authors and white male critics. But the values of literary criticism, the decisions as to what is important and excellent and true, have been appropriated by white men in hegemonic ways that have denied that appropriation. Valuing the universal (read "white") over the particular (read "black"), they have virtually erased black characters, black authors, black themes, black issues from the central part of American literature. But just as Saxton and Roediger find white workers defining their identities against black workers, so too Morrison finds the white writers of the canon (Hemingway, Faulkner, and others) defining the major issues, indeed the national character, in relationship to blackness. She argues that "the meta-phorical and metaphysical uses of race occupy definitive places in American literature, in the 'national' character, and ought to be a major concern of the literary scholarship that tries to know it."[16]

The Wages of Whiteness, *Playing in the Dark*, and *The Rise and Fall of the White Republic*, then, are foundational examples of what is good about whiteness studies. Morrison, Roediger, and less explicitly Saxton, analyze whiteness in order, one might say, to decenter it, to make it less hegemon-ical, to reduce its power. Other useful examples of white studies abound.

Theodore Allen joined the discussion with *The Invention of the White Race*. Instead of the nineteenth century as the critical time for white racial formation, Allen looks to America in the seventeenth and eighteenth cen-turies. He posits a time before the categories white and black had social meaning, when national labels such as English and Irish were the modes of identity. He argues with polemical ferocity that the white race was invented no later than the middle of the eighteenth century by the planter elite of the Chesapeake colonies, as a deliberate measure of social control. The laboring classes were divided, white and free on one side, black and slave on the other.[17]

Tomás Almaguer expanded the discussion beyond the black-white dichotomy in *Racial Fault Lines*. Roediger had made some mention of white workers defining themselves against Chinese workers in the West, but otherwise the authors described up to this point all saw race as a binary rela-tionship between black and white. Looking at the construction and uses of whiteness in California in the second half of the nineteenth century, Almaguer paints a more complicated picture. Here there were not just white and black people, but Asians, Mexicans, and Native Americans as well.[18] Almaguer found white people coming to the West with pre-existing convictions about white racial superiority and then creating a new racial hierarchy out of local materials.

For Almaguer, as for Saxton, Allen, and Roediger, race making is critically intertwined with class making. But unlike them he argues for "the primacy of race. . . . Beginning in 1870 and intensifying dramatically in the 1880s, an economy based on wage labor eclipsed that based on the unfree labor system of the Mexican period. Once unleashed, this proletarianization absorbed both the indigenous Mexican population and the numerous white and nonwhite immigrant groups that settled in the area." "Racial status" played a "central role" in co-creating the new class structure:

> *Far from being merely an ideological construct or an anachronistic status designation, race became the key organizing principle structuring white supramicist economic, as well as political, institutions that were introduced in California. White male immigrants became farmers, proprietors, professionals, and white-collar employees, while the Mexican, Japanese, Chinese, and Indian male populations were securely ensconced at the bottom end of the class structure as unskilled manual workers.*[19]

The multiple sides to Almaguer's analysis may tempt some to conclude that *Racial Fault Lines* is something other than whiteness studies. Although he is sensitive to the existence and issues of other groups, the actors in his story are white people, and the story is about the ways they drew lines between themselves and various peoples of color—the ways they defined and used whiteness.

Neil Foley echoed Almaguer's description of a multiple-sided racial encounter in *The White Scourge*. Set in the cotton country of Central Texas, mainly in the first decades of the twentieth century, *The White Scourge* examines the relationships between blacks, Mexicans, and poor whites. Where Almaguer focused on whites making racial distinctions, Foley treats all three of the groups under study as actors, and attends to the ways they negotiated their identities and class positions. For Foley, the critical item under negotiation was whiteness. As cotton farming grew into agribusiness at the dawn of the century, former sharecroppers and tenant farmers became proletarian field workers. Foley finds that, for a time, poor whites lost some of their racial privilege relative to black and especially Mexican agricultural workers. Conversely for a brief period Mexicans were able to negotiate a place for themselves part-way between black and white, taking on, Foley says, a measure of whiteness.[20]

George Lipsitz turned a harsh lens on white privilege in an influential essay and book, both titled, *The Possessive Investment in Whiteness*.[21] Lipsitz offers a brilliant tour of American racial history, showing how, in each era from Jamestown up to the present, and in various sectors of the economy and polity, powerful whites have chosen to establish structures that favored European-derived Americans over peoples of color, and then masked those decisions behind the language of individualism. "From the start," says Lipsitz, "European settlers in North America established structures encouraging possessive investment in whiteness. The colonial and early-national legal systems authorized attacks on Native Americans and encouraged the appropriation of their lands. They legitimated racialized chattel slavery, restricted naturalized citizenship to 'white' immigrants, and provided pretexts for exploiting labor, seizing property, and denying the franchise to Asian Americans, Mexican Americans, Native Americans, and African Americans."[22]

This drawing a line between whites and people of color, and favoring the former over the latter, did not end with slavery, however. Lipsitz offers example after example, from the racist quality of the American seizure of the Philippines, to the Bakke decision against affirmative action, to FHA housing policies that helped create all-white suburbs. Nonetheless, he concludes, almost hopefully: "The problem with white people is not our whiteness, but our possessive investment in it. Created by politics, culture, and consciousness, our possessive investment in whiteness can be altered by those same processes, but only if we face the hard facts openly. . . . How can we account for the ways in which white people refuse to acknowledge their possessive investment in whiteness even as they work to increase its value every day? We can't blame the color of our skin. It must be the content of our character."[23]

One of the most sophisticated examples of the merits of white studies is Matthew Frye Jacobson's *Whiteness of a Different Color: European Immigrants and the Alchemy of Race*.[24] Jacobson attempts to chart the entire history of the European immigrant peoples of the United States and to examine the relationships among those peoples. Jacobson divides American racial history into three periods. The first was 1790–1840, when "free white persons" as designated in the first naturalization law was an amorphous category that had some element of hierarchy within it, but that did not sharply delineate among varieties of European-descended peoples. For Jacobson, the crucial tool that made these peoples a common white race was republican ideology—an estimate of their fitness for self-government. In the second period, 1840–1924, Jacobson finds the white race broken up into some groups that are white and some that are less so—perhaps even some that are not white (he is not consistent on that point)—under the force of more varied immigration, the rise of industry, and pseudoscientific racial theorizing. That hierarchy among whitenesses explains the Anglo-centric quota system at the heart of the 1924 immigration act. In the third period, 1924–1965, white people were mushed together again into an amorphous group called Caucasians.[25]

The strength of *Whiteness of a Different Color* is that it takes seriously the hierarchies that existed among white people, and tries to account for them. There are some problems near the book's core, however. For one thing, although on nearly every page Jacobson speaks of the "racial" character of this or that distinction, at no place does he define what "racial" means for him.[26] So when he says that the differences among Anglo-Americans, Irish, and Jews were racial, we are not quite sure what he means. He seems to want to set up various European immigrant peoples as racially separate from the dominant group of whites, especially in his middle period. Surely, there was hierarchy among whites (and surely, by his own evidence but contrary to his schema, it existed in all three periods). But that does not mean that the disabilities suffered by Irish or Italians or Jews in the United States achieved the same scale as those suffered by peoples of color. Some people may have used race language in that middle period to describe what they called "ethnic" differences in another period, but that does not mean that the groups were more sharply divided in that middle period; it may only mean that the language fashion changed.

Jacobson very seldom even mentions African or Native or Mexican or Asian Americans, but on those few occasions when he does, it is clear that the disabilities suffered by subordinate white "races" pale by comparison. He writes:

> *Reconstruction collapsed in the South, raising new questions about the relations among whites and blacks in an era of black Emancipation and the reintegration of the South into national political life. In the aftermath of Custer's demise . . .*

the Great Sioux Wars ended with the defeat of the Minneconjou Sioux; Sitting
Bull escaped to Canada, and Crazy Horse surrendered to federal troops. A vocal
and often violent anti-Chinese movement coalesced in the West, particularly in
California, where white workers decried the labor competition of "Mongolians"
and insisted upon a "white man's republic." The East and Midwest, meanwhile,
were wracked by labor unrest which raised questions *in some quarters about*
the white immigrant working class itself.[27]

"Raised questions" versus killed, enslaved, imprisoned on reservations, and excluded from the country. Yes, there were groups of whites who were set off from the dominant group, and they had less privilege, but that does not mean that they were racially separate from dominant-group whites, nor that their disadvantage came close to that experienced by peoples of color. They could vote, they were eligible for naturalization, and no one was killing them on account of their ethnicity. Theirs was, as the title suggests, not non-whiteness, but "whiteness of a different color." Yet Jacobson's book is premised in part on their being more separate and disadvantaged than that, and the evidence just will not support such a claim.

Despite some such shortcomings, *Whiteness of a Different Color*, like *The White Scourge*, *The Wages of Whiteness*, and similar books, is a significant help to our understanding of the ways that race has been constructed and used. The best white studies are like these, historically grounded studies of how the white group was formed, and how power has been employed to enhance and maintain it.[28]

There is a related movement—critical race theory—that is worth mentioning as an adjunct to whiteness studies. Critical race theory is an intellectual movement primarily within the circles of legal scholarship. Some progressive legal scholars saw the modest gains experienced by people of color during the civil rights movement disappearing in the 1970s. They grew impatient with the standard liberal approaches to racial justice. Turning to neo-Marxist and postmodern ideas, they fashioned a new approach to legal interpretation surrounding racial issues.[29] Critical race theory intersects with whiteness studies through one of its offshoots: critical white studies. The branching began with an article by Cheryl Harris in the *Harvard Law Review*, "Whiteness as Property". There, she made from a legal point of view much the same argument that Lipsitz would later make in terms more broadly cultural and political. In *White By Law*,

Ian Haney López broadened Harris's analysis to show how whites used the law to draw lines around their whiteness and reinforce their privilege. Richard Delgado and Jean Stefancic widened the discussion of critical white studies in a massive compendium of writings by legal scholars and others on the ways that white people have created and maintained white privilege.[30]

If these are the many strengths and important achievements of whiteness studies, are there weaknesses, too? Alas, there are. The problems stem from what seem to be the motivations behind much of the white studies movement. One factor seems to be embarrassment on the part of some white people who regard themselves as sensitive to racial issues—embarrassment that they are white. Jonathan Rutherford, in the passage quoted early in this chapter, used that word to describe the root of his desire to study whiteness.[31] No one wants to be part of the problem. People of sensitivity and good will want to be part of the solution. However, that desire may shade over into a longing to be at the center of action racially speaking. Like the young man whose story opened this chapter, whiteness studies people want to be on the side of progressive social change in racial matters.

Embarrassment and a desire to be at the center of action lead some people to want to flee their whiteness. Rutherford writes of a longing to "disown . . . white English ethnicity" and Ignatiev and Garvey call on progressive whites to "defect" from, in fact to "abolish" the white race.[32] That would neatly solve the embarrassment problem and perhaps put one at the center of the action, but how can one do that? Black theologian James Cone put a positive spin on the dilemma in 1970, long before the white studies movement: "There will be no peace in America until whites begin to hate their whiteness, asking from the depths of their being: 'How can we become black?'"[33]

One way, perhaps, to lessen the tension is to suggest that one is not an oppressor because one is not quite so white as those bad whites who are the main oppressors. This leads to the We Are Other Too fallacy that is a significant sub-theme in the whiteness studies movement. Some white people, in desiring to flee or disavow their whiteness, retreat into the comforting assertion that they (or some other whites with whom they identify) are not, or were not always, quite so white as the main white oppressors.

They begin with the accurate observation that there has long been a hierarchy among white Americans along lines of ancestral nationality, and that it has sometimes assumed a racial tone (that is, the language people have used to describe it has sometimes referred to supposedly innate characteristics and phenotype). This hierarchy within whiteness can be illustrated by the following exercise. More than 100 audiences in the last two-plus decades—students, church groups, and audiences at public lectures—have been asked to rank ten American ethnic groups "according to how closely they approximate the core of what it means to be an American." In every single case, the audience, on average, gave a ranking that looked about like this:[34]

1. English
2. Swedish
3. Irish
4. Polish
5. Jewish
6. Black
7. American Indian
8. Japanese
9. Mexican
10. Arab

Something very like this hierarchy was coded into the Immigration Act of 1924, which set strict quotas on Eastern and southern European immigrants and banned Asians outright. Such a hierarchy was assumed by Florence Ewing, a kind white woman from Missouri, who early in the twentieth century wrote the names of all her high school friends next to their pictures in her scrapbook. The ethnicity of her Anglo-American, German, and Scandinavian Protestant and Irish Catholic friends went unmarked, but she felt compelled to write "Jewish" next to the names of those to whom that appellation might be applied. It did not mean that she was not equally their friend, only that their Jewish identity made them something less than other whites.[35]

Starting from the observation of such a hierarchy among white people, some students of whiteness take it a step further into the assertion that Jews or Irish or Italians or some other group of white people once were not white. Thus we now see books and articles about How Whomever Became White. The unspoken assertion is, "We have race, too, the same as people of color. We are not part of the problem because we are Other, too."

The standard-bearer in this trend is Noel Ignatiev, in an influential book with the provocative title, *How the Irish Became White*. Intrinsic to Ignatiev's argument is an idiosyncratic definition of whiteness. He begins with the observations that race is not biological in origin, but rather that people are assigned to races, and that there is an intimate "connection . . . between concepts of race and acts of oppression." One is not white in one's person, and a group of people are not a white group in their being. Rather, they are white insofar as they participate in oppressing others who are defined as the racial target for subordination. For Ignatiev, "[T]he white race consists of those who partake of the privileges of white skin." This provides him the conceptual foundation from which to argue that, for Irish Americans in the nineteenth century, "To enter the white race was a strategy to secure an advantage in a competitive society."[36] That is, by the quirks of Ignatiev's definitions, the Irish were once not white, and then they worked to become white, by drawing a distinction between themselves and people who were not white and actively oppressing those people.

Ignatiev argues there was a time in Ireland when Irish people were oppressed in something like racial terms. English people colonized Ireland, took away people's lands and livelihoods, and created an ideology of Irish innate, quasi-biological inferiority—not quite black, but not like English people either. Irish people came to America and were slotted into low class positions—though not as low as slaves or free blacks. Here, according to Ignatiev, instead of making class solidarity with African Americans, the Irish chose to be white—that is, to be oppressive—in order to distance themselves from blacks and improve their social and economic possibilities. Through the Catholic church, labor unions, and the Democratic Party they claimed a place in what was becoming the white republic.

The important contributions of Ignatiev's polemic are his insistence on examining relations between white and black members of the working class, and his conclusion that adopting anti-black attitudes and activities was essential to Irish Americans making a place for themselves above the bottom rung in the United States. His broader contention highlighted in the title, that the Irish were once not white and then chose to become white, is intelligible—but only if one recognizes and accepts his idiosyncratic definition of whiteness not as biology or group identity, rather as choosing to act oppressively toward African Americans.

Yet the impact of the title and argument is quite different. Very few people comprehend Ignatiev's definition of whiteness, and fewer still accept it as normative. This writer has heard dozens of times since Ignatiev's book was published, from white laypeople and scholars alike, some version of the following statement: "You know, the Irish weren't always white. Once they were not white and then they became white." The implication is that the kind of mobility that Irish Americans are said to have experienced is readily available to people of color in the United States. It is an easy step from there to the racist conclusion that if blacks or Latinos or Indians or Asians have chosen not to become white it is out of perversity on their own part. Like the Irish, they could have become white, and escaped the disabilities that are their lot.

Ignatiev would not own that interpretation. In *Race Traitor* and in *How the Irish Became White* he shows how vehemently he opposes white privilege and oppressiveness. That is why he wants to disown whiteness. It is a noble urge, but ultimately a misguided one. Ignatiev and other whites (including the author of this essay) cannot effectively disown our whiteness, much as we might like to do so. We necessarily carry white privilege whether we want to do so or not. To illustrate: try as I may, I cannot change the fact that I can get a cab easily in midtown Manhattan, while a middle-aged black or Latino man wearing similar clothing cannot. More consequentially, we will be seen differently when applying for a loan, seeking a job, or confronting a police officer. Whites as a group have better life chances than African Americans or other people of color. We can hate white privilege, we can denounce it, but until race is irrelevant in America—a distant day indeed—we cannot be not privileged. We can fight against racial hierarchy and oppression daily, but we cannot abolish the white race. We still enjoy the fruits of whiteness, whether we want them or not.

The We Are Other Too trend is carried further by Karen Brodkin in *How Jews Became White Folks and What That Says About Race in America*.[37] One hesitates to cast aspersions on a book as good as *How Jews Became White Folks*. Brodkin began the study as an attempt to understand how race, class, and gender interpenetrate each other in American society. Gradually it turned, however, first into an exploration of changes in the nature of Jewishness, and then into a kind of family history of racial identity. *How Jews Became White Folks* in fact does a superb job of illuminating how gender and class work together with race in the formation of identities and hierarchies in the American economic and political systems.

But in the more expansive theme that gives the book its title, Brodkin loses her way. Her central contention on this theme is that there was a time in American history when Jews were nonwhites. When she hews closer to her evidence, she describes Jews as being "not-quite white" or having "a whiteness of our own."[38] Here she refers to the fact that Jews have long held a lower position in the American ethnoracial hierarchy than white Gentiles (although that position has improved in the last generation and though it was never so low as any of the nation's peoples of color). But more frequently than such nuanced phrasings, Brodkin boldly asserts, again and again, and without any supporting evidence, that Jews were in fact nonwhite.

This is an example of whiteness studies run amok. If this trend continues, one can expect to see books before long on How the Italians Became White, How the Swedes Became White, perhaps even How the English Became White. It is pretty silly, and disrespectful of the genuine disabilities faced by people of color in America's racial system.

The ultimate absurdity on the theme We Are Other Too is John Gennari's 1996 article, "Passing for Italian." On the cover of the trendy cultural studies journal *Transition* is that title across a picture of Denny Mendez, Miss Italia 1996—an apparently black woman. One might expect Gennari's article to be a meditation on the complexities of Italian identity in an age when immigrants (including the Dominican-born Mendez) are remaking the ethnic map of places that are frequently thought to be racially homogeneous. That would be a worthy subject. Instead, we are treated to a self-indulgent essay whose central contention is that there is "a distinct tradition of interethnic identification. . . . the black/Italian crossover fantasy" which Gennari calls "'goombah blackness'—an affective alliance between Italian and African Americans based on mutual desires and pleasures, and grounded particularly in a tradition of boisterous male assertiveness." Blacks and Italians, says Gennari, are natural pals.

Gennari's evidence? He has almost none, beyond assertions that Marvin Gaye admired Frank Sinatra, that Sinatra admired Billie Holiday, and that Sinatra and some gangsta rappers had similar attitudes toward women. The suspicion lingers that Gennari is just a white guy attempting to appropriate blackness in order to make himself look more hip. It does not work. Sinatra's attitudes may have been similar to those of some hip-hop artists, and there surely have been times and places where blacks and Italians (and others) have interacted. But I know of no black neighborhood in the 1940s and '50s where more than a tiny handful of people even listened to Frank Sinatra, much less thought him one of their own. There is no evidence at all of a special affinity between the black and Italian American populations at large. "Passing for Italian" is pernicious silliness.[39]

Thus, many white studies authors assert, without adequate foundation, a parallel between racial divisions and the situations of white ethnic groups. And almost none ask the comparative questions that would be needed to prove their assumptions true. For example, precisely how *are* the disabilities suffered by Jews or Italians like—and how are they unlike—those suffered by blacks and Indians? Do those disabilities stem from the same causes? Are they equally susceptible to remediation? These and questions like them are worth asking, but one will not find them asked in whiteness studies.

There is another theme to some studies of whiteness by white feminists, and it borders on an assertion that We Are Other, Too. It is the implication that femaleness blackifies, that because a white person or group is female that person or group does not partake of white privilege to the same degree as do white males. I take that to be a nearly spoken subtext in the interchange between Catharine MacKinnon and Martha Mahoney in the *Yale Journal of Law and Feminism*.[40] I do not wish to contest or discount the very real disabilities faced by white women in a sexist society—quite the contrary. Nonetheless, there is something pernicious about adopting, even by subtle implication, the oppression of members of a group to which one does not belong. Salient refutations of such an assertion of common otherness are made by a number of feminists of color, among them bell hooks, Hazel Carby, Haunani-Kay Trask, and Donna Awatere.[41]

Finally, the We Are Other Too vector in whiteness studies extends to skinhead chic. The taking off point here is a smart, funny, subversive collection of essays called *White Trash*, edited by Matt Wray and Annalee Newitz. The editors describe their project thus: "Poor or marginal whites occupy an uncharted space in recent identity studies, particularly because they do not easily fit the model of whiteness-as-power proposed by many multiculturalist or minority discourses. Associated in mainstream culture with 'trashy' kitsch or dangerous pathologies rather than with the material realities of economic life, poor whites are treated as degraded caricatures rather than as real people living in conditions of poverty and disempowerment."[42]

Thandeka, in a *Tikkun* essay called "The Cost of Whiteness", echoed that analysis: "I am not denying 'white privilege.' All whites . . . benefit from their wage of whiteness. Such talk of privilege, however, is incomplete unless we also speak of its penalty. For poorer wage earners without power, money or influence, their wage of whiteness functions as a kind of workers'. . . . 'consolation prize' to persons, who, although not wealthy, do not have to consider themselves losers because they are, at least, white. . . . These workers are, in effect, exploited twice: first as workers and then as whites . . . . Whiteness functions as a distraction from the pervasive class problem."[43] This is a convoluted way of saying that Thandeka wants the real problem to be class, not race. But it is also a serious attempt to address the disabilities faced by poor people who are white.

Where are the lines between (1) exploring whiteness, (2) rescuing white working-class culture from abuse by outsiders, (3) celebrating whiteness as a positive identity, and (4) embracing white supremacist racism? It is not always clear. A tour of who-bought-what-else from Amazon.com led from excellent whiteness studies books by Roediger, Ruth Frankenberg, Allen, and Jacobson to white trash books like Wray and Newitz's. Then the trail went on to Jim Goad's *Redneck Manifesto: How Hillbillies, Hicks, and White Trash Became America's Scapegoats*. Finally, it landed in the heart of Aryan Nation: *They Were White and They Were Slaves* by Michael Hoffman and *The South Was Right!* by James Ronald Kennedy.[44] Where exactly was it that the anti-racist intent of whiteness studies shaded into advocacy of white racism?

Brodkin, Ignatiev, and nearly all the authors of the We Are Other Too school express a desire to undermine white privilege. These authors, as much as Lipsitz, Rodeiger, and the other more successful writers on the theme, seem to be trying conscientiously to do what James Bevel instructed that white man to do in 1966: go back and teach white people about their bigotry. The best examples of whiteness studies achieve that goal. Still, even the best authors in this field spend nearly all their time talking about white people. And there are so many authors, writing so much about whiteness these days.[45] Each of them surely makes a contribution to the understanding of whiteness. And white studies has opened up space for some very creative and insightful riffing on activities around race.[46] But they place white people at the center of investigation, saying by implication, "It is white people who are the important ones."[47]

The sheer volume of whiteness studies overwhelms the senses. Even in the study of race, all the attention these days seems to be going to white people. Not long ago I was standing on a street corner talking with a Filipino scholar about whiteness studies. He asked, "Don't you white guys have enough already? You are the subject matter of almost all the departments on campus. Now you want ethnic studies, too?" His observation was not far off the mark. How sad that some of the makers of white studies should, in attempting to dethrone whiteness, end up examining it obsessively and placing it at the center yet again.

LESTER YOUNG
Master of Jive

DOUGLAS HENRY DANIELS

Tenor saxophonist Lester "Pres" Young looms large as a hero among jazz fans and writers as well as among musicians. Known as "president" of the tenor saxophone, he gained recognition for his musical genius while playing with leading swing bands of the 1930s, including the 13 Original Blue Devils and the King Oliver and Count Basie bands. Amiri Baraka (Leroi Jones), Ted Joans, and Al Young have written poems about him; novelist John Clellon Holmes featured a musician modeled after him in The Horn; bassist and composer Charles Mingus composed "Goodbye, Pork Pie Hat" in his memory; and multi-instrumentalist Rahsaan Roland Kirk recorded Mingus's piece with lyrics. Even the abstractionist painter Stuart Davis was said to have been influenced by the tenor saxophonist.[1]

The tenor saxophone is an instrument deeply embedded in Afro-American culture. And yet, except for its use in military bands and by vaudeville performers, it was relatively neglected by musicians until the advent of Coleman Hawkins. Hawkins "originated something on tenor saxophone that had never been heard before," inspiring a school of tenor sax playing dominated by a full, rough sound. When Lester Young replaced Hawkins in the Fletcher Henderson band in 1934, his contrasting tone and style found little favor among the Henderson reed section, and the bandleader had to let him go, replacing him with Ben Webster, a Hawkins man.[2] Despite this setback, Young was quite popular in Kansas City, the city most commonly associated with his name and that of the Count Basie band. Eventually his tone and style came to rival Hawkins's, and today he is ranked as one of the most seminal contributors to jazz.

Fletcher Henderson, for example, described him as "the best saxophonist I ever heard," and Count Basie characterized his music as "like nothing we'd ever heard." At the time of Young's death in 1959, Basie recalled him as "a precious jewel." Teddy Wilson, the pianist who led a number of recording sessions that included Young and singer Billie Holiday, maintained that Pres was "one of the great landmarks in jazz"; and recently Harry Edison contended "there's nobody more influential on tenor players today." Critic Ralph J. Gleason noted that musicians regarded Young with "a reverence shared only by Charlie Parker, Duke Ellington, and Count Basie." Another writer claimed that Young was "probably the biggest influence in jazz, outside Louis Armstrong."[3]

Young's influence was not restricted to music and to musical activities. His impact on poets and other nonmusicians would seem to suggest that his importance also stemmed from extramusical aspects of his role. A humorist, philosopher, and storyteller, Young's effect on musicians, fans, and hangers-on was unique and long lasting. One of his most significant contributions was as a master of jive, combining wisdom with wit and humor in a language partly of his own making. His language, shared by musicians, entertainers, and the knowledgeable or hip public, considerably influenced American slang. Basie trumpeter Wilbur "Buck" Clayton pointed out: "Lester could make up a name for something, it would stick whatever you'd call it. I know a lot of things that people don't know that Lester started. . . . I never heard these words before he said them, and then five years later, everybody's saying them, and nobody knows who started them." In this respect, Young was similar to Louis Armstrong and bandleader Cab Calloway. His use of jive, a phenomenon rarely treated by scholars, sheds light on his role as humorist and philosopher within the jazz world.[4]

This essay will focus on the cultural milieu of the artist rather than his music. By tracing Young's ideas about humor, music, and language, I hope to achieve and convey a better understanding of this unique performer, who seems "inscrutable" and baffling to many critics and observers of the jazz scene. And by examining Young's own statements in interviews as well as the opinions of his associates and the musicians with whom he played, I will attempt to place this complex and controversial artist within his proper cultural context and tradition.[5]

Young was not very adept at verbally communicating his ideas about music to strangers. His shyness and reticence in speaking to people outside his own close circle were as much a part of his personality as was his unique sound on the tenor saxophone. Those who knew him well, however, commented on his intelligence, wit, unfailing sense of humor, and his role as an elder statesman of jazz after World War II. The drummer Connie Kay recalled Lester as "a brilliant man" with "a good sense of humor," one who "learned something from whatever he did. . . . He was that type of person."[6]

Guitarist Barney Kessel claimed that Pres was a philosopher whose humor leavened his statements. Lester Young, furthermore, "had great insights into the forces of life and the elements of daily living, and his commentaries were not only rich in wisdom, but outrageously humorous. There was always a lesson in what he said, and always that superb wit. His words are still passed from musician to musician, especially the humorous things he said."[7] Pres thus fulfilled his role as a teacher of musicians in two ways: by profoundly commenting on the nonmusical, but no less important, aspects of life and by providing young musicians with an apprenticeship in the combo he led beginning at the outset of World War II.

Young, nonetheless, found words a poor substitute for ideas that could be presented musically, and he often would play a phrase from a song instead of speaking. When surprised on one occasion with a birthday party, he played "I Didn't Know What Time It Was." If a Basie band member became angry, "He'd blow the first bar of Runnin' Wild." When a musician made a mistake at rehearsal, he rang a bell he kept handy for just this purpose.[8]

A virtuoso such as Pres might not even feel a need to be verbally articulate. His brother, Lee, explained that there were "times [Lester] didn't like to mess with words at all." When it came to leading his combo, again Pres was a man of few words. Kansas City musician Sir Charles Thompson echoed a fact corroborated by other Young sidemen when he recalled that "Lester led the band with his eyes. He hardly said anything except 'Hey, baby.' He had nothing to say hardly at all except through his horn, but you could look at his eyes and tell what he was thinking if you were with him."[9]

When Young elected to speak, however, his statements seemed to take on a greater importance and meaning. In oral as well as musical communication, silences were punctuations that helped his ideas to stand out more clearly, enabling him to convey feeling with greater intensity. For Young, getting his point across was very likely secondary to making the statement. As has been said about Basie, another musician known for witty comments and pithy humor delivered with a deadpan expression, "If it goes unheard or is lost on the listener [Basie] doesn't seem to care. The satisfaction in a witticism, for a true wit, lies more in the thought than in its expression."[10]

Some of Young's humorous remarks stand out as classics in the oral tradition of his fellow musicians. In a seemingly lighthearted fashion, he made comments that had serious undercurrents. For example, Young wore a porkpie hat with a wide brim and a flat crown that he shaped to his personal tastes. It was invariably black. His color preference and possibly his racial consciousness were hidden by the understated humor expressed in the idea that "black is such a beautiful color, you can do so much with it."[11]

One of the more frequently quoted tales has Pres calling Kenny Kersey long distance to inform him that, if he could get to Detroit, he could earn twenty-five dollars. When Kersey pointed out that travel cost twice that amount, Pres, unruffled, responded, "You know, Kenny, you gotta save your money so you can make these gigs."[12] A constant traveler from the age of ten, Young hated to fly: "You've got to give me four lungs before I can do some skywriting." And concerning bills sent through the mail, he remarked, "I don't ever open envelopes that have windows."[13]

Aside from his use of one-liners, Pres was known among musicians for a comic wit that sometimes led to overt action. When the Basie band was on Broadway, waiting for the "big chance," the bandleader called for a production number titled *I Struck a Match in the Dark*. When the lights went out, saxophonist Earle Warren was to sing while everyone in the band struck a match. Pres, who disliked Warren's singing, "struck a match, held his part up, and set fire to it!" Harry Edison added that Young "always imitated singers and made a comedy out of it."[14]

Humor in jazz is not unusual, given its roots in minstrelsy and vaudeville. For example, the comedian Bert Williams, known for his influence on blackface comics and such personalities as W. C. Fields and Eddie Cantor, had an impact on jazz that is yet to be assessed. Pres's humor was of a distinctly different order—the sly humor of the wit expressed in a deadpan manner rather than the backslapping buffoonery of the minstrel or clown. In this respect, Pres represented a break with the kind of humor usually associated with black musicians, and he paved the way for musicians of the 1940s, such as Warren "Baby" Dodds, Jo Jones, Sonny Rollins, and others, who regarded their music as serious art, something not to be confused with music of the era of minstrelsy and Jim Crow.

Many black musicians have commented on the spiritual dimension of their art and, in words that occasionally seem to adumbrate African cosmology, have viewed it as a vital life force that permeates one's very flesh and blood.[15] The critic Robert Perlongo quotes Young in this regard: "Just all music, all day and all night music. Just any kind of music you play for me, I melt with all of it." And shortly before his death, the artist who had made his way through the world solely through music from the age of ten said, "Music's my thing. My business is the musical thing. All the way."[16]

These values and actions are comprehensible if we view these musicians as standard-bearers of patterns deeply embedded in Afro-American culture. The role of music and language in Afro-American culture clarify the link between Young's ideas, his music, and his jive.

The African antecedents of Afro-American music express "life in all of its aspects through the medium of sound." African music "grows out of the intonations and rhythmic onomatopoeias of speech." Indeed, the human voice is the instrument most frequently used by Africans, and "vocal music is truly the essence of African art." Correspondingly, "the prime motive of the instruments is to reconstitute spoken or sung language."[17]

In Africa and Afro-America, speakers glide almost imperceptibly from speech to song and back again. In the nineteenth century James A. Harrison commented on the singing or chanting quality of Louisiana Creole. In black American churches ministers sermonize in eloquent but nonmusical speech patterns and then intone their phrases and sentences in a singsong fashion before singing a hymn. The black American has transformed standard English "into a singing language whose intonations resemble his ancestral tongues. Shifting of the tonic accent, the ellipse of certain syllables, and the use of percussive onomatopoeias . . . have given us the jazz idiom as well as the declamatory preaching style."[18]

Afro-American musicians frequently "speak" with their instruments—not always in a humorous vein—and this "speaking" quality highlights the importance of words and storytelling traditions in both West African and Afro-American music and culture. This mode of playing became widespread in popular music. Brass men Joe "King" Oliver of New Orleans and Bubber Miley and Joseph "Tricky Sam" Nanton of the Ellington band characteristically "spoke" through their instruments, using mutes to growl and slur their messages and to attain exotic or humorous effects.

Pres's tenor saxophone playing mirrored these cultural patterns. It, too, "seemed to have much of the quality of the human voice." Significantly, Young played in King Oliver's band in the early 1930s and arrived at these effects through constant study and practice. Saxophonist Jimmy Heath observed Young's fingering and the way he produced different textures: "There's certain notes that Lester fingered two different ways in order to get a talking or more communicative sound."[19]

Jazz musicians, in fact, regard their music as a language. Duke Ellington claimed that music "has striven in a world of other values, to get across its own message." His saxophonist Harry Carney maintained that jazz is "a language that is spoken everywhere." Sir Charles Thompson compared jazz to "a language, and you have to speak that language to understand it."[20]

Young admired singers and was especially influenced by Billie Holiday. The influence was mutual. Holiday, for example, noted the influence of horn on voice and vice versa: "I always try to sing like a horn—a trumpet or tenor sax, and I think Lester is just the opposite. He likes to play like a voice. . . . Lester sings with his horn. You listen to him and can almost hear the words." Connie Kay maintained, "He used to say, 'I like to sing . . . ,' so when he was playing he was actually singing that song, man, just like a vocalist." Jo Jones contended that Lester "would literally talk on his horn." There was one time you could actually hear him play, "I want some money."[21]

When he played a ballad, this effect was particularly striking. Barney Kessel observed that Young achieved the desired effect not merely through the fingering and rhythm but through the very sound he made on the horn. Furthermore, "there was something about it that always had a tinge of sadness, melancholy, and wistfulness . . . bittersweet." Unlike the followers of Coleman Hawkins, Pres "didn't sound as if he were trying to blow as loud as possible to produce a big sax sound but rather as if he were projecting his own human voice through the horn."[22]

Besides trying to sing while he played, Young would tell his sidemen to "sing me a song" before they soloed. He also valued knowing a song's lyrics. Discussing his "dream band" in the 1950s, he asserted, "One of the rules of the band would be that everybody would know the lyrics of anything they played." So while sometimes he preferred, as his brother claimed, to leave words alone, this was not the case with song lyrics.[23]

In much the same way that his ideal was to "sing" while playing, he aimed at telling a story, a metaphor central to the musical tradition of

which he was a part. The storytelling tradition shaped the solo as well as
the songs. While it is fairly obvious that song lyrics might tell a story, this
is not as clear with instrumentals. It should be stressed that after his big-
band days (from the early 1940s) Young's band often lacked singers, but for
him and his musicians the goal remained the same. Buck Clayton explained
that, with respect to a solo, telling a story simply meant that it must have
a logical structure, a beginning, middle, and conclusion, melodically and
harmonically.[24]

Other musicians gave more descriptive explanations when asked about
the connection between the black oral or storytelling tradition and
soloists. Jimmy Heath observed, "If they are good soloists, they speak the
language that is understood by Afro-American people . . . the language of
slavery, or spirituals, of . . . church music, the blues."[25]

Similar to the West African griots, black American musicians insist on
the importance of telling a story. Drummers as well as saxophonists make
this claim. Drummer Denzil Best maintained that "all drummers have a
story to tell, but they do it in different ways." Bassist Gene Ramey of
Kansas City claimed that in the southwest the storytelling tradition was as
strong in music as it was in speech. When he explained how Young
dethroned Coleman Hawkins in a legendary tenor-saxophone battle at the
Cherry Blossom, he said that the Kansas City musician played "more creative things." In that city, the "adage was—still is—say something on your
horn . . . not just show off your versatility and ability to execute. Tell us a
story, and don't let it be a lie. Let it mean something. If it's only one note,
like Louis Armstrong, like Duke would do."[26]

Tenor saxophonist Dexter Gordon explained the significance of Pres
over his rival, Hawk, in similar terms. "Hawk had done everything possible and was the master of the horn, but when Pres appeared we all started
listening to him alone. Pres had an entirely new sound, one that we had
been waiting for, the first one to really tell a story on the horn." In the
hands of a virtuoso, as Ramey claimed, a story could be told with one note,
and that would be with sufficient emotion to move people. Basie trombonist Vic Dickenson maintained the same thing: "Louis could tell a story
with one note. He didn't have to have a whole lot of notes or nothing—
just that one note would swing people."[27]

Significantly for these musicians, one note could say more than one
word, as the former possessed the ability to "swing" people—that is, to

move them emotionally. This is at the heart of African and Afro-American music. It is more obvious in church music, rhythm and blues, and ballads than it is in instrumental jazz, but it is still true. Storytellers affect the listener's emotions and expectations, and so do soloists, but more efficiently than their word-oriented counterparts. Musicians shape their solos according to the song, their feelings, the audience, and the circumstances. As Jimmy Heath explained, a soloist who had been to church might insert "Sometimes I Feel Like a Motherless Child" in the solo. Lester Young, in fact, used such quotes to convey his message. Furthermore, "whether he played the actual notes of a spiritual or . . . just the feeling of being raised in this country, he portrayed that feeling in his solos." Lester was always "portraying life, happiness and sadness, the dues we pay."[28]

Young's musical values and the traditions he shared with Afro-Americans profoundly influenced the manner in which he talked. Referred to by one critic as "the great epigrammaticist of jazz," Young, forever the artist, improvised when he spoke. His impact was such that "today his aphorisms are so widely diffused that many of those who plagiarize him are unaware they are doing so."[29] His spontaneity in speech, however, should not overshadow the fact that, as in his music, he worked within a well-established tradition—one that mirrored his experiences.

As a child and adolescent Young played in the family band composed of his father, Willis (or Billy) H. Young, his stepmother, brother, sister, and others. They performed at minstrel shows and for the carnival of which they were part, and they also played at fairs, socials, and dances. In addition to becoming acquainted with the humor of this milieu, Lester also learned pig Latin and carney talk. The circuit they traveled was known as T.O.B.A. (Theatre Owners Booking Association), and it featured black acts for black audiences. His experiences were by no means unique, as Jo Jones, Louis Jordan, and numerous other musicians played carnivals and traveled the T. O. B. A. circuit.

Lee Young recalled the use of a "special language" on the circuit. "Most everybody on the circuit could talk" in this vernacular. "It's not like hip-slang, it's entirely different." At least one expression, "fuzz" for policemen, the origin of which is attributed to Lester Young, is known to have been used by circus people.

Lee and Lester enjoyed talking this way, both as youngsters and as mature adults. "When we were young, Lester and I used to stand round for an hour and talk and no-one would know what we were saying. My sister and I still do it on long-distance phone calls." Jo Jones, who shared the same carney origins and language, corroborated Lee's account. Of Lester, he said, "Nobody could talk to him." Moreover, "when he and I talked, the way we talked nobody knew what we were saying."[30]

Young's preference for a different mode of talking lasted until the end of his life. During his last interview in Paris, Pres spoke in a modified form of jive talk before asking, "Can I talk nasty? I talk nasty . . . can you clean it up?" After the interviewer's assurances that he could censor for publication, Pres used the language in which he was most comfortable.[31]

It is important to keep in mind that numerous traditions were tapped by Lester Young when he created his own style of speaking. The underworld he was exposed to provided words and probably a measure of inspiration. His playing in nightclubs afforded ample opportunity to associate with various kinds of businessmen, including narcotics dealers and hustlers. While he avoided the company of hard drug addicts, Pres himself smoked marijuana regularly, and in the 1930s "vipers," as smokers were known, used their own slang to refer to their habits. Popular during the 1930s were such songs as "The Reefer Man" and "A Viper's Song."[32]

Before marijuana was made illegal, musicians smoked openly and received gifts of it from well-wishers. A saxophonist in Louis Armstrong's band sang at least one song in the viper's language. Armstrong told how the band played "Sweet Sue" and how before the chorus he would say, "Now I want my little tenor player to come up here and sing it in the viper's language." The musician later explained "this was a little language that we made up on the road. And, that we used to talk." He sang the song in this language and, years later, said it was remembered and requested in Europe.[33]

Musicians' jive, based on a variety of different argots, emerged in its modern form in the 1920s. It became popular on the radio, in trade journals, in clubs, ballrooms, and newspapers as the swing fad emerged. According to the New York *Amsterdam News*, it was "a by-product of swing [that] first saw the light of day within the Savoy." Also known as "swing slang," or "jive talk," "it had myriad variations and countless thousand definitions started originally by musicians playing" this famous New York ballroom. Dancers and fans picked it up quickly "until today Savoy Swing Slang is an accepted form of speech even in best society."[34]

Musicians such as John Lewis, a Young sideman at one time, contended that this way of talking came from a milieu larger than the Savoy or New York City. It represented a collective effort of black speakers from throughout the United States. Lewis did not find Young's manner of speaking a way of hiding—as some interviewers claimed. Nor was it an entirely conscious phenomenon. Lewis had heard swing slang "in Albuquerque from my older cousins, and there were variations of it in Oklahoma City and Kansas City and Chicago in the late twenties and early thirties." A style of dress, including the porkpie, was also affected by users of this idiom. "So speech and dress were natural things he picked up. They weren't a disguise—a way of hiding. They were a way to be hip—to express an awareness of everything swinging that was going on."[35]

Connie Kay also pointed out that Young's contemporaries spoke this idiom. "Cats like Jo Jones, Basie and them, and Buddy Tate, cats like them, they all spoke like that." In fact, he added, "Jo Jones today has a little bit of it. Today he still talks like that, but I know he doesn't do it as much because the cats ain't around for him to keep it up." Kay stated he never asked Young about the origins of jive talk, an idiom that took Kay a few days to understand. It mystified "squares," of course, partly because that was its object. It was also meant to confuse whites. Kay never really thought about it because he understood how it functioned "just like signals" and "probably [originated] from the days of being in the band and being on the road."

These musicians, almost like train men or telegraph operators, used their special code to reach out to one another. Instead of *physical* distances, however, their signals were sent out to cover *social* distances. They bound band members invisibly but no less tightly into a fraternity of sojourners who had to travel vast distances regularly and whose constant movement united them and allowed them to forge a verbal as well as a musicial idiom from their common experiences. It was a means for public figures to maintain their privacy. Kay explained, "You know, you're in a club . . . you've got a band and all the cats got a language that they talk to keep people out of their business . . . cause when you're out there on the road, you know, you've always got hangers-on and people following you around and whatnot. There might be things you want to say and don't have no time to say it in private, so you say it so they don't—so it will go over their heads."[36] As with all signal systems, swing slang covered vast distances and, inevitably, was a means of saving time, a precious commodity for people on the road, rushing from one one-nighter to another.

Literary materials also suggest the importance of jive. Autobiographies were written in variants of this vernacular, and some included glossaries at the end. Dan Burley's Original Handbook of Harlem Jive analyzed jive and presented examples of Shakespearean soliloquies and popular rhymes in jive. Burley also wrote a column on the Harlem scene for the *Amsterdam News* that included jive and jitterbugging. On the West Coast, a reviewer wrote that Lee and Lester Young's combo were "doing 'solid' swinging these nights at the Club Troutville in Hollywood." It "really does have some nice 'grooving' . . . so all of you persons who like to hear that 'solid swing jive' tune in on Lee and Lester [radio station KHJH] . . . and get your 'kicks.' "[37]

Bandleader Cab Calloway and others, together with Pres, shared with their most avid fans and public a rich oral tradition that was profoundly influenced by music. Ralph Ellison noted that waiters in one club at 136th and Lenox in Harlem sang and improvised lyrics as they served drinks. Saxophonist Dexter Gordon mentioned that there were "cats at the corner candy store [who] would make up lyrics to Prez's solos and jam." Saxophonist Buddy Tate claimed that fans knew their favorite musicians' solos so well they would stand around the bandstand humming them "note for note . . . when you played," forcing the artists to perform their solos differently from how they played them on the records their listeners studied. The emphasis on improvisation and the dominance of the voice influenced and counterinfluenced both song and music, musician and listener, thereby blurring the distinctions between artist and audience, as well as between lyrics and melody and rhythm.[38]

Lester Young was a talented creator in both the swing and jive idioms. John Lewis referred to him as "a living, walking poet." Some sense of his contribution can be acquired from the tape-recorded version of his Paris interview in 1959, in which he gave one of the most relaxed accounts of his life and philosophy in jive. As he speaks, one is struck by several things, for example, sounds that remind us of the drums he played as a child (he often used the word "boom!" in his statements). Thus, of his early years in New Orleans, he said, "Anything I was doing . . . they'd start playing some music . . . BOOM I'd run there." Similarly, Jimmy Heath recalled that Pres used "doom!" to announce the end of a conversation. Then there were such expressions as "bells" and "ding dong." When asked by a Boston drummer how he should play behind Lester, the response was "Just go tiddy-boom." Other explosions of sound reminiscent of drums and music, such as "ivey divey," "oobey doobey," and "rooty pooty" are heard in the Paris interview. He also imitated the weak sound of a tenor player he disliked.[39]

Besides employing onomatopoeia, Pres almost sang one statement in the Paris interview. Describing his approach to the saxophone, he started his sentence high: "So I developed my saxophone to make it sound just like an alto." Then he dropped his voice to say: "Make it sound just like a *tenor*." And as he concluded with "make it sound like a bass," his voice modulated to a deeper register.

Some of his sounds are the verbal counterparts to scat singing, the syllables strung together by vocalists to produce the rhythms and cadences of riffs and melodies in swing and in bop. Like scat, they do not have any verbal meaning but are pure sound and rhythm, stripped of all the usual references. Given the exchange between music and speech in Afro-America, this onomatopoeia has its own sense.

Another characteristic of Young's speech was his habit of assigning titles to people as well as to things, elevating them within the unique world in which their distinctive tongue was used. He started calling Billie Holiday "Lady Day," not merely a name, but an appellation of dignity that has stayed with her from the late 1930s to the present. She, in turn, gave him the title of President of tenor saxophone playing, thus making him a titled rival to Coleman Hawkins: "I named him the President and he named me Lady and my mother Duchess. We were the Royal Family of Harlem." Then she modified her title, explaining, Lester "was the President and I was Vice-President."[40]

Numerous other musicians received titles and names from Pres, and these, too, stayed with them. Trombonist Dicky Wells said that "when Pres named anybody the name stuck." Pres gave Charles Thompson the title "Sir," which was promptly accepted and is still a part of the pianist's name, although most people do not know or have forgotten its origins and connection with Pres. Thompson recalled Pres saying, as he bestowed the title, "You look like royalty anyway."[41]

There was also a leveling influence to counterbalance the titles and other names of distinction. It was almost as if there were two conflicting trends at work—one mirroring the jazz world's and the nation's enchantment with aristocracy and one reflecting the democratic impulse suggested by the name Pres. Thus everyone in Pres's world became both a titled person and a president, sharing both his and Lady Day's exalted station. Collectively, he often referred to the musicians as "ladies" or, when they were younger, as "kiddies."[42]

Pres was not the only Afro-American to rename people, but he seems to have done so with greater consistency and permanence. "Sweets" Edison, whose nickname came from Pres, as well as Billie Holiday possessed this power. The drummer Zutty Singleton called people "Suit Face," "Tie Face," and "Boat Face," as well as "Boot Nose" and "Gizzard." Mezz Mezzrow recalled in his autobiography that "later on everybody started using the expression 'Face' as a greeting: you'd say "Watcha know, Face." And the common nickname "Gate" as well as others came from Armstrong.[43]

The use of nicknames for entertainers was part of the code by which the larger Afro-American community, as well as musicians, communicated. The *Amsterdam News* used a number of these names or, when nicknames were lacking, designations that reflected specific talents in much the same way that Afro-Americans employ specific terms such as *deacon, brother,* and *sister* in church.[44]

This penchant for nicknames is not unique to the jazz world or Afro-America. The custom, however, seems to be more consistent among people of African descent than among others in the Americas. In the West Indies and in West Africa, it is common for individuals to have nicknames—"Big Man" might be assigned to someone who is short, or "Captain" to someone whose appearance suggests a lower station in life. These are methods that people use to elevate and dignify individuals whose inner qualities make them worthy of these distinctions but whose outer appearance suggests otherwise.[45]

Through his creative use of names, the employing of onomatopoeia, and the development of other codes, Lester Young expressed his ideas, while confounding outsiders and initiates. Pianist Jimmy Rowles pointed out that Pres did not give translations. One had to study him intently and listen for clues from the sidemen. "You had to break that code to understand him. It was like memorizing a dictionary. Sometimes it took months."[46]

In reviewing some of the substitute words that Pres used, it is easy to see why listeners were confounded. Characteristic word substitutes include "hat" for "woman," as well as "homburg" and "Mexican hat" for other females. "Pound cake" referred to an attractive young girl, while "startled doe" was used on spotting a doe-eyed woman. "Catalina eyes," "Watts eyes," and "bulging eyes" meant immense appreciation or admiration. "No eyes" was used for dislike or displeasure. A rehearsal was a "molly trolley," applause was "little claps," a pianist's hands were "right people" and "left people" respectively. A "needle dancer" was a heroin addict, while the police were "Bob Crosby." Something unpleasant or depressing was a "von Hangman." Whites were "grey boys," blacks "Oxford greys."

Young put these words together, a few at a time, in brief statements and questions. Some typical examples with translations follow:

"I feel a draft." (I detect racism in our midst.)

"How's your feelings?" (How are you?)

"Can madam burn?" (Can you/he/she cook?)

"Startled doe, two o'clock." (There's an attractive doe-eyed woman off to the right.)

"Those people will be here in December." (My second child is scheduled to arrive this winter.)

"George Washington." (Play or solo on the bridge of the song.)

"How do the bread smell?" (How much does the job pay?)

References to songs were customarily used as a kind of shorthand. The popular song "I Only Have Eyes for You" probably supplied him with the abbreviation "eyes," meaning liking or wanting something or someone. "I Didn't Know What Time It Was" gave him the expression "You don't know what time it is," meaning someone is naive or otherwise unknowing. And Young used abbreviations and showed his wry humor when calling for songs on the band stand. "Just Us" referred to "Just You, Just Me." "Poker Chips" meant "Polka Dots and Moonbeams." And the original "Afternoon of a Basie-ite" became "Afternoon of a Baseball Player."[47]

Pres's use of swing slang is significant for a number of reasons. While he chose to use it consistently, he recognized the distinctions of polite and profane society, and he sanitized his language when necessary. Young's question of his Paris interviewer, "Can you clean it up?" shows his sensitivity to this issue. Another tape recorded interview, with Chris Albertson, was broadcast as it was recorded, and Young refrained from using words that were not acceptable on the air. These distinctions also indicate that swing slang was rich enough to be modified for the occasion.

Lester Young and his colleagues were cultural standard-bearers who upheld black musical and oral traditions and, at the same time, found them rich enough to sustain the creative impulse. They spread their argot through American society with a thoroughness that is impressive. Moving from carnivals, minstrel shows, and circuses to vaudeville, nightclubs, teas, balls, radio, stage shows, and films, they took their argot with them. When a word or expression effectively expressed their experiences or sentiments, they retained it and passed it on; otherwise it was forgotten or discarded. Swing slang emerged from these different traditions and was utilized by musicians and entertainers as the best means of expressing their values as well as their insights and experiences.

Serving to bind musicians and show folk together, jive gradually joined them with still others. Unlike swing music, the argot could be readily learned by nonmusicians. Jive popularized the music, meshed with the Afro-American idiom, and bound together hip black folk and whites in entertainment. A few newly acquired words permitted speakers to immediately identify with the popular phenomenon whether they were musicians or knew nothing about music.

This Afro-American idiom resembled pachuco, spoken by Hispanic youth in the southwestern cities at the same time. In Los Angeles and El Paso, a distinctive style of dress, the zoot suit, was linked with pachuco and the swing fad in the 1940s. The Hispanic parallel suggests that swing slang results from the encounter of an oral tradition with radio, jukeboxes, and phonograph records.[48]

Lester Young vitalized American culture by blending idioms from carnivals, nightclubs, the underworld, and jazz. Both swing music and argot gave musicians and jazz fans, including such youths as Malcolm X and Cesar Chavez, a chance to show their creativity, affirm their cultural values, and forge bonds with like-minded city dwellers of Kansas City, New York, Los Angeles, and other metropolises.[49]

Significantly, a number of artists besides Young—Armstrong, Holiday, Calloway, and Frank Sinatra—are known for their endeavors in song and speech. They set new styles in language as they did in music, fashion, and mannerisms.[50] Rarely are connections with an ancient past seen as clearly as in Young's conceptions of music and speech and in his dual role as a musician's musician and a purveyor of wit and wisdom. Earning a meager existence on the fringes of a society whose ethos is work and whose tone is secular, artists like Young serve as evidence of the strength of black cultural traditions.

HOLDING CENTER STAGE

Race Pride and the Extracurriculum at Historically
Black Colleges and Universities

Patrick B. Miller

Writing at the turn of the century as scholar, teacher, and prophet, thus drawing a line from his historical studies through his experiences as a professor to his vision for the future of blacks in the United States, W. E. B. Du Bois described the African American colleges of the South as "pillars of fire." The allusion was to the Book of Exodus, which depicted the flight of the Jews from Egypt and captivity into the Promised Land and freedom. As one of many references in *Souls of Black Folk* (1903) that underscored Du Bois' faith in the libratory potential of education, the image opened out to the crucial role that historically black colleges and universities (HBCUs) would play in the quest for racial justice during the twentieth century. Such institutions as Howard and Fisk and Atlanta were not merely training sites for individual uplift but also temples for the cultivation of race pride and social change. Ultimately, those centers of learning, Du Bois avowed, stood among the few means available for black people to become full participants in the economic, political, and cultural life of the nation.

Souls of Black Folk remains compelling as both lamentation and lyric manifesto. After its publication, however—and beyond the Niagara Movement and the creation of the National Association for the Advancement of Colored People (NAACP) in 1909—Du Bois sought a different stage for the enactment of his hopes and platforms. In this endeavor, he was joined by other social commentators who assessed black colleges and universities with an eye toward the subtle processes of cultural adaptation and innovation that would establish the groundwork for broad-based racial reform. The matter was complex, and there was no single program for assimilation and uplift. Assertions of black advancement through higher education were highly contested within Afro-America; what is more, they were often resisted or contained by white authorities on both sides of the Mason and Dixon line.

With respect to the kind of education proposed by Booker T. Washington, for instance, and the more expansive ideal advanced by Du Bois, nearly a half-century of scholarship has ably elaborated the turn-of-the-century debates over the mission and methods of HBCUs, whether privately endowed or publicly sustained. As a result we know quite a lot about the curricular controversies setting bricks and brooms against the French text or geography lesson and the contrast between the Hampton/Tuskegee model of agricultural and mechanical education and the notion of the "Talented Tenth."[1] For their part, institutional histories have surveyed the growth and development of HBCUs, both within the limitations often mandated by northern white philanthropy and in the face of steady southern white antagonism to any notions of higher education for blacks. Significantly, however, most accounts have largely neglected the creation of a vital student culture and the ways it expanded upon what "race men" wrote and said, or what the catalog of courses included or excluded. The omission is regrettable. For in many respects, the *extracurriculum* also animated the black colleges of the segregated South, embracing an array of organizations and leisure pursuits that in their own ways represented race pride and argued for social equality.[2]

Student activities, though sponsored or supervised by academic authorities, provided a variety of outlets for undergraduate initiative and talent. They established a certain *esprit* on campus and from time to time projected the image of a striving and successful southern black population to the world beyond. From the last quarter of the nineteenth century through the first half of the twentieth, the associational endeavors of African American students attested to their vitality, ambition, and resourcefulness beyond the classroom. Significantly, these activities were nurtured in an environment that was in some respects insulated from the day-to-day scrutiny of southern officialdom, out of sight from the hostile gaze of white supremacists. Here was a certain kind of freedom from the impositions of Jim Crow. Just as tellingly, though, what occurred on black college campuses marked substantial differences between those who were being trained to lead the race and the masses who labored as 'croppers or domestics, and who found few opportunities to display the full range of *their* talents.[3] Nevertheless, working within—and against—a dominant culture that was fairly obsessed by the doctrine of Social Darwinism, the cultivators of an expansive extracurriculum provided powerful examples of the "fitness" of African Americans for first class citizenship.

Perhaps the most popular, and widely-recognized, representatives of black collegiate culture were the Fisk Jubilee Singers. Starting in 1871, students sent out from that financially beleaguered institution raised funds on tours that extended from old abolitionist strongholds in Ohio to the royal courts of England and Germany. Their choral program may have begun with European classical music and popular American ballads, but where the Fisk singers made a distinctive mark was in their solemn rendering of cabin melodies and the sacred songs of their parents. Although the performance of the spirituals was occasionally criticized for evoking the ordeal of slavery at a time when blacks were striving to achieve the ideal of equality, those "Sorrow Songs," as Du Bois called them, nevertheless offered a formidable response to the antics of blackface minstrelsy, and both the Fisk sponsors, like George White, and the most prominent singers, such as Ella Shepherd, fully understood their larger mission. The dignity that always characterized the Jubilee performances ran counter to all the stereotypes and ethnic notions contrived by the ruling race during the postbellum era.[4]

Aside from the many rivals and imitators of the Jubilee Singers on other college campuses, many less familiar aspects of student culture engaged the African American experience and at the same time suggested a sense of belonging to the mainstream culture. From the camera clubs established at Hampton and Tuskegee—among other institutions—emanated precise visual chronicles of life in the turn-of-the-century South as well as portraits of the campus scene, illustrating the discipline and energy that framed black educational enterprise.[5] Likewise, in organizing various Paul Lawrence Dunbar societies across the South and in writing numerous poems and stories, black students inscribed themselves squarely within the regional literary landscape. The project of "uplifting the race" could take many forms. And the notion of uplift itself would contain problematical elements. Yet it is significant that in their contributions to the arts—whether traditionally conceived in the sonnet form or in the technically innovative medium of photography—African American college students were in some sense making political statements about their place in American society.[6] From a very different vantage, it was a long way from the accommodating phrases of Booker T. Washington's Atlanta Exposition Address of 1895 to the tennis courts that the Wizard of Tuskegee ordered to be constructed on campus a short time thereafter. The Tuskegee regimen of work and study precipitated a huge rate of attrition among matriculants; paradoxically it also permitted a little bit of play.[7]

The classroom, library, and laboratory continued to be the centerpieces of higher education for African Americans in the South. Instructors and deans and the principal or president would remain authority figures, the ultimate arbiters of good conduct and academic success. And with regard to many issues—from smoking and drinking on campus, to the music played on phonograph machines, to discussions of politics and current events, as well as the nature and extent of off-campus excursions—these regimes could be discouragingly authoritarian and repressive.[8] Still, in their associational activities, African American students helped shape social arrangements and the ideal of community on campus—inventing traditions and fashioning a particular identity for their respective institutions while at the same time assimilating black academe to a national collegiate culture. The Greek system, intercollegiate athletics, student dramatics and organized debate all made the extracurriculum a robust counterpart to the formal offerings of black higher education. Often these initiatives became contending forces within the larger collegiate landscape, rivals competing for the loyalty or the time of the student body. In some instances, they divided as much as they unified campus culture or they pitted students and alumni against academic officials. But they also might establish solid and long-lasting ties to alma mater as well as webs of commitment to the larger programs of racial reform.

Significantly, many extracurricular activities were patterned after the associations and organizations that had been founded earlier at predominately white colleges and universities. Yet these initiatives were never simply acts of imitation. The creation of fraternities and sororities offers a telling example of the distinctive features that characterized organized leisure, self-improvement, and racial consciousness on black college campuses. In 1907, within a year after Alpha Phi Alpha was established by seven black men at Cornell, a chapter was established at Howard University. There too, in 1911 several undergraduates—with the help of Professor Ernest E. Just—created Omega Psi Phi, and three years later Phi Beta Sigma established a presence on the hilltop campus in the District of Columbia. The founding of black sororities began in 1908 when Alpha Kappa Alpha became a part of the Howard campus scene. Five years later, Delta Sigma Theta was launched at Howard, introducing what would become a tradition of social service and a long string of contributions to broader fields of activism. Within two months of the founding of the chapter in 1913, Deltas took part in the largest suffragist parade ever staged to that date. Critically, they resisted the forces of segregation in the same manner as the legendary anti-lynching crusader, Ida B. Wells, that day, by stepping out from their assigned spot at the back of the group and moving up to places alongside other feminists throughout the line of march.[9]

The further development of the Greek system on many black campuses ran parallel to the establishment of chapters among the few, socially isolated, African American students at nominally-integrated schools above the Mason-Dixon line, in the Midwest, or along the Pacific slope. The distinctive element in the black Greek movement was the setting of high scholastic standards and the notion of social service. By 1919, for instance, Alpha Phi Alpha was sponsoring a "Go to High School, Go to College" campaign to counter the high dropout rate among black students. Deltas, for their part, raised funds for bookmobiles and were involved, through the "Vigilance Committee" in various lobbying efforts on behalf of health education, women's rights, and anti-lynching legislation. During the Depression, proceeds from Greek-led fundraising drives at Lincoln University (Missouri) lent support to Missouri and Arkansas sharecroppers and tenants who were fighting to unionize. Meanwhile, Delta sorors competed with AKAs for the best grade point average at schools as far-flung as Wilberforce in Ohio and Atlanta's Clark College. According to one historian, "Delta women of the period declared that they studied night and day to maintain superiority in numbers on the university's honor roll" although it was also said "that special kudos awaited the member of one sorority who managed to attract the boyfriend of a student belonging to another"[10]

What was also important were the lifelong attachments often nurtured in the black Greek system. The extension of undergraduate affiliations took several forms. One involved participation in programs of racial uplift, in contributions to the NAACP and to the National Urban League, for instance, or in the creation of networks of communication that included the National Association of Colored Women and the National Association of College Women. The other was the shaping of a self-conscious black elite beyond the campus setting. Black people of prominence in cities such as New York, Chicago, Washington, and Atlanta sustained collegiate loyalties in cotillions and banquets, and even in the establishment of their own summer resorts. The exaltation of "our kind of people" might cross Greek boundaries and alumni ties: AKAs from Howard and Fisk might intermingle in high society functions; this elite might also unite graduates from black colleges and universities with those who had made their way through Penn, Columbia, Berkeley, or Kansas University. And it would *ultimately* feed into the establishment of other groups: the Links and the Girl Friends, the Boulé, and the Guardsmen.[11]

The evolution of a Who's Who on black college campuses may have pulled many undergraduates together in communities of support that could be vitally important for individuals and, in later incarnations, might also further the cause of the race. Yet for several decades, the major Greeks refused admission to students attending Land Grant institutions (state-supported schools directed toward agricultural and mechanical educations) such as Alcorn A & M or West Virginia State. The debate at the annual national conventions—*ultimately* resolved in favor of inclusion—revolved around prestige and "standards." What is more, the social hierarchies on campus could dampen college spirit or divide the student body. As Paula Giddings writes, "against the long experience of discrimination and exclusion in the broader society, and color and class distinctions within the race itself, debates regarding the various criteria for membership have, historically, been particularly emotional and intense." Fraternities and sororities "having the most prestigious memberships" often made those distinctions with regard to skin color. So too did the elite social clubs in the Atlanta system, the Wolves and Owls. The Wolves, Helen Edmonds writes, "had fair complexions, while the receding shades were found in the Owls." As early as the mid-1920s Langston Hughes had been appalled by the color consciousness at Howard. Thereafter, the paper bag test or the blue vein test for skin color, or the ruler test for hair length became symbols of a system that could be as exclusionary in its own way as were the first-class cars on municipal trains and trolleys.[12]

What many white Americans think they know about black fraternities and sororities derives from Spike Lee's *School Daze*, a film that probably reveals more about the twists and turns of Lee's reflections on being a Morehouse Man than about the structure and culture of the system earlier in the century. Then again, for most African American students at HBCUs, the Greek system represented influence and power. The organizational skills of the Greeks, combined with traditions of loyalty that were cast—emphatically—in terms of kinship, meant that fraternities and sororities dominated the campus social scene. Simply stated, by the time HBCUs had initiated modest models of student government or created elaborate halftime pageants, outsiders were not likely to be elected class president or homecoming queen. This could be a cause of resentment before the era of civil rights and black liberation, but it was not raised in public by those who had not been selected by the Greek system, or who chose to stay independent.

What would not be tolerated, even when a powerful fraternity tried it, was tampering with the selection of the starting eleven for the football team; one did not mess with football. Intercollegiate sporting competition among historically black institutions represented both an emblem of school pride and participation in *national* pastimes. It represented the ideal of muscular assimilationism. In 1894 a student writer for the Fisk University *Herald* declared, "We do not agree with Pindar, who said, 'No man is great who is not great with his hands and feet'; but we do believe that not only the brain but also hands and feet ought to be cultivated. For well has it been said that only strong arms can make men and nations free."[13] "Athletics is the universal language," an editorialist asserted in the Howard University newspaper thirty years later. "By and through it we hope to foster a better and more fraternal spirit between the races in America and so to destroy prejudices; to learn and to be taught; to facilitate a universal brotherhood."[14]

The first facts regarding black college athletics customarily pinpoint the date and location of the initial forays by college teams into extramural competition, whether it was the ball games played between the students of Hampton Institute and clubs from several towns in southeastern Virginia, or the contests between Howard and visiting squads from northern colleges. The 1892 football competition in North Carolina, matching Biddle (now Johnson C. Smith) and Livingstone, was the first black intercollegiate game on record for that sport. Within two years Howard and Lincoln as well as Tuskegee Institute and Atlanta University had commenced their rivalries. By the turn of the century, Morgan College, Atlanta Baptist (later Morehouse), and Virginia Union had also entered the intercollegiate athletic fray. With notable pride, Wiley College boasted in 1901 of the introduction of "football, as it is played at Yale and other Eastern colleges." Variations on the theme of precedence abounded. Though the inauguration of off-campus athletics was often in reality quite a modest affair—just as it had been at New England colleges and the institutions of higher learning established in the Midwest—through memory and nostalgia the first football game became a prominent part of the early histories of schools from Prairie View in Texas and Talladega in Alabama to Bluefield, West Virginia, and Langston, Oklahoma.[15]

College sport engendered an enormous outpouring of school spirit. In adopting familiar team colors and nicknames, African American students in the New South hoped to give their schools a prominent place on the collegiate map. Thus, from the menagerie of ferocious mascots available to them, black collegians at Atlanta Baptist chose to become Tigers while at Livingstone they adopted the nickname Bears. Other schools distinguished themselves as the Lincoln Lions, Wiley Wildcats, and Howard Bisons, though the Tornadoes of Talladega and the Trojans of Virginia State departed from the dominant zoological theme. The early teams from Fisk were named after President Erastus Milo Cravath and played as the Sons of Milo. They would become, in later years, simply Bulldogs. And inevitably perhaps, numerous Agricultural and Industrial schools started out as Aggies on and off the field. To join a national intercollegiate culture, African American students created small distinctions between their institutions and selected rivals, but they also conformed to patterns of self-representation already well established.[16]

Concerning the exhilaration and pageantry surrounding black college sport, it would be difficult at a distance to measure the jubilation on campus following an invitation to the Penn Relays, a vast—and racially mixed—track-and-field carnival, widely known during the 1920s as the Negro Olympics. From current affairs perhaps, one might get a sense of the college spirit (and spirits) that once animated the bonfire rally on the eve of a dramatic contest between archrivals Lincoln and Howard or between Tuskegee and Atlanta. The rituals black colleges shared with their predominantly white counterparts were significant in cultural terms, but their differences were more important still. At least one rite attending football at historically African American institutions contrasted sharply with the autumn spectacles enacted on the campuses of northern and western colleges. This was the "Rabbles." A halftime pageant at several schools, the Rabbles occurred when the grandstands emptied and students, clad in their finest, some carrying their own musical instruments, danced around the field, perhaps in conscious contrast to the precision marching bands that were the pride of many predominately white universities. "The ending of the first half was the cue for 'rabble' exhibitions," reported the *Howard University Record* about the game against Lincoln in 1921: "The rabbles of both schools pounced upon the field in spite of its mud-soaked condition and the continuous rain. The "Blue and White" rabble, headed by its band, executed a wild snake dance while the Lincoln horde did its serpentine dance. The weather forbade society exhibitions . . . and kept the ladies in their seats, prohibiting the fur coat parade of last year."[17]

As another periodical, the *Howard Alumni Sentinel*, observed, athletic rituals not only attested to the exuberance that infused the black athletic experience, they also offered a way to keep alive the spirit of tradition on the college scene. By other accounts as well, sport stood at the center of campus culture. According to the President of Florida A & M University, "No school in this day can expect to attract promising men or women that does not give organized athletics a foremost place. Where there are no athletics, it is very likely true that only deadheads are attracted. Young men and women of promise desire to be connected with an institution that has spirit and force." Such ebullience would also characterize the response of some faculty members to the sporting spectacle. In 1920, for instance, Professor Clara Standish of Talladega College wrote proudly to her friends that "our football team has won every game so far and is considered one of the finest in the South." Describing a crucial contest against Tuskegee, not merely as the triumph of skill over superior weight but also with a strong sense of academic status, Standish boasted that it was a "decided victory for higher as compared with industrial education."[18]

But there was another side to the intercollegiate athletic pageant. Throughout the 1920s and 1930s, the athletic programs of numerous black colleges came under criticism for their unfair recruiting practices and indifference to academic standards of eligibility, as well as for the subsidization of their best passers, pitchers, and runners. Accusations about violations of rules filled the mails traveling from one campus to another. Such allegations also flowed from the pages of the *Crisis*, where W. E. B. Du Bois, and his protégé, George Streator, periodically railed against a long litany of abuses in sports, breaches of the spirit if not always the letter of the rules then defining amateurism. Claflin College admitted athletes without reviewing their transcripts, Streator reported in one lengthy article, while South Carolina State College fielded several athletes who had seen considerable action around Orangeburg during the preceding eight years and several more who had played collegiate ball elsewhere. The indictment ran to several fact-filled pages, and Streator even ranked black colleges according to the extensiveness of their athletic transgressions.[19]

Numerous practices of this sort not only called into question the sportsmanship of some schools, Du Bois contended; such conduct also suggested the need for substantial reform. A vital student culture was laudable, but athletic scandals indicated too great an emphasis on matters not related to the academic purposes of higher education. For many African American leaders, self-government had long been an issue of great concern, and they strove to dispel prevailing images regarding poorly-formed habits and values among black youth. Simply stated, the reputation of centers of learning needed to be protected.[20] Within a wide-ranging indictment of campus culture run amok, which he delivered at the Howard commencement of 1930, Du Bois castigated the "rabid sports lovers of the country" and emphasized the ill effects of athletic excess: "The average Negro undergraduate has swallowed hook, line and sinker the dead bait of the white undergraduate, who, born in an industrial machine, does not have to think and does not think. Our college man today, is, on the average, a man untouched by real culture. He deliberately surrenders to selfish and even silly ideals, swarming into semi-professional athletics and Greek-letter societies, and affecting to despise scholarship and the hard grind of study and research."[21]

Those who addressed the issue during the interwar period were as eloquent as any who came after. But of all the critical observations on sport, perhaps the most acute expression of doubt about athletic ideals and practices occurred in a verse published in the *Crisis* in 1928 by a young African

American scholar, whose lines, both earnest and sardonic, were addressed
to "The Second Generation" at historically black colleges:

Juggling basket-balls
And women
You won't work,
You won't study,
You won't marry

But you have four "letters"
And a fraternity pin.
College education
Of a hundred like you every year
Will bring the race along rapidly.[22]

In response to the various pronouncements about sport as the universal
language, the poem by Allison Davis—who in 1942 became the first
African American professor hired by a predominantly white university—
highlighted the problems of a student culture not directed outward to
larger social concerns. It implied, from an academic's point of view, what
higher ideals black collegians ought to strive for. And it suggested a more
profound apprehension that what African Americans had succeeded in
doing with their bodies had not communicated, for the dominant culture,
the entire range of black aspiration and capability.[23]

In 1930 the playwright and drama teacher Randolph Edmonds wrote to
the same purpose as Allison Davis, although from a slightly different
standpoint. A sense of urgency characterized his critique of sport and its
disproportionate influence on black popular consciousness. At the same
time, references to the necessity of teaching works by Aeschylus,
Shakespeare, and Ibsen clearly established the broader terms of his thinking. "We have enough physical advertising," Edmonds asserted. "Huge
stadiums and mammoth gymnasiums are built. Expensive coaches are
hired to turn out winning teams. The art of ballyhoo has been used to the
greatest degree. The results have been a steady stream of advertised brawn
from most of the colleges." In drawing a sharp line between popular culture and high culture, Edmonds not only endeavored to contrast those

who were devoted to "the Gods of Football and Track" with another "class of people"—those who worshiped "the God of Beauty." He also wanted to make the best case for his own profession and passion: the theater. Ultimately, Edmonds argued, well-funded and thoroughly-appreciated theater programs on black college campuses—like choral performances, oratorical contests, and intercollegiate debates—offered a significant "medium of cultural advertising," a way of reaching "an audience usually untouched by the sports sheets." He could not overstate the importance of this dimension of the extracurriculum, Edmonds concluded. Racial reformers needed to strengthen their support of the lively arts.[24]

Edmonds' writings, as well as his work in developing theater programs at Dillard, Morgan College, and Florida A & M, clearly reflected his concern about racial uplift and assimilation. His essay, "Some Whys and Wherefores of College Dramatics," published in the *Crisis*, was probably the clearest call for the development of the aesthetic dimension of the extracurriculum and for the notion that "cultural advertising" best served black colleges and universities. But Edmonds did not stand alone, and in many respects high culture was holding its own within black academe.

As early as 1910, the Howard College Dramatic Club, under the direction of Professor T. Montgomery Gregory, had produced Shakespeare's *The Merry Wives of Windsor* and by 1920 the same group had performed Eugene O'Neill's *Emperor Jones*, with the famed Charles Gilpin in the title role. At the same time, Lillian Cashin was writing a Columbia University M.A. thesis on the significance of a theater movement among African Americans, especially because it represented an antidote to minstrelsy. Cashin would go on to a long teaching career in English and drama, and she would help establish the Fisk University Stagecrafters. Although she was not a playwright herself, Cashin helped organize annual playwriting contests on campus, and she joined with other educators like Edmonds to organize a Negro Intercollegiate Dramatic Association as well as regional theater tournaments among the black colleges and universities. The careers of African American writers and teachers, such as Edmonds, and their white counterparts, like Cashin, are eminently suggestive of the ways the HBCUs fostered a dynamic campus community, one that linked remote southern institutions to the renaissance of Negro artistic and intellectual life associated with Harlem.

Cashin's counterpart, first at Tougaloo then at Talladega, was Lillian Voorhees. Ultimately, she would become Cashin's successor at Fisk.

Working under the auspices of the American Missionary Association (AMA), which had founded many HBCUs, Voorhees spent the school year as a teacher, summers earning her Master's degree and taking in plays in New York City, and on several tours, in Europe as well. Though she labored over her students' writings on a daily basis, and succeeded in publishing *The Brown Thrush*, an anthology of verse by black college students, her first love was the theater. From the early 1920s until the 1950s, Voorhees staged plays, wrote about theater design and lighting, and maintained a wide-ranging correspondence with like-minded individuals teaching in historically black colleges. After establishing the Paul Robeson Drama Club at Tougaloo College in 1925, Voorhees supervised the production of a number of performances. Her autobiographical fragments tell us about the exhilaration of putting together elaborate stagings of classical works of drama and more modern pieces. Along with one of her students, Olive Hunter, Voorhees arranged *An De Walls Came Tumbling Down*, which was a musical dramatization featuring forty-five of Paul Lawrence Dunbar's poems as well as several of his stories, with music by African American composers.[25]

At Talladega Voorhees reinvigorated the Little Theatre, directing a range of performances both on campus and in nearby cities. The playbills that mounted up in her files, like her professional correspondence, are informative not just regarding the large number of undergraduates who were involved in these productions, but also about the enormous energy that those students concentrated on the shows. One of Voorhees' proudest memories was the production of *MacBeth*, specifically the contribution of one student who spent more than 50 hours wiring the college chapel for the special lighting effects of the banquet scene. Another occurred in the 1938 premiere performance of *The Amistad* by the African American playwright Owen Dodson, commemorating the 100th anniversary of the founding of the AMA "growing out of the Amistad incident." Finally, when she moved to Fisk University, her Stagecrafters mounted a range of plays from Greek tragedies to Shakespeare, from *Our Town* to *The Diary of Ann Frank*. Starting in the 1930s, the repertory expanded as the Fisk companies staged *Wanga Doll* (concerning voodoo in antebellum New Orleans), then, later *Raisin in the Sun* and *Purlie Victorious*. "The spirit of the productions," Voorhees later wrote, "was exemplified in the motto originating with Mary McLeod Bethune, which we were in the habit of reciting together as we clasped each other's hand just before curtain—'A long pull and a strong pull and a pull all together.'"[26]

When Randolph Edmonds wrote his "Whys and Wherefores of College Dramatics" in 1930, the Little Theatre movement was already well underway. To be sure, actors and actress were striving to hold center stage in the extracurriculum as rivals of the athletes who sometimes seemed to dominate the college scene. But as Edmonds' own career, and those of Lillian Cashin and Lillian Voorhees, should suggest, a vital cultural scene flourished on campus—apart from the playing fields. This was further illustrated when Frank Yerby wrote his Fisk University Master's Thesis on "The Little Theatre in the Negro College" in 1938. By that date, no fewer than 50 historically black colleges and universities could boast an array of dramatic performances from popular comedies, to mysteries, to current Broadway hits, to the classics. Students as well as teachers were writing plays. So too was the President of Cheyney Training School for Teachers, whose work depicted the life of Toussaint L'Ouverture. Yerby's thesis, moreover, drew the connection between the styles and standards of collegiate dramatics and numerous professional troupes: the Negro Art Players and the Lafayette Players of New York City, The Krigwa Players (who were sponsored in part by Du Bois), and the Gilpin players of Cleveland, among others.[27] His survey of HBCUs suggested that actors and directors of experimental plays often encountered a militant conservatism among black audiences and cautious administrators. Yet though a certain moral as well substantial racial sensitivity was always a consideration in the selection of the works to be produced, Yerby would nevertheless conclude that the Little Theatre movement was making a significant contribution to the education of future drama teachers as well as to the stimulation of interest in the lively arts both on campus and in the surrounding community. Ultimately, this element of the extracurriculum was incorporated into the formal offerings at many schools. Yerby could cite hundreds of courses in the history and interpretation of drama, in acting and directing, and set design.[28]

As they endeavored to cultivate the next Ira Aldridge or Paul Robeson—or more modestly to train their own successors—drama coaches and English teachers saw their efforts as a means of subverting racial stereotypes about Negro inferiority and to counter the prevailing representations of black people in the United States. Just as they petitioned national intercollegiate organizations to allow their students to compete in oratory contests or to participate in broad-based (that is, desegregated) theater festivals, many educators at historically black colleges and universities during the 1920s and 1930s also saw their strivings as contributions to "cultural front" of the modern civil rights movement.

Finally, perhaps even more than the outstanding actors and actresses of the Little Theatres across the South, it was the best orator on campus, or a member of the champion debate team, who was perceived as the strongest rival of the most popular athletes. So asserted James Weldon Johnson, the distinguished author and activist. Yearbook testimonials and alumni recollections tell a similar story; the power of the spoken word was never lost on black college students or their teachers. Significantly, dramatics, oratory, and debate called upon the rich oral traditions and communal rituals of Africa and the slave past. Just as importantly, those performances drew on the distinctive preaching styles of the African American clergy. To hear, once and again, the cadences, rhyming patterns, and alliteration of Dr. Martin Luther King, Jr., for instance, would have been to recall Sunday sermons in a thousand and more black churches across the South as well as his training in diction at Morehouse College.

Apart from the ways English and speech courses honed skills that would prepare students for service to African American communities, many college educators envisioned other purposes for elocution and declamation. Shaping the persuasive argument in debate, then refining it for effect, both oratory and debate involved considerable dedication and long hours of training, in substantive matters and style. Race leaders knew that the tactics of formal debate played into a broader civil rights strategy: the podium was the classroom for future lawyers. Prophetically, intervarsity debate was one of the first places where the color line was breached during the interwar years.

As a cultural forum, intercollegiate debate stood out from other activities. Unlike the touchdown or 100 yard dash, for instance, formal debate could not be discounted by those who strove to link white supremacy with exalted notions of Western Civilization. Strictly bound by time limits and longstanding rules of argumentation and rebuttal, this brand of disquisition ultimately showcased the talents of African American collegians in terms of discipline and logic as well as oratorical skill. While most of the prominent black colleges and universities featured a debate squad, one school became a phenomenon during the early 1930s. That was tiny Wiley College of Marshall, Texas. Coached "intensively and extensively" by Professor Melvin B. Tolson during the years before he claimed fame with his epic poems, Wiley emerged on the national intercollegiate scene after it had won victories, not merely over local rivals, but in competition against some of best debate teams in the entire United States. It also won a decision over a touring Oxford University team. Debating was a spectator sport in the era before television, "so popular" Tolson's son remembered, "that you could charge admission and get a full house." Topics were often noteworthy only for their banality, but sometimes issues like equal rights or major pieces of legislation made their way from the lists produced by the national society into the file cards of intercollegiate debaters.[29]

Wiley's teams of the early 1930s included a few women as well as men, and they attracted, for a time, the talents of the future civil rights leader, James Farmer. They traveled far and wide—for the most part, on Jim Crow rail cars—to face the University of Michigan in a packed theater in Chicago or the University of Southern California, the national champions, in USC's Bovard Auditorium. The Wiley student newspaper reported only one defeat during those heady years. That was to Howard University, whose coach was the legal scholar Charles Hamilton Houston, dean of the law school and mentor of Thurgood Marshall. Back in Texas, almost two decades before Marshall would argue before the Supreme Court in *Brown vs. the Board of Education*, intercollegiate debate created a bridge across the color line, setting the stage for far more wide-ranging programs of deseg-regation. For his part, Hobart Jarrett, Wiley class of 1936, reported that the greatest of his "adventures in interracial debates" occurred when his school was invited to meet Texas Christian University in Fort Worth. This "was the first time a Negro college had ever encountered a white institution on its campus in the South," Jarrett declared. The event "shattered precedent" and foreshadowed later triumphs over Jim Crow that would accumulate, albeit slowly, in the aftermath of the Second World War. About the Wiley-TCU debate, an editor of the *Crisis* noted ironically, "no race riots were reported."[30]

For those who wanted to cultivate a "Talented Tenth," the earnestness and energy of young debaters like Hobart Jarrett lent themselves to the new social ideal. During the era of Jim Crow, what occurred on the campuses of historically black colleges and universities was inevitably conceived by Du Bois and like-minded individuals with regard to racial solidarity and community building. At the same time, many black cultural commentators hoped that the accomplishments of "the College-bred Negro" would bear witness to the potential of all African Americans to achieve success in diverse realms of endeavor. Integration stood as a distant goal during the interwar years, and while some despaired about "dreams deferred" or conceived of an idealized African homeland, others wrote scripts and plotted a better future. They also organized, forging strong loyalties and organizations that continued to affirm the significance of black achievement, past and present.

Extracurricular activities on black college campuses during the interwar years thus functioned in elaborate ways. At the podium or on the playing fields stood cultural assertions no less expressive than instrumental; here were ways of reconciling notions of assimilation and uplift to racial heritage and identity, even if only in abstract terms. And here, too, folkways could be accommodated to ideals of modernity and progress. What a sorority might accomplish, at some level, would conform to the anthropologists' model of "kin-work." For "race women" this would mean fundraising, circulating a petition nationwide, or organizing a boycott. In this and in other respects, student initiatives ran well beyond the daily practices of the Greek system, or of college sports, dramatics, and debate. Just as significantly, while it helped shaped consciousness and community at HBCUs, the extracurriculum was not intended to rival the arts and sciences, preparation for the learned professions or a life's work in education. In fact, student initiatives often represented a splendid complement to the formal offerings embodied in syllabus, lecture, and textbook. Under the guidance of Sister M. Elise, students at Xavier College, New Orleans, for instance, went beyond their music classes to stage grand opera. With the assistance of Professor Charles Spurgeon Johnson, Fisk University students in sociology started a settlement house in Nashville.

There were, of course, significant limits on associational activities both before the Second World War and after. Student journalism operated within considerable institutional constraints. From the vantage of collegiate authorities, political activism needed to be measured out very carefully, especially in the Deep South. Moreover, the nurturing of a black elite, charged with the task of uplifting the race, created strains between talented-tenth blacks and working-class African Americans, even though the mission of many HBCUs was the training of a host of educators who ultimately brought reading and writing to much of the rural South. Still, among the achievements of black higher education, the development of a lively campus culture stood out. During the era when Jim Crow policies and practices were meant to reinforce white supremacy, African American educators and students formed associations and organized clubs that lent themselves in impressive ways to both race pride and the integrationist ideal. In so doing, they effectively challenged many of the impositions and containments of longstanding racist ideologies and endeavored, in the most compelling ways at hand, to expand the realm of opportunity for black people in the American social order.

Part IV

RELIGION

"BLESSED ARE THE PEACEMAKERS"

William Jay and the Drive for
International Arbitration

Stephen P. Budney

On June 12, 1849, Richard Cobden delivered a speech before the English House of Commons defending his call for the introduction of international arbitration in all future treaties between Britain and other nations. Although many members of Parliament thought his plan absurd, Cobden's plea was considered respectfully. In his delivery, Cobden noted with sadness and alarm the cost of preparing and maintaining readiness for war. He deplored the fact that inventions capable of advancing the "unalloyed" progress of humankind, such as Fulton's steam engines, were being turned instead into steam navies. He derided the concept of defensive war, and asked if Britain's honor could not instead be preserved by better means, particularly through the expedient of treaties that designated a neutral umpire to settle potential disputes between nations.[1]

What sources inspired Cobden's plea? In his speech, he noted precedents set in treaties between the United States and Great Britain, especially the Jay Treaty of 1794. The Jay Treaty was important because it did not rely upon crowned heads or neutral states to adjudicate differences, but a commission headed by an arbitrator. Although Cobden received just praise for his promotion of arbitrated settlement in Britain, the concept was not original. Cobden's ideas were part of a continuing trans-Atlantic discourse between British and American advocates of peace and reform. Pacifists earnestly promoted stipulated or compulsory arbitration to the American and European governments in the years 1842–1854. As Cobden noted, the concept owed much to John Jay, negotiator of the 1794 treaty that bore his name. The idea evolved through the writings of William Ladd, founder of the American Peace Society, and was most clearly articulated by John Jay's son, William.

The Jay Treaty grew out of America's need to remain out of the hostilities between Britain and France that escalated after the French Revolution. English seizures of American shipping ostensibly headed to France, and the continuing British presence on American borders, were among the issues that needed to be resolved. Unable to dispatch his first choice, Alexander Hamilton, to negotiate with Britain because of political opposition by the Jeffersonian Republicans, George Washington had to cast about carefully for a proper replacement to serve as envoy. Not surprisingly, he settled upon then Chief Justice of the Supreme Court John Jay. Jay's record as a negotiator and diplomat was solid. He had served as envoy to Spain during the Revolutionary War, and later had carefully charted a course through the minefield of European power politics in helping negotiate peace between the American rebel colonies and their former British masters. In those negotiations, which resulted in the Treaty of Paris, Jay had been insistent that American independence be recognized before any peace treaty with the British could be signed.[2]

In spite of Jay's notable abilities as a diplomat, Jeffersonians perhaps disliked him as much as they despised his friend Hamilton. Jay's ideological baggage consisted of a concern for the well being of the commercial interests coupled with an abiding distrust of society's lower orders, attributes that indelibly stamped him as a Federalist. If the Jeffersonians were thrilled by the leveling social implications of the French Revolution, Jay was appalled by its egalité. The Jeffersonians also pointed to the other side of Jay's diplomatic record. In their eyes, his apparent indifference to America's western interests when negotiating with Spanish Minister Gardoqui over navigation rights on the Mississippi, and his supposed pro-British bias, rendered him unsuitable.[3]

Craving Jay's failure, the Republicans could have only delighted in the inability of Jay's 1794 treaty to wring one substantial concession from the British. Payment for British depredations against American commerce was deferred until a future date, as was the removal of British outposts on American borders. Attempts to open up trade in the West Indies were granted on terms favorable to Britain, as was a concession to allow freedom of all American ports to British vessels. These and other terms were disparaged by Republican leadership, with Jefferson referring to Jay as a "rogue of a pilot" who was guiding the ship of state into an enemy port while the captain slept.[4] Such allegations permitted the Republican opposition to fan the

flames of wounded American pride. Washington became the target of slan-
derous invective, Hamilton was stoned by a mob when he attempted to
defend the treaty in New York, and effigies of Jay were hanged in village
squares throughout the young nation.[5]

If the sentiments expressed in the writings and letters of George
Washington during this trying period are examined, they reveal that he was
never sanguine about the prospects of Jay being able to wring substantial
concessions from the English. Washington hoped for the best, but he
assuredly expected the worst. In April 1794, Washington told the Senate
that he was sending Jay to "announce to the world a solicitude for a friendly
adjustment of our complaints, and a reluctance to hostility." Washington's
objective was "peace with sincerity," but he also sought to steer clear of the
dangers of European involvements.[6] Historian Merle Curti contended that
Washington endorsed the enormously unpopular Jay treaty because it contained an arbitration clause that promised to prevent future wars with
Britain through peaceful settlement of disputes between the two nations.
The arbitration clause in the Jay Treaty had grown out of the American
attempt to gain compensation for the maritime commerce seized by Britain
in her efforts to weaken Napoleon during the ongoing Anglo-French conflict. But simply to demand compensation would have only made Britain
more intractable and left the procedure to the tedious workings of the
Admiralty Courts. John Jay suggested that American complaints be reviewed
by a board of four commissioners, two appointed by the King and two
appointed by the United States President and Senate. A fifth commissioner
would be appointed upon agreement by both sides. The five commissioners would then meet in London to decide the cases on the basis of "justice,
equity, and the laws of nations." The arbitration clause was the major
accomplishment of the treaty and ultimately secured some $10 million in
compensation for American merchants.[7]

Clearly Washington chose his envoy well, and Jay's previous diplomatic
record had proven his ability to secure an honorable settlement. John Jay
could be considered a "practical man of peace," who believed that negotiation should be based upon mutual interest. As Jay embarked upon his
mission to England, he wrote to his wife Sally: "If it should please God to
make me instrumental in the continuance of peace . . . we shall both have
reason to rejoice."[8] Sixteen years later, when the Massachusetts Peace
Society solicited his support, Jay responded affirmatively—if indeed the

society's objectives were to reveal the ". . . evils of unjust and unnecessary war." He was joined in his support of the Peace Society by his old adversary Thomas Jefferson.[9]

John Jay died in 1829. His youngest son William would spend the next four years using public papers and private correspondence to write his father's biography. In that biography, William fiercely defended his father's methods and motives in negotiating the oft derided treaty of 1794. William had attended Yale, studied law, and been appointed a judge of Westchester County, New York in 1818. William later became involved in the rising reform movements that blossomed in the northeast and attempted to sway the conscience of American society in the antebellum years. Because he was deeply religious, William's first efforts at social reform were in the promotion of temperance, the inviolability of the Sabbath, and the formation of the American Bible Society. Energetic in those reform movements, he later became a visible and committed agitator for the abolition of slavery and the promotion of world peace.

In the years immediately after the War of 1812, societies promoting world peace emerged in the northeast, particularly in New York and Massachusetts. These organizations were divided, however, as to how their goals might best be achieved. Happily, in 1828, these societies were conjoined as the American Peace Society under the uniting influence of Maine sea captain and farmer, William Ladd. Ladd was an unflagging campaigner in the cause of peace and attempted to develop a workable formula for its preservation. In 1833, the American Peace Society sponsored an essay contest to solicit the best plan for a congress of nations to maintain world peace. Luminaries serving on the committee to decide the winner included John Quincy Adams, Daniel Webster, and Ladd himself. Forty essays were submitted and five published. Ladd then took then best elements of the unprinted essays and amalgamated them into his own *Essay on a Congress of Nations*. Ladd never claimed that his concept of an international congress was original. Ladd did however divide the proposed body into a Congress of Ambassadors to represent civilized nations, and a Court of Nations for arbitration. It was 1840 before Ladd's essay appeared; by 1841 he was dead. But the idea of a congress of nations would continue to live, and William Jay's knowledge of Ladd's plan would appear in his work.[10]

Increasingly, the circle of New York friends with whom William Jay associated to promote the cause of anti-slavery became receptive to the doctrine of world peace. Merchants Arthur and Lewis Tappan, who were deeply involved in anti-slavery and other reforms, contributed both time and money to the cause. Jay's friend Lewis was serving on the board of directors for the American Peace Society by 1829, and Jay himself would eventually serve as President of the society from 1848 until his death in 1858. For these men, as for Jay, slavery and war were impediments to attaining the ideal of the Christian self-made man. Lewis Tappan freely admitted that his pacifism was influenced by Jay's pragmatic views on the subject. Peace was the condition to which humankind should aspire, foremost because it was mandated by God, but also because peace permitted men to focus upon business matters while they nurtured their morality.[11]

In 1841, Joseph Sturge toured the United States. The English industrialist and Quaker abolitionist had been instrumental in cataloging the abuses of the apprenticeship system that followed slavery in the British West Indies. Sturge had also been extremely active in the cause of peace, having founded the Birmingham Peace Auxiliary in 1819. At the time of his American tour, Sturge was serving as president of the London Peace Society. Sturge dined with William Jay in May of that year and was presented with a portion of the manuscript outlining Jay's soon to be published peace plan. After he had reviewed the work, Sturge was favorably impressed and wrote back to Jay offering to get it published and distributed in England, an offer that Jay gratefully accepted. Later that summer, Sturge met with members of the American Peace Society in Boston, reviewed Jay's plan, and suggested that a convention should be staged in London for the free exchange of ideas on how best to promote world peace.[12]

Upon his return to England, Sturge presented Jay's plan to the London Peace Society, and it was approved. In the course of promoting Jay's ideas, Sturge spoke to Richard Cobden. Cobden has been justly praised as a promoter of peace and compulsory arbitration. Yet many of the ideas Cobden expressed were not his exclusive intellectual property but the work of several other contemporary thinkers, William Jay among them. Both Jay and Cobden shared the belief in a free commercial intercourse between nations, and both worked similarly for arbitration as the most useful tool in the foreign policy arsenal. It was Jay who first promoted arbitration, however, then Cobden who later kept the idea alive.[13]

In 1842, Jay's *magnum opus* on practical pacifism, *War and Peace*, first appeared in the United States. The first half of the book is prosaic, given to examinations of national honor, the cost of colonial warfare to Great Britain, and a recapitulation of the wars that arose as a consequence of the French Revolution. Jay showed a special concern for the effects of war upon the civilian populace. In the course of his historical review, Jay lauded the work of temperance advocates and anti-slavery efforts while posing this question: "If we are so close to wiping away the stains of slavery and bibulousness, could not good Christians now turn their efforts to eliminating war?"[14]

For the abolitionist Jay, war and the abominable institution of slavery were inextricably linked. War created a situation where civil rights had to be subsumed to the will of the ruler (or dictator) in order to prosecute the conflict efficiently.

> *Civil liberty requires the substitution of laws for the will of the ruler; but in war, the will of the ruler and his subordinates becomes the source of legitimate authority.* Salus populi *is acknowledged as the* supreme lex; *and the bulwarks erected around the civil rights of the citizen are leveled on the proclamation of martial law.*[15]

Two types of slavery existed in the world: the personal slavery of the coerced worker and the political slavery that wars forced upon the citizens of belligerent nations. In order to be free to fully realize its potential, humankind had to be liberated from the physical and moral constraints that the horror and darkness of war imposed. Even as Jay wrote, events were unfolding that allowed him to illuminate this linkage.[16]

On October 25, 1841, the United States brig *Creole* left Richmond bound for New Orleans. The vessel's primary cargoes were tobacco and 135 slaves. On the night of November 7, the slaves, led by one Madison Washington, mutinied and killed a member of the crew. They then commandeered the vessel and forced it to sail to Nassau, where, after considerable negotiation, they were eventually permitted to come ashore by British authorities. When the ship was finally released by British authorities and docked in New Orleans on December 2, the story of the mutiny was made public and a storm of protest against English actions in the matter consumed the South. As negotiations between the United States and Britain dragged on in an attempt to resolve the sensitive situation, southern politicians became increasingly strident in their demands for the return of American property and the surrender of the "murderous slaves."[17]

In *War and Peace*, Jay made it clear that he believed the call by southern members of the Senate for the return of the former *Creole* slaves had no legal basis. No precedent or agreement existed for the return of fugitive slaves between nations. Further, outraged southern cries to destroy Nassau and other British towns in the West Indies proved, in Jay's estimation, that governments did not always settle matters of national honor through "righteous judgement," but might instead act in a moment of "irritation and passion." When they did so, they trampled not only the rights of citizens of other nations, but the peace and security of their own. Jay utilized the *Creole* incident to illustrate the irrationality of national pride and its incompatibility with a just settlement. Jay was correct. The *Creole* incident strained Anglo-American relations, and almost derailed the signing of the Webster-Ashburton Treaty that helped define the U.S.-Canadian border in the Northeast.

How could such threats to peace be avoided? Like William Ladd before him, Jay suggested that the common interest of Europe should lead to a recognition of the need for the establishment of a court to adjudicate differences between nations. He also proposed the eventual creation of a congress of nations, even though he felt such an action was impractical at the time owing to the reluctance of European governments. An alternative that would prove more expedient, in Jay's opinion, was that future treaties between nations contain a clause for stipulated arbitration. In that manner, future disputes between potential belligerents would be decided by a third, previously-agreed-upon party.

Jay borrowed from William Ladd when he suggested the congress of nations. This was evident because he referred to the bipartite system of congress and court that Ladd was credited with having envisioned. But where did the call for arbitration as an alternative come from? Jay quoted Vattel's *Law of Nations*, stating that arbitration was a comfortable method of resolving differences that did not affect national safety. Still, Jay was forced to duly note that treaties with arbitration clauses had previously been of "rare occurrence." *War and Peace* likely owed the concept of stipulated arbitration to the Jay Treaty. But the treaty was seldom mentioned in the book, and it is apparent that the son's suggestions differed from the manner in which the father had employed the method.[18]

The question that remained to be answered was which of the world's nations was so infused with altruism and so Christian in deportment to hoist the standard and lead the way toward adopting future arbitration? Because it had been the first to abolish the slave trade, because it had taken the lead in convincing men of the dangers of liquor consumption, Jay felt that the honor should fall to the United States. His reasoning did not denote a loss of perspicacity, even though it appears a variant on the theme of Manifest Destiny. America's fitness to provide enlightened leadership was a pervasive ideal, not only promoted by journalists such as John O'Sullivan, but shared by intellectuals of the time including Walt Whitman. Perhaps Ralph Waldo Emerson most eloquently expressed this view in his 1838 *Address on War*:

> *Not in an obscure corner, not in a feudal Europe, not in an antiquated appanage where no onward step can be taken without rebellion, is this seed of benevolence laid in the furrow, with tears of hope; but in this broad America of God and man, where the forest is only now falling, or yet to fall, and the green earth opened to the inundation of emigrant men from all quarters of oppression and guilt; here, where not a family, not a few men, but mankind, shall say what shall be; here we ask, Shall it be War, or shall it be peace?*[19]

Similarly, Jay reasoned that all factors, from its expansive commerce to its extended territory, favored the United States as a world leader; no nation had "less reason to covet the possessions of others, or to apprehend the loss of her own."[20] In Jay's opinion, arbitration had the salutary effect of anticipating future disputes rather than dealing with controversy after it had boiled over. To those who would inevitably observe that the plan was impractical, or "visionary and impossible," Jay replied that it was not. The plan "violated no principle of human nature," and required no adjustment in the "passions and prejudices of mankind." It was a proposal demonstrably based upon past national policy experience, and adaptable to the current "state of civilized society." Further, and perhaps most importantly, the plan was not only "consistent with the precepts of Christianity," but "also in accordance with the selfish dictates of worldly policy."[21]

Jay also thought his plan was obviously in accord with Christian virtue. Had Jesus not proclaimed: "Blessed are the peacemakers, for they shall be called the children of God?" But how would humankind be induced to walk the path toward its inception? Like William Ladd, Jay believed that governments could not be trusted to take the lead; the appeal would have to be made to the citizens of the world. In the same manner in which he presented his anti-slavery homilies to reluctant audiences, Jay again invoked the realization of liberal self-interest through the gentle stimulus of moral suasion. The tools were available through "voluntary associations, the pulpit, and the press." "Let the friends of peace," Jay continued, "concentrate their exertions in peace societies . . . and call upon their hearers to engage in this blessed work." Petitions had to be presented to rulers, and the press convinced to illustrate unflinchingly the folly of war in order to educate humankind. The age was "propitious to the enterprise," for minds were alert and "every ear is open to the reception of new truths."[22]

Selectively borrowing from what might be considered its antecedents, William Jay's plan was widely embraced by the international peace movement. Beginning in 1843 and at each succeeding international peace congress, the promotion of the plan was one of the first orders of business. Copies of *War and Peace* were printed and distributed to every member of the English Parliament. Some, like Richard Cobden, whose impassioned 1849 plea for international arbitration echoed Jay's, tried earnestly to implement this and other pacifist strategies. But European efforts to gain acceptance for Jay's plan were overshadowed as the Crimean conflict approached.

In the United States, peace advocates worked diligently to convince politicians to accept the plan. They had considerable success in the Northeast, where several state governments adopted it and urged the Federal government to do so. The plan for stipulated arbitration was a plank in the Free Soil Party's Pittsburgh Platform of 1852. The plan's association with the anti-slavery cause doomed it on the national level, however. Increasingly truculent sectional differences over slavery and its expansion made it impossible for Americans to achieve a political consensus on virtually any topic by the 1850s. At the same time, Quakers and other peace advocates began to focus more resolutely on the politics of abolitionism. After over a decade of hopeful promotion, the appeal of stipulated arbitration diminished.

MAX WEBER IN NEW ENGLAND

Charles L. Cohen

If one had to select a poster-child to advertise Max Weber's religious sociology, Puritanism would surely loom among the favorites. Although Weber educed Pietism, Methodism, and Baptist sectarianism as theological sources for the Protestant ethic, his foremost example was "Calvinism"—which in the event meant English Puritanism—and its most prominent adumbrator Richard Baxter, a maddeningly prolific English Puritan.[1] Americans unconsciously betray the logic of equating Protestantism with Puritanism by colloquially rendering Weber's term as the "Puritan ethic." Throughout his religious sociology, Weber highlighted arguments by deploying Puritanism over against other faiths, contrasting it with Confucianism as two possible orientations toward man and God, for example, or comparing it with Judaism as types of this-worldly creeds that fostered economic activity.[2] Since Weber rests securely among the giants of twentieth-century social science, one would expect him to appear prominently in the scholarship on New England Puritanism, one of the most overgrown literatures in American historiography: specialists in Anglo-America joke that, given current rates of publication, the number of books on colonial New England will soon equal the number of inhabitants. Yet amidst this fecundity, Weber is conspicuous by his absence, his lack of influence inversely proportional to his global reputation. Given the stereotype of canny New Englanders making pound over fist in the Atlantic marketplace, this paucity of references is mightily odd.

Perhaps omitting Weber from footnotes is intended to avenge his back-handed treatment of the American Puritans (and by extension their academic champions), whom he virtually ignored—albeit with unhappy consequences for his own work. Weber froze Puritanism in mid-seventeenth-century England and pinned it to the doctrine of predestination; his treatment lacks a developmental perspective and characterizes Puritanism by a single doctrine that did not in fact dominate its dogmas. He defines Puritanism primarily as a theological and liturgical phenomenon as opposed to an experiential one, whereas most historians now consider it pre-eminently a spiritual temperament and devotional regime whose internal dynamics and sociological significance can be discerned only by investigating the evolution of its spiritual economy within the changing political, ecclesiastical, social and religious contexts of early modern England and Anglo-America.[3] Weber constructed an essentialized Puritanism that few historians find useful.

Had he lived a few years longer, Weber might have vindicated his position by pointing to contemporary American opinion, for which New England Puritanism's historical significance seemed to lie in its fortunate demise two centuries earlier. *The Sociology of Religion* appeared in 1922, two years after Weber's death, by which time Americans hopped up on Fords, Freud, and jazz had discovered the erotic potential of guttural saxophones and the back seats of cars, their behavior justified by heady draughts of popularized libido theory. Misconstruing late-Victorianism's staid strictures as seventeenth-century anti-libertinism, they mocked the godly as enemies of sense and sensuality: "Puritanism," H. L. Mencken declared, "is the morbid fear that somewhere, someone may be happy." The Saints fared little better within the academy, where professors steeped in Progressive historiography's presumption that ideas merely cloak economic interests and intent on discovering historical precursors of modern democracy dismissed the importance of Puritan ideas and wrote the Saints off as illiberal theocrats.[4] In such an atmosphere, Weber was as irrelevant as Puritanism was nauseating. When Perry Miller, fresh from an "epiphany" induced while loading oil drums in the Belgian Congo, arrived in graduate school determined to "expoun[d]" the "innermost propulsion of the United States" by "beginning at the beginning," that is, "the Puritan migration," his mentors warned him "against throwing [his] career away" on a field whose "wheat had long since been winnowed" and in which "nothing but chaff remain[ed]."[5] Fortunately, he demurred, to become American Puritanism's most insightful and hypnotic expounder. Yet even Miller, who dramatized the intricate interplay between Reformed theology and New England's rough-hewn economy, paid Weber little heed. In a chapter entitled, of all things, "The Protestant Ethic," he alluded to Weber just once— as the person who "taught us" about "this configuration of ideas."[6] In these pages Miller elaborated on the Jeremiad, a rhetorical form in which preachers chastised their congregations for endangering New England's covenant with God by committing scandalous sins, most of which—like enlarging one's income to acquire waistcoats and Madeira, seventeenth-century equivalents of platform shoes and Dom Perignon—we understand as the prerequisites for and perquisites of living in a consumer society. For Miller, the Jeremiad voiced the angst of a community in the throes of realizing that implementing its cherished values—in this case the imperative to labor diligently in one's calling—was undermining its beloved social order: the wages of sin were social mobility and declension. Miller might profitably have commented on the applicability of Weber's work—the thesis that Puritanism disintegrated as New England prospered fits comfortably with Weber's argument about the habits of rational capitalism having been planted by religious habits gone to seed—but, for whatever reason, he did not. His successors have, for the most part, followed suit.

There are good intellectual reasons why American historians might regard Weber's portrayal of Puritanism skeptically. As I shall demonstrate, many of his notions warrant qualifying. Nevertheless, the sum total of these reservations ought not amount to wholesale dismissal. As recent work has shown, Weber can help us rethink even so well-worked a topic as American Puritanism.

Weber's discussion of Puritanism and politics exemplifies his work's strengths and weaknesses. Commenting on predestination's political consequences, Weber averred that Puritan belief in the doctrine "was regarded by authorities everywhere as dangerous to the state and as hostile to authority, because it made Puritans skeptical of the legitimacy of all secular power."[7] Puritan politics indubitably displayed a radical streak, as Charles I discovered when he had his head handed to him—literally.[8] Nonetheless, Puritan hostility to secular power did not issue from the doctrine of predestination. When James I opposed Puritan hopes for reforming the English Church on Genevan lines with the epigram "No Bishop, No King," he was observing that anti-episcopalianism might be a vector for unlovely feelings about his jurisdiction, but the threat derived from Puritans' ecclesiology, not their soteriology: their dislike of England's Erastian state-church system derived from their dismay that it violated the New Testament's pattern of true apostolic church governance, not that it traduced their theology of grace. Here, as elsewhere, Weber accorded predestination too much influence, in the process missing the importance of covenantal motifs important in Puritan political thinking (and much else).

Puritans grounded the legitimacy of government in God's donation of authority to rulers coupled with a covenanted agreement between magistrates and people that the former would govern according to God's Law and the latter abide by their rulers' decisions. This theory accorded the people a modicum of responsibility for constituting and participating in the polity, but it did not enshrine the doctrine of popular sovereignty— magistrates derived their authority from God, not their constituents. Such conceptions stacked the deck in favor of the state's legitimacy without discarding the joker hidden up Reformed sleeves, the idea that resistance to tyrants was obedience to God and that the ruled had an obligation to unseat any ruler who transgressed His law.[9] Puritans did not innately distrust secular power—their political program required godly magistrates to defend the church and secure moral order, after all—but they excoriated what they considered ungodly secular power, governments that did not preserve the true church, failed to secure moral order, and flouted God's laws. Puritans were neither inherently statist nor revolutionary—depending on circumstances, they could be either.

In New England this complicated attitude toward power grounded centralized polities that were operationally supple. Puritans established governments expressly intended to impose social and moral discipline; they had fled what to them was no longer John of Gaunt's "blessed plot"[10] to escape the breakdown of community structures and obligations that had unleashed "masterless men" uninhibited by family oversight to beg, borrow, and steal their ways through a no-longer peaceable kingdom. The ultimately anti-monarchical disposition of English Puritans should not obscure the statist inclinations of their American cousins bent on creating a godly commonwealth in New England's "free aire." At the same time, the colonists were still Albion's seeds jealous of their English rights. As early as 1632, the good citizens of Watertown protested the Massachusetts General Court's imposition of a tax on them without their representatives' consent, which complaint led immediately to the institution of deputies to consult with the Court on such matters and ultimately to a bicameral legislature in which the deputies comprised the lower house.[11] Puritans were not hostile to secular authority per se; they merely wanted to hold it.

But if Weber was not entirely accurate on this score, he hit the mark by using Puritans to epitomize people who solved the "problem of the relation between religion and politics" by discerning no fundamental conflict between the two spheres: as he put it, they "represented as God's will the domination over the sinful world, for the purpose of controlling it, of religious virtuosi belonging to the 'pure' church. This view was fundamental in the theocracy of New England. . . ."[12] It certainly was—in some cases. The Massachusetts General Court in 1631 passed a law that freemen— voters and officeholders—had to be regenerate church members, a qualification that became even more rigorous a few years later when churches began requiring that candidates for full membership had to relate their personal conversion experiences publicly so that the Saints could judge whether the applicant was a sheep or a goat. New Haven, whose founders left Massachusetts in part because they deemed its moral order too liberal, followed suit. Connecticut did not, however; since the colony was more homogeneously Puritan than Massachusetts, the magistrates may have presumed that the freemen would be godly by default. The more interesting anomaly is Plymouth, founded by semi-Separatists who, unlike the first settlers of Massachusetts, denied that the Church of England constituted a true church. As insistent as any Puritans that the church is an institution gathered out of the world by the Saints—Weber's "religious virtuosi"—the Pilgrims nevertheless did not make church membership necessary for holding political power.[13] Still, Weber's insistence that ascetic movements "can compromise with the facts of the political power structures by interpreting them as instruments for the rationalized ethical transformation of the world and for the control of sin" accurately describes the Puritans' political imperative.[14]

One of Weber's pre-eminent themes is the intertwined rationalization of religious, social, and economic life that distinguished Occidental civilization from Oriental. Weber employed "rationalization" or "rationality" in at least two ways: generally, the terms intend the systematic organization of society in which "human actions should be subject to a fundamental 'hierarchy of control'"; more specifically, they mean "the elimination of magic as a means to salvation."[15] There is no question that Puritans were paragons of social rationalization: Saints' every nerve strained toward maintaining magistrates' authority, securing class hierarchies, and imposing moral discipline, tying up society's loose ends unraveled by sin. But they were not quite such archetypes of rationalism as presented in Weber's claim that "Only ascetic Protestantism completely eliminated magic and the supernatural quest for salvation"[16] Their sacramentalism did not dispense entirely with supernaturalism, magical elements persisted in their popular religious life, and the exercise of reason was not for them the primary means to salvation.

The sacramentalism of the American Puritans did display Reformed Protestantism's typical disdain for Catholic "superstition." To speak only of the Eucharist, they rejected any hint of Christ's immediate physical presence in the elements of bread and wine; the "starkness" of their "introspective spirituality," according to Brooks Holifield, "diluted the possibility of sensuous participation that had marked traditional Roman and Lutheran eucharistic devotion." Nevertheless, even New England's founding ministers, perhaps the foremost opponents of interpreting the Eucharist supernaturally, refused to reduce the Lord's Supper "to a memorial of the past." They "were intent on possessing the middle ground between Zwinglian and Lutheran extremes," and their "ambivalence" about the Supper's meanings allowed room for their successors to elaborate a more fervent sacramentalism. One aspect of the late-seventeenth-century "sacramental renaissance" was Solomon Stoddard's advocacy, against New England's practice, of opening the Lord's table to all congregants, unregenerates as well as Saints. A second was a confident, if understated, apprehension of Christ's real appearance in the sacrament; as Boston's Samuel Willard put it, Christ had to be present "in some sort here according to his Human Nature," else he would not have offered the formula, "This is my Body, and this is my blood." According to Brooks Holifield, "this recourse to mystery was itself fully reminiscent of Calvin's own sacramental piety."[17] The Puritan Supper did not efficaciously convey to communicants grace embodied in transubstantiated elements—by magic, in Weber's terms—but neither was it exactly a ceremony capable of exerting an "ethical effect" on believers "precisely because of the absence of magical and confessional controls."[18] At Puritanism's heart lies the sensation not of rational control over a deity who disburses grace as piety's wages but of awe before the majestic god with whom one can never bargain. Communion brought one closer to the King of Kings, but it did not allow the faithful to manipulate Him either magically or rationally.

Nor did Puritans banish magic from their lives. Their belief in and fear of witchcraft is well known, but to invoke only the panic at Salem touches the subject superficially; occultism mingled with orthodox piety more than scholars once suspected. We now know that Reformed Protestantism did not fully disenchant the world; believing in the efficacy of white as well as diabolic magic, devout Puritans employed charms and solicited cunning-folk to make their way through daily life as well as to deliver themselves from evil.[19] According to Weber, using predestination to "determine concrete events in history" immediately causes it "to lose its ethical, rational character," as occurred in Islam.[20] Yet although in theory Puritanism should have focused individuals on mundane signs of salvation, in practice many individuals tried to discern their fate not through spiritual or worldly evidences but by trying to determine if God had decreed their salvation, that is, by practicing a sort of spiritual fortune-telling. We know that at least some laypeople indulged in such divination because the clergy periodically urged them to stop it. Indeed, Puritans were fascinated by miracles and wonders, supernatural intrusions into the natural order whose magnitude advertised their salvific importance and required translation by the hermeneutic community of ministers and laity. One's eternal fate might be discerned by extraordinary signs whose existence owed nothing to an individual's works but rather to God's mercy in revealing providential tokens for His own reasons.[21] Weber's point that for Puritans salvation was not possible through magical manipulation is certainly correct, but he erred in suggesting that ethical manipulation replaced it. For the Saints, God disposes unpredictably according to His divine and horrible decree, whose logic lies infinitely beyond human comprehension. Ethical behavior signifies election—as might wonders—but does not solicit it.

Weber rightly cited Puritans of all classes for their devotion to thought: their "unparalleled diffusion" of biblical knowledge and their "interest in extremely abstruse and ethereal dogmatic controversies . . . even among peasant groups" encouraged "a popular religious intellectualism never found since."[22] New Englanders' habits of reading to their children and their elevated literacy rates, their early establishment of free town schools and of Harvard College, more than secure that judgment.[23] But the Puritan attitude toward reason was ambivalent and contorted. The faculty that sets human beings apart from all other mortal creatures, reason was supposed to inform the will and control the passions, but Original Sin had corrupted the soul beyond grace's capacity to purify it in this life. Even a regenerated mind could not consistently provide the will with the proper data that would allow it to choose good. Interest in theology or knowledge of Scripture were laudable, but at best, Puritans thought, salvation's accouterments, not its source. Thought cannot seduce grace.

To insist that Puritans cried up unregenerates' inability to achieve salvation by works leads us to Weber's most famous and problematic thesis, that the anxiety predestination instilled in people desperate to enter heaven's gate induced them to paroxysms of holy labor. Calvinism's "most characteristic dogma," he averred, predestination elicited "a feeling of unprecedented inner loneliness" in individuals severed by the "magnificent consistency" of its baleful logic from the comforts of Catholicism's institutional conduits to divine personages and its magical aids to grace, thereby condemning them to discover their eternal fate alone. One can know one is saved only by observing one's actions, notably the purposive obedience of God's commands. Calvinism demanded a "more intensive form of the religious valuation of moral action" than "has perhaps" ever "existed."[24] As a result, "in no other religion was the pride of the predestined aristocracy so closely associated with the man of a vocation and with the idea that success in rationalized activity demonstrates god's blessing as in Puritanism." Yet not even such Olympian "moral athletes"[25] as Puritans could sustain this tension forever; "as this doctrine continued to flow into the routine of everyday living," Weber concluded, its "dour bleakness became more and more intolerable" and collapsed, leaving as its residue a contribution "to the rationalized capitalistic temperament, the idea of the methodical demonstration of vocation in one's economic behavior."[26]

Weber's handling of predestination and its discontents is susceptible to both theological and historical critiques. His use of Richard Baxter as the single most important theoretician of how anxiety about election fosters holy work typifies his theological inexactitude, for he proposed that capitalist habits were induced by the onus of double predestination, in which God decrees both who shall be saved and who damned, whereas Baxter held that Christ's redemption may be applied to anyone who will take it, rejected the decree of damnation, and thus allowed individuals more power to assist grace than Weber imagined. Too, predestination was not Reformed Protestantism's controlling dogma. Although central to seventeenth-century polemics, where it served as a party badge, it figured little in preachers' sermons and did not, as far as we can tell from narratives of religious experience, especially concern the laity, who, when properly counseled, worried if they were saved but not if they had been elected.[27] Nor was predestination doleful when properly slotted theologically; in fact, it assuaged anxiety. The Saints could rest absolutely assured of enjoying eternal life because the doctrine of predestination pledged that they could never fall from grace. Their salvation did not depend on their ability to live without sin, a genetic impossibility, but on God's decree of election, which guaranteed that they would persevere. Those who held that good works conduced to salvation can never live peaceably, preachers explained, for any slip forfeits one's soul, whereas God's Elect can always sleep the sleep of the saved. Weber's religious psychology of work requires that Saints look to their actions for evidence of salvation, but although good deeds provide one sort of indication that one might be elect, they are neither the only nor the cardinal form; a person desperately seeking assurance need not rehearse one's deeds at all. Finally, Weber adduced fear of God's wrath and anxiety over one's fate as the primary motives for work, but powerful feelings of love for God and the Saints elicited Puritans' industry even more strongly; Saints labor primarily because they delight to do God's will, not because they cower under His wrath.[28] In sum, Weber misidentified predestination's soteriological function and so misconstrued its spiritual psychodynamics.

Weber's thesis also runs into two historical problems: rational economic activity appeared in England *before* the Saints did, and their economic behavior did not reproduce the acquisitive, profit-maximizing activity that Weber considered the hallmark of capitalistic calculation. In England, Puritanism was most prominent in market towns; rather than initiating enterprise, the godly congregated within areas already commercialized. A similar observation holds true for New England. If forms of rational enterprise had appeared only after the spiritual habits that shaped them had drained away like hot wax from a sculptor's mold, then New England mercantilism should have emerged only in the eighteenth century, after declension had banked the fires of "hotter Protestants." In fact, though, entrepreneurialism was alive and well from the outset of New England's settlement. New Haven—arguably the most strictly "puritanical" colony hived off from Massachusetts—was founded largely by people who departed Boston in 1638 because competitors had already taken the best commercial sites.[29] The economic slowdown of the 1640s, brought on when migrants who had stimulated agricultural production by bringing their capital to America and buying foodstuffs from settlers already on the ground were corked up by the English Civil War, stimulated merchants to contact markets around the North Atlantic temporarily abandoned by English traders. New England launched its commercial career during the heyday of Puritan rule.[30]

Paradoxically, however, although Puritanism did not inhibit capitalistic enterprise, neither did it ground rationalized profit-maximization. The notion of the particular calling, in which an individual worked diligently at one's task out of reverence for God and His commands, was subordinate to the general calling, one's duty to engage in *all* activity for the Lord's sake. In the particular calling, one proceeded in a godly, not a worldly way, measuring "success" spiritually, not fiscally. Puritans aimed to achieve a competence, an amount on which a family could live comfortably but without extravagance. For artisans, this ethic meant that one eschewed sharp business dealings even if they helped balance the books because God drew the ultimate bottom line and punished dishonesty with damnation; for farmers, it meant accumulating only sufficient land for the next generation to maintain their families, not vast estates; for everyone, it meant that industry had discernable limits and that godliness was gauged not by how much one produced but by how one produced.[31] The Saints' strove to maximize godliness, not profits, hence Puritanism's ebb could not have stranded a rationalized capitalist ethic on the American sands—they had never elaborated such an ethic.

Yet when all the criticisms have been launched and filed, a tickle at the back of the brain that Weber was onto something will not down. The pioneering work of Stephen Innes suggests that there is indeed a dynamic connection between Puritanism and capitalism, albeit one more mediated by social institutions than Weber's formulation of a direct influence between predestination and worldly activity presumes. Intent upon strengthening social cohesiveness by regulating behavior according to a biblically sanctioned moral code, Puritans engineered what Innes felicitously denominates a "culture of discipline" that had moral roots and economic consequences. Fearful of immiserating vices and eager to improve the time, Puritans endeavored to demonstrate godliness and enjoined their neighbors to do likewise. The high worth Puritans placed on constant, purposive activity on the Lord's behalf—self-control in the service of God and community—merged in America with common English sociopolitical concerns devoid of religious provenance but congruent with godly interests: desires to secure one's personal property and to protect oneself against prerogative government by upholding fundamental law devised by popularly legitimized local authorities. The love of liberty and property infused Boston long before Paul Revere strained to glimpse those lanterns in Old North Church. The marriage of Puritan discipline and English Whiggery gave birth to an institutional and ideological environment in which conditions favorable to capitalist enterprise—the economic liquidity of land (encouraged by liberalized inheritance practices), the absence of guilds and monopolies, state intervention to regulate product quality, and labor mobility—flourished. New England's "civil ecology" facilitated economic development with a distinctively puritanical emphasis: enterprise should not subserve personal aggrandizement—although one was certainly entitled to a "just" gain—but rather benefit the entire community. Puritan economics celebrated industry tempered by moral accountability, not unbridled individual acquisitiveness.[32]

The relationship between Puritanism and its social context was reciprocal, as Weber recognized: "it is not my aim," *The Protestant Ethic* concludes, "to substitute for a one-sided materialistic an equally one-sided spiritualistic causal interpretation of culture and history." Scholars should "investigate how Protestant Asceticism was in turn influenced in its development and its character by the totality of social conditions, especially economic."[33] Mark Peterson and Christine Heyrman have demonstrated that not only might Puritanism have fostered enterprise, its influence on—indeed, its very existence in—a community depended on a substantial level of economic activity being present, for if Puritanism discountenanced the idle poor, poverty precluded Puritanism. To keep up the Saints' religious order, which required educated ministers (with commensurate salaries), colleges to train them, schools to teach reading so the laity could read the Bible, supplies of the Good Book and other devotional works, and at least one meetinghouse in every town replete with sacramental silverware, demanded robust cash flows; the redeemed may have been justified by faith alone, but their churches needed *gelt*. So did preserving their social order. In their initial years as small fishing communities, Marblehead and Gloucester, Heyrman discovered, displayed high transiency rates, low income levels, dependence on external merchants for market access, and little organized religious activity. As the towns grew and developed, transiency dropped, income rose, a class of indigenous merchants appeared, and Congregationalists marched in, eager as always to superintend moral order.[34] Economic development satisfied the prerequisites for the church order. The spirit of capitalism gave rise to agencies of the Protestant ethic.

All of which seems neat, but economic historians are not amused. The Protestant ethic, they maintain, was essentially irrelevant to New England's capitalistic development, which is explicable in purely economic terms. Unable to manufacture needed commodities because they lacked access to trained labor and sufficient capital, New Englanders were forced to import such goods, and, inhibited from raising profitable agricultural staples by their soils, exported primarily extractive goods like whales, fish, and timber. Puritanism contributed nothing to these developments.[35] Furthermore, colonial Virginia constructed an exemplary capitalist economy that accrued greater profits in Puritanism's absence than did New England in its presence. The earliest Virginians elevated lassitude to an art and bowled in the streets when they should have hoed, but once John Rolfe proved that one could put the colony's tobacco in a pipe and smoke it—and, even better, sell it—colonists bestirred themselves to sow weed for cash. Those whom luck or pluck favored with sufficient returns invested in labor—servants and then slaves—to increase production and returns. Planters made carefully calculated economic decisions, the only difference between them and Weber's rationalistic Protestants being the Virginians' preference for disciplining their laborers rather than themselves.[36] At the Revolution, the Old Dominion was the largest and wealthiest mainland British colony. Virginia constitutes arguably the best site in colonial Anglo-America to observe rationalizing entrepreneurs animated by a desire to acquire maximum profits and accumulate great wealth, goals the province achieved without benefit of Puritans, whom Governor William Berkeley had harried from the land in the 1640s.

How relevant Weber's sociology of religion may be for understanding Anglo-America is still an open question. The founders of the southern staple sector, West Indians and Carolinians as well as Virginians, operated during the apogee of Puritanism's cultural influence, yet their fervid quest for profits owes nothing to Reformed religiosity. Economic historians may legitimately question whether the development of New England, where the Saints were thick on the ground, had anything at all to do with their spirituality. Weber misconstrued Puritan theology, overstated the Saints' self-aggrandizing qualities, and posited a direct relationship between religious ideology and economic behavior that ignored the intervening cultural context. That said, we still should not dismiss him. Capitalism is, after all, a cultural as well as an economic system, and religious ethics may have had more of a determinative impact on its evolution than we have supposed, as Innes proposes. Too, Weber intimated that the shape of certain religious formations may depend on the economic preconditions in which they emerge. To cite the history of a different creed: Quakerism as it evolved in Wales and Northwest England emphasized the importance of raising and educating children within loving but disciplining families. Sustaining parental capacity to pass on the faith to future generations required income sufficient to keep families together. Exogamy was a sin; to marry out weakened the tribe, but children would have incentive to do so if they could not find mates with whom to establish economically viable households. Quakers valued industrious work habits that allowed family units to maintain themselves and the Society of Friends. The poverty of their British homeland often frustrated their plans, but their efforts thrived in the Delaware Valley. Because Quakers completely jettisoned predestinarianism, their ethics in no sense emerged from Puritan formulas, but their valuations of discipline, work, and family paralleled those of the Saints.[37] Weber may have overgeneralized about Protestantism's role in constructing capitalism, and he was certainly wrong to posit the pre-eminence of soteriology as the theological locus for stimulating sectarian enterprise, but his insights that religious ethics can influence economic life and that levels of economic activity can stimulate or suppress religious institutions warrant continued investigation.

Max Weber visited the United States in 1904. It is time for scholars of American history to invite him back.

NOTES

Foreword, by Charles Joyner

1. Winthrop D. Jordan, *White Over Black: American Attitudes toward the Negro, 1550–1812* (Chapel Hill, 1968).

2. Jordan, *The White Man's Burden: Historical Origins of Racism in the United States* (New York, 1973); "American Charioscuro: the Status and Definition of Mulattoes in the British Colonies," *William and Mary Quarterly*, 19 (1962): 183–200; "Modern Tensions and the Origins of American Slavery," *Journal of Southern History*, 28 (1962): 462–73; Jordan and Leon F. Litwack, *United States: Conquering a Continent, United States: Becoming a World Power*, 7th ed. (New York, 1990).

3. Jordan, *Tumult and Silence at Second Creek: An Inquiry into a Civil War Slave Conspiracy* (Baton Rouge, 1993, 1995).

4. David Brion Davis, "Terror in Mississippi," *New York Review of Books*, 40: 18 (November 4, 1993).

"The Erotic South: Civilization and Sexuality in American Abolitionism," by Ronald G. Walters

1. Julia Grifiths, ed., *Autographs for Freedom*, II (1854: rpt. Miami, 1969), 231. The connection between "disinterested benevolence" and immediatism was given its earliest sustained formulation in Gilbert Hobbs Barnes, *The Antislavery Impulse: 1830–1844* (1933: rpt. New York, 1964).

An earlier version of this essay, under a different title, was presented at the Annual Meeting of the Organization of American Historians in April 1971. Commentators at that session were Professors William O'Neill and Anne F. Scott, the latter of whom dissented strongly from the paper's conclusions and methodological assumptions. Other drafts, before and since, received helpful criticism from friends and colleagues, most especially from Professors David Hollinger, Winthrop D. Jordan, Tom and Carol Leonard, Leon Litwack and from members of the Institute of Southern History seminar at the Johns Hopkins University, particularly from David Donald.

2. Charles K. Whipple, *The Family Relation as Affected by Slavery* (Cincinnati: American Reform Tract . . . Soc. [1858]), 7; [Theodore Dwight Weld], *American Slavery as It Is: Testimony of a Thousand Witnesses* (New York, 1839), 7; *Philanthropist*, Apr. 14, 1840.

3. *Liberator*, Mar. 1, 1850; Whipple, *Family Relation*, 23; [Weld], *American Slavery as It Is*, 115.

4. John White Chadwick, ed., *A Life for Liberty: Anti-Slavery and Other Letters of Sallie Hollie* (1899: rpt. New York, 1969), 123.

5. Those abolitionists who were not non-resistants—Christian anarchists—had difficulty determining where authority and power should be used. See, for example, Weld's *American Slavery as It Is*. Weld seems to have spoken of the property aspects of slavery largely as a way of distinguishing between slavery and "legitimate" uses of power, as in family relations. Lewis Curtis Perry, "Antislavery and Anarchy: A Study of the Ideas of Abolitionism before the Civil War," Ph.D. Diss., Cornell University, 1967, 101–2, et passim, shows how attacks on slavery easily became attacks upon authority. See also Lewis Perry, "Versions of Anarchism in the Antislavery Movement," *American Quarterly*, 20 (1968), 772, 781.

6. *Emancipator*, July 21, 1836. Perry, "Antislavery and Anarchy," 12 ff, depicts slavery as a metaphor for denial of freedom.

7. Child, *An Appeal in Favor of Americans Called Africans* (1836: rpt. New York, 1968), 101; Bernard Bailyn, *The Origin of American Politics* (New York, 1968), 56; Woolman, conveniently quoted in William H. and Jane H. Pease, eds., *The Antislavery Argument* (Indianapolis, 1965), 7; Adams quoted in Ernest Lee Tuveson, *Redeemer Nation: The Idea of America's Millennial Role* (Chicago, 1968), 21.

8. *Liberator*, Feb. 5, 1831; for another early example see LaRoy Sunderland, *Anti-Slavery Manual, Containing a Collection of Facts and Arguments on American Slavery*, 2nd ed. (New York, 1837), 132–33.

9. Gerritt Smith to the Jerry Rescue Committee, Aug. 27, 1859, in Octavius Brooks Frothingham, *Gerrit Smith: A Biography*, 2nd ed. (New York, 1879), 240; [George Bourne], *Slavery Illustrated in Its Effects upon Woman and Domestic Society* (Boston, 1837), 73. Hints that rape would be a consequence of insurrection were generally delicately phrased. Thomas Wentworth Higginson, *Black Rebellion* (New York, 1969), 126–27, 175–76, seems to dismiss the possibility. But Higginson was concerned to demonstrate the nobility of slave rebels and was unlikely to acknowledge rape as a consequence of their assault on slavery.

10. [Louisa J. Barker], *Influence of Slavery upon the White Population* (New York, 1855–56), 6; [Bourne], *Slavery Illustrated*, 71; John Rankin, *Letters on American Slavery, Addressed to Mr. Thomas Rankin, Merchant at Middlebrook, Augusta Co., Va.* (1838: rpt. New York, 1969), letter 11. Rankin also quoted in *Liberator*, Oct. 20, 1832, and in LaRoy Sunderland, *The Testimony of God against Slavery. . . .*, 2nd ed. (New York, 1836), 87.

11. Whipple, *Family Relation*, 8; "Influence of Slavery on Slaveholders," *Quarterly Anti-Slavery Magazine*, I (1836): 326; Rankin, *Letters on Slavery*, 62–63 (which also contains comments on the corrupting influence of communication between slave and white children); Puritan. *The Abrogation of the Seventh Commandment by the American Churches* (New York, 1835), 5; Thome quoted in *Liberator*, May 17, 1834. Thomas F. Harwood, "The Abolitionist Image of Louisiana and Mississippi," *Louisiana History*, 7 (1966): 298, 299, 300, notes abolitionist concern for Southern sexuality.

12. *Liberator*, May 10, 1834 (comments on Thome's address by "G. B.," undoubtedly George Bourne); Jan. 29, 1858; *Pennsylvania Freeman*, July 4, 1834; Higginson quoted in Tilden G. Edelstein, *Strange Enthusiasm: A Life of Thomas Wentworth Higginson* (New Haven, 1968), 100; *Liberator*, Oct. 8, 1858.

13. [Barker], *Influence of Slavery*, 6. William R. Taylor, *Cavalier and Yankee: The Old South and American National Character* (New York, 1961), 139, notes that the planter, as a literary figure, was often depicted as lacking vitality and manliness. Taylor felt (I think correctly) that this may reflect the image of John Randolph as well as the nineteenth century's fascination with Hamlet. In the case of Mrs. Barker, and perhaps in the case of the languid, erratic and unstable Southerner of other antislavery writings, the implications are sexual; the worn-out, enfeebled planter is not Hamlet but the age's concept of a man who has committed sexual excess.

14. Birney to R. R. Gurley, Dec. 3, 1833 (also, Birney to Gurley, Sept. 24, 1833), in Dwight L. Dumond, ed., *Letters of James Gillespie Birney, 1831–1857* (New York, 1938), I, 97, 90: James G. Birney, *Letter on Colonization, Addressed to the Rev. Thornton J. Mills, Corresponding Secretary of the Kentucky Colonization Society* (New York, 1834), 44; Amos A. Phelps, *Lectures on Slavery and Its Remedy* (Boston, 1834), 209; Rankin, *Letters on Slavery*, 108.

Sunderland, *Anti-Slavery Manual*, 11–12. *Liberator*, Aug. 13, 1841, noted that by the Census of 1840 blacks showed less than "a fair rate of increase." It was then impossible to maintain that the South was in danger of being overwhelmed. The *Liberator*, alert to an argument, explained that the new figures now proved that slavery had murdered a quarter of a million people who might otherwise have lived.

15. *Emancipator*, Sept. 14, 1833; Aug. 10, 1837 (see also Aug. 19, 1834, and issues throughout the summer of 1834 for denials that abolitionists aimed at miscegenation). Leonard L Richards, *"Gentlemen of Property and Standing": Anti-Abolition Mobs in Jacksonian America* (New York, 1970), 31–32, et passim, notes the intense fear of miscegenation that anti-abolitionists projected onto antislavery.

16. Sunderland, *Anti-Slavery Manual*, 13; *Liberator*, May 7, 1831 (also, Nov. 17, 1832). Child, *Appeal*, 133, and Phelps, *Lectures on Slavery*, 236, argue that in the future interracial unions might not be scorned and that the present has no right to determine who should marry at a later date. Gerrit Smith, *Letter of Gerrit Smith to Hon. Henry Clay* (New York, 1839), 36, asserts that legal marriages between blacks and whites would increase after freedom, but that these were preferable to licentiousness. See also, Bertram Wyatt-Brown, *Lewis Tappan and the Evangelical War against Slavery* (Cleveland, 1969), 177.

17. Winthrop D. Jordan, *White Over Black: American Attitudes toward the Negro, 1550–1812* (Chapel Hill, 1968), 137.

18. W.G. (undoubtedly William Goodell), in *Emancipator*, Sept. 1835.

19. Anonymous, *The Lustful Turk*. . . . (1828, 1893, rpt. New York 1967), 71; Bernard Wishy, *The Child and the Republic: The Dawn of Modern Child Nurture* (Philadelphia, 1968), 40, notes the belief that servants were corruptors and cites George Combe, a phrenological author respected and personally known by many abolitionists; Philip Rieff, *Freud: The Mind of the Moralist* (1959: rpt. Garden City. N.Y., 1961), 166. On Victorian pornography generally see Steven Marcus, *The Other Victorians: A Study of Sexuality and Pornography*

in Mid-Nineteenth-Century England, rev. ed. (New York, 1967). Marcus relates the cult of sensibility, which appeared among antislavery writers, to sexuality. Milton Rugoff, *Prudery and Passion: Sexuality in Victorian America* (New York, 1971), is scantily researched but does include a section on the image of the South.

20. Bourne, letter to Rhode-Island Anti-Slavery Society, in *Liberator*, Feb. 6, 1836; [Bourne] *Lorette: The History of Louise, Daughter of a Canadian Nun, Exhibiting the Interior of Female Convents*, 3rd ed. (New York, 1834), 37–40, 45, stresses the absolute power of the priest, a theme of the whole novel. Bourne was also a supporter of the notorious Maria Monk and editor of an anti-Catholic newspaper.

21. *Philanthropist*, quoted in *Emancipator*, Dec. 6, 1838.

22. [Theodore Dwight Weld], *The Bible against Slavery: An Inquiry into the Patriarchal and Mosaic Systems on the Subject of Human Rights*, 4th ed. (New York, 1838), 7; James G. Birney MS Diary, May 9, 1850, Birney MSS., Library of Congress; Gilbert Haven, *National Sermons: Sermons, Speeches and Letters on Slavery and Its War* (Boston, 1869), 3. Daniel Walker Howe, *The Unitarian Conscience: Harvard Moral Philosophy, 1805–1861* (Cambridge, 1970), 60: "Unitarians were led to espouse the view that sin consisted of a breakdown in the internal harmony, an abdication by the higher faculties of their dominion over the lower." The theme of control clearly was not confined to antislavery. For other examples see Wishy, *Child and the Republic*, 17; Clifford S. Griffin, *Their Brother's Keepers: Moral Stewardship in the United States, 1800–1865* (New Brunswick, 1960); and Nathan G. Hale Jr., *Freud and the Americans: The Beginnings of Psychoanalysis in the United States, 1876–1917* (New York, 1971), 24–26. Joseph Ambrose Banks, *Prosperity and Parenthood: A Study of Family Planning among the Victorian Middle Classes* (London, 1954), 198, notes that about 1830 members of the English middle class began "applying the theme of control to their own way of life." They did this, in part, by advocating sexual self-restraint. I am aware that the word "passions" had a technical psychological sense that lingered into the nineteenth century. But both the context of comments and a check of the *Oxford English Dictionary* have convinced me that abolitionists generally used the word in its more modern sense of "intense emotions," largely sexual. There is information on topics discussed on the following pages, as well as on Victorian sexuality, in John R. Betts, "Mind and Body in Early American Thought," *Journal of American History*, 54 (1968): 787–805.

23. Parker to Robert White, Oct. 7, 1849, in John Weiss, *Life and Correspondence of Theodore Parker, Minister of the Twenty-Eight Congregational Society, Boston* (New York, 1864), I, 386; *Liberator*, Jan. 12, 1838; Green to Weld, July 11, 1841, in Gilbert H. Barnes and Dwight L. Dumond, eds., *Letters of Theodore Dwight Weld, Angelina Grimké Weld, and Sarah Grimké, 1822–1844* (New York, 1934), II, 868. On the religious meaning of slavery, sin and bondage see Jordan, *White Over Black*, and David Brion Davis, *The Problem of Slavery in Western Culture* (Ithaca, 1966).

24. *Radical Abolitionist*, I (1856): 101; *Emancipator*, Aug. 24, 1833. See Green to Theodore Dwight Weld, July 11, 1841, in *Weld-Grimké Letters*, II, 868: "We are not fit to plead the cause of Freedom, until we get free from the tyranny of our own passions." Bertram Wyatt-Brown, "Prophets Outside Zion: Career and Commitment in the Abolitionist Movement," paper delivered at the American Historical Association annual convention, Dec. 30, 1970,

notes many abolitionists who recalled childhood struggles with self-control. Professor Wyatt-Brown has recast some of his ideas in slightly different form in "The New Left and the Abolitionists: Romantic Radicalism in America," *Soundings*, 44 (1971): 147–63.

25. Weld to Angelina Grimké, Mar. 12, 1838; Angelina Grimké to Weld, Feb. 21, Mar. 4, 1838 (see also Weld to Angelina and Sarah M. Grimké, Feb, 16. 1838; and Weld to Angelina Grimké, Feb. 18, 1838), in *Weld-Grimké Letters*, II, 602, 565, 587, 556, 560; Birney MS Diary, Mar. 14, 1840, Birney MSS., Library of Congress. Birney also thought the Welds and Sarah Grimké to be "the happiest people I know." Weld achieved a Victorian triumph when he was able to exclaim to Miss Grimké "I forgot utterly that you were not of my own sex." Feb. 8, 1838, in *Weld-Grimké Letters*, II, 534.

26. *Liberator*, Jan. 29, 1858; Higginson, "Holiness Unto the Lord," *Harbinger*, 3 (1847): 28; *Liberator*, Sept. 17, 1836; *Emancipator*, Jan. 14. 1834; Stephen Pearl Andrews. ed., *Love, Marriage. and Divorce, and the Sovereignty of the Individual. . . .* (New York, 1853), 17.

27. The best introduction to the literature on antebellum economic change is still Stuart Bruchey, *The Roots of American Economic Growth, 1607–1861: An Essay in Social Causation*, new ed. (New York, 1968). Population trends can be spotted in J. Potter, "The Growth of Population in America, 1700–1860," in *Population in History: Essays in Historical Demography*, eds. D. V. Glass and D. E. C. Eversley (London, 1965), 672–73, 677–78. Wishy, *Child and the Republic*, 28, notes a reappraisal of family life after 1830, and the best introduction to the literature of American family history, although now somewhat dated, is Edward N. Saveth, "The Problem of American Family History," *American Quarterly*, 21 (1969): 311–29. Keith E. Melder, "The Beginnings of the Women's Rights Movement in the United States, 1800–1840," Ph.D. Diss. Yale University, 1963, 13–14, 19, 34, remarks on the change in woman's economic role, a point several abolitionists also perceived. See Sarah M. Grimké, *Letters on the Equality of the Sexes, and the Condition of Woman. . . .* (Boston, 1838), 54; and Theodore Parker, *Sins and Safeguards of Society*, ed. Samuel B. Stewart (Boston, n.d.), 182–83.

28. *National Era*, May 17, 1849.

29. Stephen S. Foster, *The Brotherhood of Thieves: Or, A True Picture of the American Church and Clergy: A Letter to Nathaniel Barney, of Nantucket* (Boston, 1844), 9.

30. Richards, *"Gentlemen of Property and Standing,"* deals with the motivation of anti-abolition mobs. David Donald, "The Proslavery Argument Reconsidered," *Journal of Southern History*, 37 (1971): 3–18, analyzes defenders of slavery and makes the point that the proslavery argument bears similarity to abolitionism and other antebellum movements.

31. *Sins and Safeguards of Society*, 203. Melder, "Beginnings of the Women's Rights Movement," 88, notes the coincidence of moral reform and antislavery in time; Robert Samuel Fletcher, *A History of Oberlin College from Its Foundation through the Civil War* (Oberlin, 1943), I, 296–308, gives material on the appeal of moral reform at Oberlin and Western Reserve. The Magdalen Society affair is recounted several places, most directly in Lewis Tappan, *The Life of Arthur Tappan* (New York, 1870), 110–20. Data on abolitionist connections with the American Society for Promoting the Observance of the Seventh Commandment can be found in Fletcher, *History of Oberlin*, I, 297, 305; *Emancipator*, Feb. 18, 1834; *Weld-Grimké Letters*, I, 130–31, 136. Otelia Cromwell, *Lucretia Mott* (Cambridge,

1958), 106, relates the story of Lucretia Mott and the Moral Reform Society. For additional interest in moral reform by abolitionists see the *Friend of Man*, particularly the issues of Dec. 1, 1836, and Jan. 12, 1837; William Lloyd Garrison to Helen Benson. Dec. 17, 1836, Garrison MSS., Boston Public Library; and Henry Steele Commanger, *Theodore Parker* (Boston, 1936), 177.

32. Stanton to Susan B. Anthony, Mar. 1, 1853, in Theodore Stanton and Harriot Stanton Blatch, eds., *Elizabeth Cady Stanton as Revealed in Her Letters, Diary and Reminiscences* (New York, [1922]), 11, 48–49. Stanton to Anthony, June 14, 1860, in Stanton and Blatch, eds., *Elizabeth Cady Stanton*, II, 82: "Woman's degradation is in man's idea of his sexual rights." For interesting parallels with English reform see J. A. Banks and Olive Banks, *Feminism and Family Planning in Victorian England* (Liverpool, 1964).

33. Wright, *Marriage and Parentage: Or, The Reproductive Element in Man, as a Means to His Elevation and Happiness*, 5th ed. (Boston, 1866), 265, 100; Andrews, ed., *Love, Marriage and Divorce*, 20. Wright's book was reviewed by C. K. Whipple in *Liberator*, Sept. 29, 1854, in general, favorably. Perry, "Antislavery and Anarchy," 229–34, discusses Wright's views on marriage and family. Perry plans to analyze Wright's complicated personal attitudes in his forthcoming biography of Wright.

34. Tappan, *Life of Arthur Tappan*, 121; *Liberator*, Jan. 16, 1846; Catharine E. Beecher and Harriet Beecher Stowe, *The American Woman's Home: Or, Principles of Domestic Science* (New York: Ford, 1869), 286. The sisters warned that auto-erotic activity might "terminate in disease, delirium, and death" and that "certain parts of the body are not to be touched except for purposes of cleanliness, and that the most dreadful suffering comes from disobeying these commands."

35. Weld to Theodore Grimké Weld, July 26, 1860, Weld MSS, Clements Library, University of Michigan. The episode also appears in Gerda Lerner, *The Grimké Sisters from South Carolina: Rebels against Slavery* (Boston, 1967), 345–49.

36. Sarah M. Grimké to [Elizabeth Smith Miller], June 1, 1873, Weld MSS., Clements Library. For statements blaming either American women or Southern women for maintaining slavery see E. L. Follen, *To Mothers in the Free States* (New York, 1855–6), 1; Puritan, *Abrogation of the Seventh Commandment*, 3; George Bourne, quoted in *Liberator*, Feb. 6, 1836; Angelina Grimké, *Appeal to the Christian Women of the South*, 3rd ed. (New York, 1836), 25. For examples of "conservative" abolitionists conceding woman's redemptive influence see *Emancipator*, Dec, 21, 1833; James A. Thome, *Address to the Females of Ohio, Delivered at the State Anti-Slavery Anniversary* (Cincinnati, 1836), p. 4; and Haven, *National Sermons*, 627.

37. William B. Walker, "The Health Reform Movement in the United States: 1830–1870," Ph.D. Diss., Johns Hopkins University, 1955, 124; H. B. Stanton and others to Theodore Dwight Weld, Aug. 2, 1832, in *Weld-Grimké Letters*, I, 85; Fletcher, *History of Oberlin*, I, 318–39; *Graham Journal, of Health and Longevity*, 3 (1839): 185; 1 (1837): 5: and 2 (1838): 209. Thomas H. LeDuc, "Grahamites and Garrisonites," *New York History*, 20 (1939): 189–91, reprints with commentary an amusing document about abolitionists who believed in Graham's system.

38. Walker, "Health Reform Movement," 276; Benjamin P. Thomas, *Theodore Dwight Weld, Crusader for Freedom* (New Brunswick, 1950), 39; Henry Villard, *The Memoirs of Henry Villard, Journalist and Financier: 1835–1900* (Boston, 1904), II, 52; Thomas Wentworth Higginson, *Out-Door Papers* (Boston, 1863), 142; Sallie Holley to Mrs. Samuel Porter, Feb. 28, 1859, in Chadwick, ed., *A Life for Liberty*, 166–67. Edelstein, *Strange Enthusiasm*, 26, writes of Higginson: "The issue of manliness would be very close to many of the social causes he would champion." Walker, "Health Reform Movement," 285–87, considers the "vigorous life" of the late nineteenth century to have been an outgrowth of the health reform movement.

39. Higginson, *Out-Door Papers*, 139. Walker, "Health Reform Movement," contains information on Trall, Lewis, Graham and Alcott.

40. "First Annual Report of the Oneida Community" (1848), in Norman E. Himes, *Medical History of Contraception* (1936: rpt. New York, 1970), 269–74; Alice Felt Tyler, *Freedom's Ferment: Phases of American Social History from the Colonial Period to the Outbreak of the Civil War* (1944, 1962), 185ff.

41. Wright, *Marriage and Parentage*, 18, 227.

42. Stanton to Susan B. Anthony, Mar. 1, 1853; Stanton to Elizabeth Smith Miller, Sept. 11, 1862, in *Elizabeth Cady Stanton*, II, 48–49, 91; Andrews, ed., *Love. Marriage and Divorce*, 20. There was an interesting and significant strain of hereditarian thought expressed by early advocates of Woman's Rights like Wright and Stanton. Note also that Orson Fowler, who published some of Wright's works, was both a phrenologist and author of *Love and Parentage, Applied to the Improvement of Offspring*. Making the connection even more intriguing, Fowler also published the first edition of *History of Woman Suffrage*.

43. Birney MS Diary, Dec. 10, 1850, Birney MSS., Library of Congress. Anne L. Kuhn, *The Mother's Role in Childhood Education: New England Concepts. 1830–1860* (New Haven, 1947), 114–18; and Walker, "Health Reform Movement," 27–29, see phrenology coupled with an interest in improvement. On phrenology itself see John D. Davies, *Phrenology, Fad and Science: A Nineteenth-Century American Crusade* (New Haven, 1955).

44. Henry C. Wright, for instance, advocated a form of birth control when he advised abstinence from sexual relations except for procreation and procreation at intervals of no less than three years. Yet Wright railed against physicians who promoted artificial birth control instead of telling couples to control their passions. *Marriage and Parentage*, 1–6, 132–33.

45. Parker, *Sins and Safeguards*, 53; Stowe, "Bodily Religion," *Atlantic Monthly*, 18 (1866): 92. LaRoy Sunderland, at the time a Methodist minister, argued that religious duty required people to preserve health, *Graham Journal of Health and Longevity*, 3 (1839): 186–87. For a similar feeling, expressed in a different reform, see Charles F. and Carroll S. Rosenberg, "Pietism and the Origins of the American Public Health Movement: A Note on John H. Grissom and Robert M. Hartley," *Journal of the History of Medicine and Allied Sciences*, 13 (1968): 16–35.

46. Conway, *Autobiography, Memories, and Experiences of Moncure Daniel Conway* (Boston, 1904), II, 350; Stanton to Robert Dale Owen, Apr. 10, 1866, in Elizabeth Cady Stanton, II, 113; Parker Pillsbury, *Acts of the Anti-Slavery Apostles* (Boston, 1884), 489–90.

"Ministerial Misdeeds: The Onderdonk Trial and Sexual Harassment in the 1840s," by Patricia Cline Cohen

1. Julia Hull Winner, ed., "A Journey Across New York State in 1833," *New York History*, 46 (Jan. 1965): 60–78.

2. William Stevens Perry, *The History of the American Episcopal Church, 1587–1883*, 2 vols., (Boston, 1885), 269–282.

3. Norma Basch, "Marriage, Morals, and Politics in the Election of 1828," *Journal of American History* 80 (1993): 890–918.

4. See entries on both brothers in the *Dictionary of American Biography*; and Elmer Onderdonk, *Genealogy of the Onderdonk Family in America* (New York, 1910), 104–05.

5. *The Proceedings of the Court Convened Under the Third Canon of 1844, on Tuesday, December 10, 1844, for the Trial of the Right Rev. Benjamin T. Onderdonk, D.D. Bishop of New York, on a presentment made by the Bishops of Virginia, Tennessee, and Georgia* (New York, 1845), 15.

6. Ibid., 30–39.

7. Ibid., 40.

8. Ibid., 39–62. James Richmond, *The Conspiracy Against the Late Bishop of New-York, Unravelled by one of the Conspirators* (New York, 1845), 10.

9. *Proceedings*, 7, 139–40.

10. Ibid., 63, 64, 73.

11. Ibid., 64.

12. Ibid., 65, 66.

13. Ibid., 8.

14. James Richmond, *Mr. Richmond's Reply to the "Statement" of the Late Bishop of New York* (New York, 1845), 9–10.

15. Benjamin Onderdonk, *A Statement of Facts and Circumstances Connected with the Recent Trial of the Bishop of New York* (New York, 1845), 7.

16. Richmond, *The Conspiracy Unravelled*, 5, 6, 8–9. "James Cook Richmond," *Appleton's Cyclopedia of American Biography* (New York, 1888).

17. Richmond, *The Conspiracy Unravelled*, 7.

18. Anon., *An Appeal from the Sentence of the Bishop of New York, in Behalf of his Diocese; Founded on the Facts and Improbabilities Appearing on Both Sides in the Late Trial* (New York, 1845), 7, 14.

19. Quoted in both the *New York Herald*, Jan. 11, 1845, and *The Advocate of Moral Reform* 11 (Feb. 1, 1845): 20.

20. *Advocate of Moral Reform*, 11 (Feb. 1, 1845): 20–21.

21. *The Churchman*, Dec. 21, 28, 1844; Jan. 11, 1845.

22. Spectator, *The Verdict Sustained at the Bar of Public Opinion* (New York, 1845), 10; *Proceedings*, 291.

23. *The New York Herald*, Jan. 31, 1845; *The Verdict Sustained*, 9.

24. Paul de Kock [George Thompson] *New-York Life, or the Mysteries of Upper-Tendom Revealed* (New York, n.d.), 54.

25. *De Darkies Comic Al-Me-Nig for 1846* (Philadelphia, 1845).

26. Smith, *Sunshine and Shadow*, 584–85.

"Stallions in the Churchyard: Sexuality and Privacy in Rural Mississippi," by Susan Ditto

1. *Laws of the State of Mississippi* (1892), #1220; As Lawrence Stone warns, historians must not accept statutes as evidence of actual behavior. However, "there is a reciprocal relationship between the enacted law, current theories of justice, and the social, economic, and cultural background" from which they are derived *Road to Divorce: England, 1530–1987* (New York, 1990), 10. Court cases, on the other hand, tell us how at least some people actually behaved. Peter Bardaglio notes that appellate opinions "are especially valuable because the supreme courts established guidelines for the lower courts adjudicating cases in these areas of the law." *Reconstructing the Household: Families, Sex, & the Law in the Nineteenth-Century South* (Chapel Hill, 1995), xviii.

2. *Laws of the State of Mississippi* (1892), Chapter 23, Article 15.

3. Sarah Lois Wadley diary, 19 June 1861, Sarah Lois Wadley Papers, Southern Historical Collection, University of North Carolina, Chapel Hill (hereafter UNC).

4. Wadley Diary (UNC).

5. Eighth Census of the U.S. (1860), Mortality and Miscellaneous Statistics.

6. Eighth Census of the U.S., 1860, Population.

7. Based on inventories dated after 1865 with a total property value between $500 and $2500. Only those inventories which included some farm implements, had fewer than five slaves, and which itemized bedding were counted. "Inventory Records of Estates," Monroe County, Miss. (1858–61, 1870–74); "Inventories and Appraisements," Rankin County, Miss. (1854–58, 1863–65, 1865–72); "Chancery Court Records," Lafayette County, Miss. (1837–39); "Inventories," Haywood County, Tenn. (1856–66); "Inventories of Estates," McNairy County, Tenn., (1865–67).

8. Eighth Census of the U.S. (1860), Population, Lafayette, Monroe, and Pontotoc Counties.

9. Stephanie McCurry has shown that slaves owned by yeomen were most likely to be women or children. In 70 percent of South Carolina upcountry households that contained only one slave, that one was female. *Masters of Small Worlds: Yeoman Households, Gender Relations, & the Political Culture of the Antebellum South Carolina Low Country* (New York, 1995), 48–49.

10. The proportion of cribs in households containing separate beds for young children may have been higher than can be judged from probate inventories, since such accounts were taken only upon the death of the household head, usually well after his or her children had outgrown the need for a crib. Eighth Census of the U.S.: Mortality, Property, & c. (1866), 35.

11. Karin Calvert, *Children in the House: The Material Culture of Early Childhood, 1600–1900* (Boston, 1992), 37.

12. Elizabeth Collins Cromley, "A History of American Beds and Bedrooms, 1890–1930" in Jessica H. Foy and Thomas J. Schlereth, eds., *American Home Life: A Social History of Spaces and Services* (Knoxville, 1992), 123.

13. Mary P. Ryan, *Cradle of the Middle Class: The Family in Oneida County, New York, 1790–1865* (Cambridge, 1981), 168.

14. Orson Squire Fowler quoted in Christopher Edward Clark, Jr., *The American Family Home, 1800–1960* (Chapel Hill, 1986), 40.

15. Sally McMurry, *Families and Farmhouses in 19th-Century America* (New York, 1988), 194.

16. McCurry, *Masters of Small Worlds*; Jacqueline S. Reinier, *From Virtue to Character: American Childhood, 1775–1850* (New York, 1996), 178.

17. *The Rural Southerner: Agricultural and Home Literature*, vol. 4, no. 1 (Jan. 1871): 13.

18. McCurry, *Masters of Small Worlds*, 75–76.

19. E. B. Fox, Williamson County Tennessee in Elliott, Colleen Morse and Louise Armstrong Moxley, eds. *The Tennessee Civil War Veterans Questionnaires* (Easley, South Carolina, 1985, vol. II), 843.

20. In "The Spermatic Economy: A Nineteenth-Century View of Sexuality" (in Michael Gordon, ed. *The American Family in Social-Historical Perspective*. New York, 1978, 374–402), G. J. Barker-Benfield uses the term *spermatic economy* in reference to the belief that the literal conservation of sperm was crucial to the success of the self-made Victorian man. Sexual self-control both fueled the vigorous industry of bourgeois men and contributed to the declining birthrate among northern middle-class women. On yeoman farmsteads, an opposite phenomenon was in play. The pressure on rural farming couples and livestock alike was to produce large numbers of offspring. Because, in yeoman farming families, the economic and physical burden lay on "self-working" females rather than "self-made" men, I prefer the opposite-gendered term "ovarian economy."

21. McCurry, *Masters of Small Worlds*, 57–60.

22. Sally McMillen, *Motherhood in the Old South: Pregnancy, Childbirth, and Infant Rearing* (Baton Rouge, 1990), 32.

23. *Code of Mississippi: Analytical Compilation, 1798–1848*. Chapter 34, Section 10, (June 29, 1822).

24. Ibid., Article XII, Title 3, Section 25, (February 15, 1839).

25. Victoria E. Bynum, *Unruly Women: The Politics of Social and Sexual Control in the Old South* (Chapel Hill, 1992), 118.

26. *Code of Mississippi: Analytical Compilation, 1798–1848*, Section 22. The penalty for rape of this kind was set at 10 years in the state penitentiary.

27. Eighth Census of the United States, 1860, Agriculture and Population.

28. McMillen, *Motherhood*, 118, 122.

29. John D'Emilio and Estelle B. Freedman, *Intimate Matters: A History of Sexuality in America* (New York, 1988), 17.

30. Olmsted, *A Journey in the Backcountry* (New York, 1860).

31. Frank L. Owsley, *Plain Folk of the Old South* (Baton Rouge, 1949), 111–14; Joe Gray Taylor, *Eating, Drinking, and Visiting in the South* (Baton Rouge, 1982), 50; Ted Ownby,

Subduing Satan: Religion, Recreation, and Manhood in the Rural South, 1865–1920 (Chapel Hill, 1990), 90–94.

32. Taylor, *Eating, Drinking, and Visiting*, 50.

33. Vance Randolph, ed., *Pissing in the Snow & Other Ozark Folktales* (Urbana, 1976), 77–79, 97–98, 191–92.

34. Ownby, *Subduing Satan*, 95–99.

35. D'Emilio and Freedman, *Intimate Matters*, 16.

36. *A Digest of the Laws of Mississippi* (1939), "An Act Concerning Divorce and Alimony," Article 11, Section 4 (June 15, 1822).

37. Lawrence B. Goodheart, et al., "An Act for the Relief of Females . . . : Divorce and the Changing Legal Status of Women in Tennessee, 1796–1860, Part 1," *Tennessee Historical Quarterly* 44 (Fall 1985): 318–339; Bardaglio, *Reconstructing the Household*, 34.

38. Keith Thomas, "Women and the Civil War Sects," *Past and Present* 13 (1958): 49–50.

39. Gaillard v. Gaillard, *Mississippi Reports* (1851), 152–54.

40. *Code of Mississippi: Analytical Compilation, 1798–1848*, "An Act for the Punishment of Crimes & Misdemeanors," June 14, 1822.

41. *Crutcher v. Crutcher*. 86 Miss. (1905), 231.

42. *Crutcher v. Crutcher*, 233.

43. *Crutcher v. Crutcher*, 235.

44. *Crutcher v. Crutcher*, 233.

45. *Armstrong v. Armstrong, Reports of Cases, High Court of Errors and Appeals*, vol. 3 (1856), 281, 289.

46. *Stroud's Legal Dictionary* defines condonation as "the complete forgiveness and blotting out of a conjugal offense."

47. *Armstrong v. Armstrong*, 290, 280, 289.

48. Ted Ownby, "Evangelicalism and Male Culture in the Rural South, 1865–1920," PhD Diss., Johns Hopkins University, 1987; Jean E. Friedman, *The Enclosed Garden: Women and Community in the Evangelical South, 1830–1900* (Chapel Hill, 1985), 14–15.

49. *Joe Carotti et al. v. State of Mississippi*. High Court of Errors and Appeals (October 1868), 336.

50. *Kenley v. Kenley*. 2 Howard (1838), 751.

51. *Waskam v. Waskam*, 31 Miss. (1856), 154, 155.

52. Business Research Station, School of Business and Industry, *Statistical Abstract of Mississippi, 1952*. (State College, Miss., 1952), Table 3; the U.S. Bureau of the Census did not begin to classify households as either rural or urban until 1874. At that time, the definition of an urban area included a population of 8,000 or more. Six years later, the Bureau lowered the urban standard to 4,000. In 1910 the census defined any area of over 2,500 people as urban.

53. Twelfth Census of the United States (1900), Agriculture and Population.

54. *Annotated Code of Mississippi* (1892), Chapter 47, #2041–2403.

55. *Annotated Code of Mississippi* (1892), Chapter 47, #2054; for the classic interpretation of southern fencing laws, see Stephen Hahn, *The Roots of Southern Populism: Yeoman Farmers and the Transformation of the Georgia Upcountry* (New York, 1983).

56. Twelfth Census (1900).

57. Laster Short of Tishomingo County, Mississippi said of a house in the Bay Springs community, "The only thing I know of that they added to it, there was a little porch back there, they boxed that in." Steven D. Smith, et al., *Ethnoarcheology of the Bay Springs Farmsteads: A Study of Rural American Settlement* (Nashville, 1982), 145.

58. Two hundred eighty-seven of 309 houses surveyed had grown by at least one room by 1910; three hundred sixty-one additions on 287 houses. Of the 309 houses surveyed, only three one-room houses and 22 two-room houses remained unaltered throughout the study period.

59. "Inventory Records of Estates", Monroe County, Miss. (1884–97, 1896–1906); "Accounts & Reports of Probate," Rankin County, Miss. (1872–94).

60. Smith, et al., *Ethnoarcheology*, 121–22.

61. Smith, et al., *Ethnoarchaeology*, 145–47.

62. Eight out of 151 houses surveyed were built after 1880 were one-room dwellings. By 1910, all eight had been expanded in some way to include at least two rooms.

63. Charles Reagan Wilson, *Baptized in Blood: The Religion of the Lost Cause, 1865–1920* (Athens, 1980), 8; Samuel S. Hill, Jr., "South's Two Cultures," in Hill, ed. *Religion in the Solid South* (Nashville, 1972), 37.

64. Wilson, *Baptized in Blood*, 46–48.

65. *Ferguson v. State.* 71 Miss. (1894), 807–08.

66. *Mississippi Code of 1904 of the Public Statute Laws of the State of Mississippi*, Chapter 28, #1358.

67. *Mississippi Code of 1904.*

68. Winthrop D. Jordan, *White Over Black: American Attitudes Toward the Negro* (Chapel Hill, 1968), 34–35, 473; Joel Williamson, *A Rage for Order: Black-White Relations in the American South Since Emancipation* (New York, 1986), 84–85; See also W. Fitzhugh Brundage, *Lynching in the New South: Georgia and Virginia, 1880–1930* (Urbana, 1993); Philip Dray, *At the Hands of Persons Unknown: The Lynching of Black America* (New York, 2002); and Grace Elizabeth Hale, *Making Whiteness: The Culture of Segregation in the South, 1890–1940* (New York, 1998).

69. Edward L. Ayers, *The Promise of the New South: Life After Reconstruction* (New York, 1992), 156–57; Neil R. McMillen, *Dark Journey: Black Mississippians in the Age of Jim Crow* (Urbana, 1989); Gerald David Jaynes, *Branches Without Roots: Genesis of the Black Working Class in the American South* (New York, 1986).

70. Ayers, *Promise of the New South*, 156–157, 496.

"Relations Which Might Be Disastrous: Natchez Indians and African Slaves in French Louisiana," by David J. Libby

1. Ian W. Brown, "Natchez Indians and the Remains of a Proud Past," in *Natchez Before 1830*, ed. Noel Polk (Jackson, 1989), 20.

A different version of this essay appears as chapter 1 of *Slavery and Frontier Mississippi: 1720–1835* (Jackson, 2004). Several friends and colleagues have provided useful comments. They include Anne Hardgrove, Stephen Rosecan, Joe Wojak, Jay Gitlin, and Stephen

Stowe. I am especially indebted to Alan Gallay, who shared insights from his then-unpublished study on the Indian slave trade, and Paul Spickard, who provided good advice on turning this chapter into a discrete essay. Finally Winthrop Jordan set me off in the right direction as I began this essay as a chapter of my dissertation. His guidance, criticism, and inspiration call for a special debt of gratitude.

2. Patricia Woods, "The French and the Natchez Indians in Louisiana: 1700–1731," *Louisiana History* 19 (Fall 1978): 416.

3. Jack D. Elliot, Jr., "The Fort of Natchez and the Colonial Origins of Mississippi," *Journal of Mississippi History* 52 (August 1990): 165.

4. On the process of consolidation see Brown, "Natchez Indians," 20–21; Brown, "An Archaeological Study of Culture Contact and Change in the Natchez Bluffs Region," in *La Salle and His Legacy*, ed. Patricia Kay Galloway (Jackson, 1982), 179. On diseases, see Patricia Kay Galloway, *Choctaw Genesis: 1500–1700* (Lincoln, 1995), 134–143.

5. Woods, "The French and the Natchez," 414. Father Paul du Ru quoted in same.

6. McWilliams, ed., *Pénicault Narrative*, 83.

7. Several works discuss the French goals in settling the Mississippi Valley, and especially Natchez, including Woods, "The French and the Natchez," 418–419; Woods, *French-Indian Relations on the Southern Frontier, 1699–1762* (Ann Arbor, 1980), 55–63; Elliot, "Fort of Natchez," 164–165; Daniel H. Usner, Jr., *Indians, Settlers and Slaves*.

8. On Choctaw society, authority structures, and matrilineage, see Charles Hudson, *The Southeastern Indians* (Knoxville, 1976), 202–205, 229, and passim; also Patricia Kay Galloway, *Choctaw Genesis*.

9. Grayson Noley, "The Early 1700s: Education, Economics, and Politics," in *The Choctaw Before Removal*, ed. Carolyn Keller Reeves (Jackson, 1985), 32.

10. An excellent discussion of the cultural differences between the French and the Choctaw is Patricia Galloway, "'The Chief Who Is Your Father': Choctaw and French Views of the Diplomatic Relation," in *Powhattan's Mantle: Indians in the Colonial Southeast*, ed. Peter H. Wood, Gregory A. Waselkov, and M. Thomas Hatley (Lincoln, 1989), 254–278. Galloway suggests that the inability of the French to conduct diplomatic negotiations effectively with the Choctaw was rooted in the differing social construction of male authority in the two cultures.

11. Usner, *Indians, Settlers, and Slaves*, 18–19.

12. On Chickasaw slaving raids, see Galloway, "Henri du Tonti du Village des Chacta, 1702: The Beginning of the French Alliance," in *La Salle's Legacy*, 159.

13. This assertion is by no means certain, but considering other cultural similarities among Southeastern Indian groups, it is a fair inference. The question of Natchez methods of assimilation is currently under study. See Brown, "Culture Contact and Change," 186. While he speaks in terms of adoption of other cultural groups, the distinction between adoption and enslavement is not as pronounced in Indian societies as in European.

14. Hudson, *Southeastern Indians*, 254

15. Abstract of letter from Bienville to Ponchartrain, July 20, 1706, *Mississippi Provincial Archives: French Dominion* (hereafter *MPAFD*), Dunbar Rowland, Albert Sanders, and Patricia Kay Galloway, eds., II, 23.

16. Louis XIV to DeMuy, June 30, 1707, *MPAFD* III, 53.

17. In 1717, the French proprietor of Louisiana, Antoine Crozat, transmitted the colonial charter to the Company of the West, headed by the Scots investor John Law. Shortly thereafter the concern was renamed the Company of the Indies. See Elliot, "Fort of Natchez," 167.

18. In reparation for the murder of four French traders the French demanded that the Natchez construct a fort. See Elliot, "Fort at Natchez," 166–167; also Woods, "The French and the Natchez," 418–420.

19. Woods, "French and the Natchez," 423; Elliot, "Fort at Natchez," 172. Daniel Usner estimates only 105 settlers lived in Natchez in 1726, alongside 65 black slaves and 9 Indian slaves. *Indians, Settlers, and Slaves*, 48.

20. These issues are debated in two essays, James J. Cooke, "France, The New World, and Colonial Expansion," 81–92, and Glen R. Conrad, "Reluctant Imperialist: France in America," 93–105, both in *La Salle's Legacy*.

21. James D. Hardy, Jr., "The Transportation of Convicts to Colonial Louisiana," *Louisiana History* 7 (Summer 1966): 207–220.

22. René Le Conte, "The Germans in Louisiana in the Eighteenth Century," trans. Glenn R. Conrad, *Louisiana History* 8 (Winter 1967): 67–84.

23. Hall, *Africans in Colonial Louisiana*, chapter 2, especially 29–34.

24. These distinctions are illustrated in Phillip D. Curtin, *Economic Change in Precolonial Africa: Senegambia in the Era of the Slave Trade* (Madison, 1975), 34–35; and James F. Searing, *West African Slavery and Atlantic Commerce: The Senegal River Valley, 1700–1865* (Cambridge, 1993), 49.

25. Ibid., 35, 115.

26. du Pratz, *History of Louisiana*, 376–377.

27. Daniel H. Usner, Jr., "From African Captivity to American Slavery: The Introduction of Black Laborers to Colonial Louisiana," *Louisiana History* 20 (Winter 1979): 33.

28. Hall, *Africans in Colonial Louisiana*, Chapter 3.

29. The cultural context for this resignation provided the framework in which slaves complied with their enslavement. Even as they took on the external demeanor of subordination, they did not necessarily internalize the fact of their subordination. See Bertram Wyatt-Brown, "The Mask of Obedience: Male Slave Psychology in the Old South," *American Historical Review* 93 (December 1998): 1228–1552.

30. Slavery in the Louisiana colony may have been similar to Caribbean slavery, but it was in fact almost foreign to France. Having abandoned slavery centuries earlier, the French took pride in the claim "there are no slaves in France," even as they reintroduced the practice in the New World. Whatever qualms they may have had were easily overcome as they established brutal and strikingly efficient slave operations in the Caribbean. Sue Peabody, *There Are No Slaves in France* (New York, 1996).

31. Dawson Phelps, trans, "Narrative of the Hostilities Committed by the Natchez against the concession of St. Catherine, October 21, November 4, 1722," *Journal of Mississippi History* 7 (January 1945): 3–10. Quote on page 10.

32. Minutes of the Superior Council, September 16, 1723, *MPAFD* III, 375–376.

33. Minutes of the Council of War, January 7, 1724, ibid., 387.

34. Minutes of the Superior Council, November 4, 1724, ibid., 439.

35. Woods, "The French and the Natchez," 429–430.

36. Memoir on the Services of Sieur de Bienville, Commandant General of Louisiana, 1725, *MPAFD* III, 493.

37. Memoir on Louisiana, the Indies and the commerce that can be carried on with them, 1726, ibid., 510–524. The two major slaveowners in Natchez were Mr. Le Blanc (a company representative) and Mr. Kolly (a partner with Hubert).

38. Committee of Louisiana to Directors of the Company, November 8, 1824, *MPAFD* II, 399.

39. Minutes of the Superior Council of Louisiana, April 7, 1725, ibid., 427.

40. Minutes of the Superior Council of Louisiana, March 23, 1725, ibid., 421.

41. Superior Council of Louisiana to Directors of the Company of the Indies (Abstract), August 28, 1725, ibid., 492, 494.

42. When the council appointed Sieur Du Tisné in 1725, he was immediately characterized as "not at all suited to command." Memoir from the Council of Louisiana to the Council of the Company of the Indies, April 23, 1725, ibid., 459. Several years later the actions of the commander Sieur de Chepart precipitated a major uprising among the Natchez, as described below.

43. Memoir from the Council of Louisiana to the Council of the Company of the Indies, April 23, 1725, *MPAFD* II, 459.

44. Périer and De La Chaise to Directors of the Company of the Indies, January 30, 1729, ibid., 639.

45. Périer to [Abbe Raguet], May 12, 1728, ibid., 573.

46. du Pratz, *History of Louisiana*, 79, 89.

47. Périer to Maurepas, March 18, 1730, *MPAFD* I, 63.

48. Périer to Maurepas, December 5, 1729, ibid., 54.

49. Hall devotes an entire chapter to Bambarra resistance in *Africans in Colonial Louisiana*, 96–118. Her interpretation is somewhat problematical. While the evidence of resistance is convincing, Hall relies on French characterizations of these slaves as Bambarras when their ethnicity may have been a French designation. Curtin's discussion of the difficulty of interpreting the term "Bambarra" from the sources is a good antidote to Hall's generalizations. See *Economic Change*, 178–179. A more skeptical treatment of Bambarras in French Louisiana is Peter Caron, "'Of a nation which the others do not Understand': Bambara Slaves and African Ethnicity in Colonial Louisiana, 1718–60," *Slavery and Abolition* 18 (1997): 98–121.

50. Beauchamp to Maurepas, November 5, 1731, *MPAFD* IV, 82.

51. Périer to Maurepas, March 18, 1730, *MPAFD* I, 65. It is quite possible that these slaves were Bambarra, as it was common in Senegambia for captured Bambarras to escape and return to their previous master. See Curtin, *Economic Change*, 115.

52. Several French colonists suspected this was the case. Governor Perier believed that the Choctaw advised the Natchez to attack, giving them the opportunity to counterattack on behalf of the French and receive rewards for their tribute. Périer to Maurepas, April 10,

1730, *MPAFD* I, 118. Others believed that the Natchez improperly coordinated their attack, and that a properly timed attack by several nations would have wrought havoc on the French. See du Pratz, *History of Louisiana*, 88–93.

53. Grayson Noley, "The Early 1700s," 102; Jesse O. McKee and Jon A. Schlenker, *The Choctaws: Cultural Evolution of a Native American Tribe* (Jackson, 1980), 32. Patricia Galloway has questioned the usefulness of Choctaw identity prior to 1700, suggesting that prior to the eighteenth century, no such tribe or ethnicity existed. See *Choctaw Genesis*.

54. Diron d'Artaguette recorded that "about fifty negroes" had been recovered, while Périer claimed they recovered "one hundred of our negroes." d'Artaguette later wrote that le Seur and the Choctaw brought back "one hundred and fifty negroes and negresses whom they took from the enemy." The precision with which the officials recorded the number of French women and children, and the absence of any in counting the slaves is most probably rooted in both the value they placed on each as well as the fact that the Choctaw retained the slaves, awaiting payment for the revenge they exacted. d'Artaguette to Maurepas, February 10, 1730, *MPAFD* I, 61; Périer to Maurepas, March 18, 1730, ibid., 68; d'Artaguette to Maurepas, March 20, 1730, ibid., 78.

55. Périer to Maurepas, March 18, 1730, ibid., 68.

56. Périer to Maurepas, March 18, 1730, ibid., 64.

57. French and Choctaw forces killed most of the Natchez and captured the survivors, shipping them off to Caribbean slavery. The few who remained slowly joined the neighboring Chickasaw. See Usner, *Indians, Settlers, and Slaves*, 75.

58. Descriptions of these demands and exchanges can be found in Périer to Maurepas, March 18, 1730, *MPAFD* I, 68 also Lusser's Journal, March 16, 1730, ibid., 110, and du Roullet's Journal, March 29, 1730, ibid., 179.

59. Perier to Maurepas, March 18, 1730, *MPAFD* I, 68.

60. The French may have counted the goods that arrived in Natchez before the uprising. While these goods never got the to Choctaw, the French no longer had them and may have considered them to have been traded. On the emergence of the Choctaw as a regional power, see Galloway, *Choctaw Genesis*, 352–360.

61. Lusser's Journal, March 16, 1730, *MPAFD* I, 110.

62. Galloway, "The Chief Who Is Your Father."

63. Lusser's Journal, March 10, 1730, *MPAFD* I, 103.

64. du Roullet's Journal, March 29, 1730, *MPAFD* I, 179.

65. du Roullet's Journal, April 27, 1730, ibid., 180.

66. du Roullet to Périer, March 16, 1731, *MPAFD* IV, 66. Such abuse was not surprising, as the slaves had no social protection within Choctaw society. See Stephen Rosecan, "Valuable Captives: Louisiana Slaves among the Choctaw Indians during the Early 1730s," (Master's thesis, University of Mississippi, 1996), 53–64.

67. du Roullet to Périer, March, 16, 1731, ibid., 67.

68. Périer to Ory, November 15, 1730, ibid., 54.

69. Lusser's Journal, March 16, 1730, *MPAFD* I, 109–110.

70. du Roullet to Périer, March 16, 1731, *MPAFD* IV, 66–67.

71. du Roullet's Journal, May 10–23, 1731, ibid., vol. 1, 186–187.

72. McKee and Schlenker, *The Choctaws*, 27–28, 33–34; du Roullet's Journal, July 21, 1731, ibid., 187.

73. Rosecan, "Valuable Captives," 74–81; Hudson, *The Southeastern Indians*, 193–194.

74. While there is little evidence concerning such bands in the wake of this uprising, examples in nearby locales tend to justify speculation that a group could survive. The French discovered fifteen African and Indian fugitives near Natchez in 1727. On a much larger scale, the maroon community living in the swampy lowlands south of New Orleans survived for years. In South Carolina, British colonists discovered "an outlaw band composed of a Spaniard, and Indian, a Negro and a mulatto, known to have made forays against whites and Indians alike." See Usner, *Indians, Settlers, and Slaves*, 58; Hall, *Africans in Colonial Louisiana*, 205–235; and Wood, *Black Majority*, 263.

"Christ in Chains: Slavery's Negative Impact on the Conversion of African American Slaves" by Daniel L. Fountain

1. Charles Joyner, "'Believer I Know': The Emergence of African-American Christianity," in *African-American Christianity: Essays in History*, ed. Paul E. Johnson (Berkeley, 1994), 37. Statement by Charlie Van Dyke in epigram quoted from Rawick, Vol. 6, Series 1, Alabama and Indiana, 398.

2. Peter Kolchin, *American Slavery, 1619–1877* (New York, 1993), 137–138. Kolchin suggested that the reaction to Phillips and Elkins led historians to overstate evidence for the "slaves' resiliency and autonomy" and subsequently he pointed to the need for "modifications" in the interpretation of slave life. Philip Morgan seconds Kolchin's dissent. Philip Morgan, *Slave Counterpoint: Black Culture in the Eighteenth-Century Chesapeake and Lowcountry* (Chapel Hill, 1998), 442–443.

3. "Destitution of Religious Knowledge," *Alabama Baptist Advocate* 20 March 1850, p. 2.; "Address of the Bishops," *Journal of the General Conference of The Methodist Episcopal Church, South* (May 1858): 392; "Georgia," *The Southern Baptist Missionary Journal* (June 1849): 18.

4. Winthrop D. Jordan's study of a Civil War slave conspiracy provides a nice overview of the religious "destitution" that existed even in an established Old Southwestern cotton county in Mississippi. Winthrop D. Jordan, *Tumult and Silence at Second Creek: An Inquiry into a Civil War Slave Conspiracy* rev. ed. (Baton Rouge, 1995), 189–195.

5. *Proceedings of the Southern Baptist Convention* (Richmond: H. K. Ellyson, 1853), 11. in Southern Baptist Historical Library and Archives, Nashville, Tennessee.

6. *Proceedings of the Southern Baptist Convention* (Richmond, 1859), 11. in Southern Baptist Historical Library and Archives, Nashville, Tennessee.

7. Grady McWhiney, Warner O. Moore, Jr. and Robert F. Pace, eds. *"Fear God and Walk Humbly": The Agricultural Journal of James Mallory, 1843–1877* (Tuscaloosa, 1997), 8, 32, 101, 199; J. B. Cain, *Methodism in the Mississippi Conference, 1846–1870* (Jackson, 1939), 190; "Report on North and South Santee Mission," *Christian Advocate* 19 (September 1834): 14; W. P. Harrison, *The Gospel Among the Slaves* (Nashville, 1893), 265–266; See also Milton Sernett, *Black Religion and American Evangelicalism: White Protestants, Plantation*

Missions, and the Flowering of Negro Christianity, 1787–1865, ATLA Monograph Series, No. 7 (Metuchen, N.J., 1975), 65.

8. "From Our Missionaries," *The Southern Baptist Missionary Journal* (November 1846): 1; See also *Proceedings of the Southern Baptist Convention* (Richmond, 1845): 33–35, in Southern Baptist Historical Library and Archives, Nashville, Tennessee; "Report on Domestic Missions," *Minutes of the Twenty-Seventh Anniversary of the Alabama State Convention* (M.D.J. Slade, 1850): 15–17. Typescript from Una Roberts Lawrence Collection, Southern Baptist Historical Library and Archives, Nashville, Tennessee.

9. Kenneth J. Zanca, ed. "Letter from Mother Hyacinth LeConnait to her brother, March 24, 1856" in *American Catholics and Slavery: 1789–1866 An Anthology of Primary Documents* (Lanham, MD, 1994), 161.

10. "A Call from Texas," *Christian Advocate* 3 April 1835, p. 194; "Need of Domestic Missionaries," *Proceedings of the Southern Baptist Convention Eighth Biennial Session* (Richmond, 1861), 57, in Southern Baptist Historical Library and Archives, Nashville, Tennessee; "Demand for Labor," *Southern Baptist Missionary Journal* (July 1848): 46; "Reformation of the Colored Population," *South-Western Baptist* 2 (March 1854): 2; "Delaware and MD. a Missionary Field," *Christian Observer* 20 (June 1845): 97; "Speech of Rev. Dr. Newton," *Christian Observer* 11 (November 1854): 177–178; "Southern Aid Society," *Christian Observer* 25 (November 1854): 185; "Address of the Bishops," *Journal of the General Conference of The Methodist Episcopal Church, South* (May 1858): 392.

11. "The Domestic Mission Board," *The Alabama Baptist* 12 (September 1846): 2; See also *Minutes of the Bethel Baptist Association (Kentucky), 1847,* 11, in Southern Baptist Historical Library and Archives, Nashville, Tennessee; *Minutes of the Bethel Baptist Association (Alabama), 1850,* 11, in Southern Baptist Historical Library and Archives, Nashville, Tennessee; Harrison, *The Gospel Among the Slaves,* 302.

12. "Men and Means Wanted," *Christian Observer* 29 (October 1853): 174.

13. *Minutes of the Thirty-Second Anniversary of the Alabama Baptist State Convention, Held at Montgomery, May 9th and 10th, 1855, and of the Alabama Baptist Bible Society Held at the Same Time and Place* (n.p.: n.d), 2. Typescript from Una Roberts Lawrence Collection, Southern Baptist Historical Library and Archives, Nashville, Tennessee; "Important City Missions," *Home and Foreign Journal* (April 1855): 1; Joe Gray Taylor, *Louisiana Reconstructed, 1863–1877* (Baton Rouge, 1974), 440; Zanca, "Letter from Bishop William Elder of Natchez, MS to Propagation of the Faith, 1858" in *American Catholics and Slavery,* 236.

14. William A. Clebsch, "Journal of the Proceedings of an Adjourned Convention of Bishops, Clergymen and Laymen of the Protestant Episcopal Church in the Confederate States of America (1861)," in *Journals of the Protestant Episcopal Church in the Confederate States of America.* (Austin, 1962), II-42.

15. "Delaware and MD. a Missionary Field," *Christian Observer* 20 (June 1845): 97.

16. "[From the Richmond *Christian Advocate*] Religious Instruction of Negroes," *The African Repository and Colonial Journal* (July 1856): 215; Anne C. Loveland, *Southern Evangelicals and the Social Order 1800–1860* (Baton Rouge, 1980), 230–232.

17. Zanca, "Letter from Bishop Bishop Augustin Verot of St. Augustine, Florida to Propagation of the Faith, July 14, 1860," in *American Catholics and Slavery,* 241.

18. "Pon Pon Mission," *Christian Advocate* 1 (January 1845): 82; Harrison, *The Gospel Among the Slaves*, 268–269; Rodger Baudier, *The Catholic Church in Louisiana* (1939, New Orleans, 1972), 433.

19. Nancy T. Ammerman, *Baptist Battles: Social Change and Religious Conflict in the Southern Baptist Convention* (New Brunswick, 1990), 32; Ted Ownby, *Subduing Satan: Religion, Recreation and Manhood in the Rural South, 1865–1920* (Chapel Hill, 1990), 126–127.

20. Rawick, Vol. 16, Series 2, Kansas et al., 22 (Fleming Clark).

21. Rawick, Vol. 2, Series 1, South Carolina Pt. 1 & 2, 100 (Josephine Bristow).

22. Rawick, Vol. 10, Supp. Series 1, Mississippi Pt. 5, 2075. (Hattie Sugg); Rawick, Vol. 14, Series 2, North Carolina, 4–5 (Louisa Adams).

23. James W. C. Pennington, *The Fugitive Blacksmith*, 2nd ed. (London, 1849), 43.

24. Rawick, Vol. 11, Series 2, Arkansas Pt. 7 & Missouri, 53 (Betty Brown); See also Ibid., 155 (Columbus Williams); Rawick, Vol. 10, Supp. Series 1, Mississippi Pt. 5, 1938 (Simmons Smith); Charles L. Perdue, Jr., et al., eds. *Weevils in the Wheat: Interviews with Virginia Ex-Slaves* (Charlottesville, 1976) 82, 130 (Baily Cunningham, Della Harris); Clayton, *Mother Wit*, 38, 44, 147 (Henrietta Butler, Manda Cooper, Hannah Kelly); Sernett, *Black Religion and American Evangelicalism*, 63.

25. For instance, Jane Thompson's master made her go outside when his family held family prayers. John Bates's master stopped taking his slaves to church with him and confiscated a literate slave's Bible once the slaves connected Christianity to freedom. See also Rawick, Vol. 11, Series 2, Arkansas Pt. 7 & Missouri, 353 (Jane Thompson); Rawick, Vol. 2 Supp. Series 2, Texas Pt. 1, 214 (John Bates); Jordan, *Tumult and Silence*, 193–195.

26. Daniel L. Fountain, "Long on Religion, Short on Christianity: Slave Religion 1830–1870," Ph.D. Diss., University of Mississippi, 1999. Masters who allowed slaves to attend church once a year were counted as permitting slaves to attend worship.

27. Rawick, Vol. 6, Series 1, Alabama & Indiana, 26 (Callie Bracey).

28. Ibid., 237 (Emma Jones).

29. Rawick, Vol. 16, Series 2, Kansas et al., 40 (David Hall); Rawick, Vol. 14, Series 2, North Carolina, 94 (John Becton).

30. Rawick, Vol. 2, Series 1, South Carolina Pt. 1 & 2, 192 (Sylvia Cannon).

31. Rawick, Vol. 6, Series 1, Alabama & Indiana, 295 (Sally Murphy); See also Rawick, Vol. 10, Supp. Series 2, Texas Pt. 9, 279 (Willis Woodsen).

32. Rawick, Vol.6, Supp. Series 1, Mississippi Pt. 1, 157 (Manda Boggan); See also Rawick, Vol. 10, Series 2, Arkansas Pt. 5 & 6, 182 (Tom Neal); Rawick, Vol. 10, Supp. Series 1, Mississippi Pt. 5, 241 (Robert Weathersby).

33. Rawick, Vol. 19, Series 2, Fisk University Narratives, 188 (Sixty-Five Years A Washer and Ironer).

34. Rawick, Vol. 16, Series 2, Kansas et al., 32 (Rev. Silas Jackson); See also Rawick, Vol. 17, Series 2, Florida, 67 (Charles Coates).

35. Rawick Vol. 16, Series 2, Kansas et al., 7 (Susan Bledsoe); Rawick Vol. 6, Series 1, Alabama & Indiana, 160 (Ella Grandberry).

36. Rawick Vol. 11, Series 2, Arkansas Pt. 7 & Missouri, 143 (Mrs. Lou Griffin).

37. Rawick Vol. 6, Series 1, Alabama & Indiana, 68 (Henry Cheatam).

38. James Williams, *Narrative of James Williams, an American Slave; Who was for Several Years a Driver on a Cotton Plantation in Alabama* (New York, 1838), 71.

39. Rawick Vol. 18, Series 2, Fisk University Narratives, 121 (Joseph Farley); Rawick Vol. 13, Series 2, Georgia Pt. 3 & 4, 142 (Green Willbanks); See also Peter Randolph. *Slave Cabin to the Pulpit* (Boston, 1893).

40. Rawick Vol. 8, Series 2, Arkansas Pt. 1 & 2, 117 (Spencer Barnett).

41. Rawick Vol. 17, Series 2, Florida, 199 (Randall Lee).

42. Rawick Vol. 16, Series 2, Kansas et al., 67 (Millie Simpkins).

43. Rawick Vol. 6, Series 1, Alabama & Indiana, 39–40 (Siney Bonner); See also Rawick, Vol. 5, Supp. Series 1, Indiana & Ohio, 166 (Nelson Polk).

44. Rawick Vol. 17, Series 2, Florida, 279 (Anna Scott); See also Perdue, et al., *Weevils in the Wheat*, 71 (Samuel Chilton); Rawick Vol. 6, Series 1, Alabama & Indiana, 26 (Callie Bracey).

45. March 1846, "Elkton Baptist Church Minutes, Elkton, Kentucky 1825–1909," in Southern Baptist Historical Library and Archives, Nashville, Tennessee.

46. Rawick Vol. 6, Series 1, Alabama & Indiana, 416 (Mingo White).

47. Ibid., 162 (Ella Grandberry).

48. For example, Thomas Jones credited secret, independent readings with giving him his first notions about God and inspiring him to seek Christian conversion. Thomas H. Jones, *The Experience of Thomas H. Jones, Who was a Slave for Forty-Three Years* (Boston, 1862), 22; See also John W. Blassingame. *Slave Testimony: Two Centuries of Letters, Speeches, Interviews, and Autobiographies* (Baton Rouge, 1977), 466 (Richard Parker).

49. "Report on the instruction of the Colored Population," *Southern Baptist Missionary Journal* (July 1849), 39; Southern Baptists were not alone in this belief. Eugene Genovese, *A Consuming Fire: The Fall of the Confederacy in the Mind of the White Christian South* (Athens, 1998) 1, 23; See also "The Bible Among the Slaves," *Christian Observer* 15 (April 1848): 62; "Instruction of Slaves," *The African Repository and Colonial Journal* (January 1856): 16–17; "Report of the Directors of the Society of the United Brethren for Propagating the Gospel Among the Heathen," *The United Brethren's Missionary Intelligencer and Religious Miscellany* 5 (No. 6, 1835): 245–246.

50. "Religious Instruction of the Colored Population," in *Proceedings of the Southern Baptist Convention* (Richmond, 1866), 85–86. in Southern Baptist Historical Library and Archives, Nashville, Tennessee.

51. Eugene Genovese, *Roll, Jordan, Roll: The World the Slaves Made* (New York, 1974), 562.

52. Sernett, *Black Religion and American Evangelicalism*, 65.

53. Ibid., 563.

54. "Report of the Directors of the Society of the United Brethren for Propagating the Gospel Among the Heathen," *The United Brethren's Missionary Intelligencer and Religious Miscellany* 5 (No. 6, 1835): 245–246.

55. Marli Weiner, *Mistresses and Slaves: Plantation Women in South Carolina, 1830–1880* (Urbana, 1998), 80–81.

56. Beth G. Crabtree and James W. Patton, eds. *"Journal of a Secesh Lady":The Diary of Catherine Ann Devereux Edmondston 1860–1866* (Raleigh, 1979), 21.

57. Mary Boykin Chesnut, *A Diary from Dixie* ed. Ben Ames Williams, (Boston, 1949), 171.

58. Rawick, Vol. 11, Series 2, Arkansas Pt. 7 & Missouri, 365–366 (Minksie Walker).

59. "Report on the instruction of the Colored Population," *Southern Baptist Missionary Journal* (July 1849): 39.

60. Catherine Edmonston described using Dr. Watt's catechism to instruct her slaves. Crabtree and Patton, *"Journal of a Secesh Lady"*, 21; Isaac Watts, *Dr. Watt's Plain and Easy Catechism for Children to Which are Added Forms of Prayer, Adapted to the Smallest Capacities* (Cambridge, 1806) ; See also (Methodist) William Capers, *A Catechism for Little Children, the Missions of the Methodist Episcopal Church in South Carolina* (Charleston, 1833); (Baptist) Alexander W. Chambliss, *The Catechetical Instructor* (Montgomery, 1847); (Presbyterian) Charles C. Jones, *Catechism of Scripture, Doctrine, and Practice, for Families and Sabbath Schools, Designed also for the Oral Instruction of Colored Persons* (Savannah, 1844).

61. Rawick,Vol. 10, Series 2, Arkansas Pt. 5 & 6, 190 (Ervin Smith); See also Perdue, *Weevils in the Wheat*, 241 (Sister Robinson).

62. Rawick, Vol. 12, Series 2, Georgia Pt. 1 & 2, 77 (Arie Binns).

63. Charles C. Jones, *Religious Instruction of the Negroes in the United States.* (Savannah, 1842), 21; See also Genovese, *Roll Jordan Roll*, 204–205; Olli Alho, *The Religion of the Slaves: A Study of the Religious Tradition and Behavior of Plantation Slaves in the United States 1830–1865.* FF Communications No. 217, (Helsinki, 1980), 164.

64. Matthew 7:13–14.

65. Stanley Elkins offered a portrait of slavery as a closed system that was comparable to the concentration camps of Nazi Germany. His work helped spawn countless studies by other historians determined to prove him wrong. Stanley Elkins, *Slavery: A Problem in American Institutional and Intellectual Life* 3rd ed. (Chicago, 1976), 81–82.

66. Lawrence Levine, *Black Culture and Black Consciousness: Afro-American Folk Thought from Slavery to Freedom* (New York, 1977); Roger D. Abrahams, *Singing the Master: The Emergence of African-American Culture in the Plantation South* (New York, 1992).

67. Charles Ball, *Fifty Years in Chains; or The Life of an American Slave* (New York, 1859), 15; Perdue, *Weevils in the Wheat*, 181 (Mr. Beverly Jones).

68. Genovese, *Roll, Jordan, Roll*, 186–187; Albert Raboteau, *Slave Religion: "The Invisible Institution"in the Antebellum South* (New York, 1978), 152.

69. Harrison, *The Gospel Among the Slaves*, 150–151; Charles C. Jones, "Suggestions on the Religious Instruction of the Negroes in the Southern States," *The Princeton Review* (January 1848): 1–30; William M. Wightman, *Life of William Capers, D.D., One of the Bishops of the Methodist Episcopal Church South; Including an Autobiography* (Nashville, 1859), 295–296.

70. Genovese, *Roll, Jordan, Roll*, 190–192; Raboteau, *Slave Religion*, 152.

71. For a similar view on sermons to slaves see Margaret Washington Creel, *A Peculiar People: Slave Religion and Community Culture Among the Gullahs* (New York, 1988), 7.

72. Genovese, *Roll, Jordan, Roll*, 166–167; See also John W. Blassingame, *The Slave Community: Plantation Life in the Antebellum South* (New York, 1979), 86.

73. Ball, *Fifty Years in Chains*, 15.

74. Peter Randolph, *Slave Cabin to the Pulpit*; See also Bibb, *Narrative of the Life and Adventures of Henry Bibb*, 24.

75. Rawick, Vol. 10, Series 2, Arkansas Pt. 5 & 6, 332 (Emma Tidwell).

76. Rawick, Vol. 11, Series 2, Arkansas Pt. 7 & Missouri, 303 (Alice Sewell); For evidence of the widespread non-salvation-based messages see also in Rawick; Vol. 5, Series 1, Texas, 208–217 (Jenny Proctor); Vol. 6, Alabama & Indiana, Series 1, 397–400, 158–161 (Charlie Van Dyke, Candus Richardson); Vol. 17, Series 2, Florida, 54, 139–145, 250–256 (Aunt Bess, Clayborn Gantling, Margaret Nickerson); Vol. 10, Supp. Series 1, Mississippi Pt. 5, 1978–1987, 2358 (Berry Smith, Frances Willis); Vol. 12, Supp. Series 1, Oklahoma, 78–81 (Robert Burns); Vol. 2, Supp. Series 2, Texas, 397–404 (Wes Brady); Perdue, *Weevils in the Wheat* , 320 (Nancy Williams); Rawick, Vol. 18, Series 2, Fisk Narratives, 45 (Slaves Have No Souls).

77. Rawick, Vol. 12, Series 2, Georgia Pt. 1 & 2, 20 (Hannah Austin).

78. Rawick, Vol. 13, Series 2, Georgia Pt. 3 & 4, 201 (Henry Wright); See also Perdue, *Weevils in the Wheat*, 305. (Bacchus White); Rawick, Vol. 18, Series 2, Fisk Narratives, 82 (Massa's Slave Son); Rawick, Vol. 7, Supp. Series 1, Mississippi Pt. 2, 373 (Ned Chaney).

79. Rawick, Vol. 12, Series 2, Georgia Pt. 1 & 2, 131 (Tom Hawkins).

80. Rawick, Vol. 3, Series 1, South Carolina Pt. 1 & 2, 194–195 (Cureton Milling).

81. Rawick, Vol. 15, Series 2, North Carolina Pt. 2, 270. (John Smith).

82. Rawick, Vol. 14, Series 2, North Carolina Pt. 1, 217 (Mattie Curtis).

83. Rawick, Vol. 12, Series 2, Georgia Pt. 1 & 2, 12 (Leah Garrett); See also Benjamin Drew, *A Northside View of Slavery* (Boston: John P. Jewett & Co., 1856), 91, 105–106, 334, 338 (David West, Charles Peyton Lucas, William Humbert, Lydia Adams); Sernett, *Black Religion and American Evangelicalism*, 86–91.

84. Frederick Douglass, *Narrative of the Life of Frederick Douglas an American Slave*, ed. Houston Baker, (1845, Middlesex, UK, 1986), 153–154.

85. Moses Roper, *A Narrative of the Adventures and Escape of Moses Roper from American Slavery* (Philadelphia, 1838), 51.

86. Harriet Jacobs, "Incidents in the Life of a Slave Girl" in *The Classic Slave Narratives.* Henry Louis Gates, ed. (New York, 1987), 403; Her mistress's lack of Christian sympathy also did not impress Jacobs. See pg. 347.

87. Ball, *Fifty Years in Chains*, 32.

88. Octavia Albert, *The House of Bondage or Charlotte Brooks and Other Slaves* (New York, 1988), 68–69 (Lorendo Goodwin).

89. Isaac Mason, *Life of Isaac Mason as a Slave* (Worcester, 1893), 27.

90. For recent discussions of white and black shared religious experiences, See James, "Biracial Fellowship in Antebellum Baptist Churches," and Hall, "Black and White Christians in Florida, 1822–1861," in John Boles, ed. *Masters & Slaves in the House of the Lord: Race and Religion in the Antebellum South, 1740–1870* (Lexington, 1988), 37–57, 81–98; Wayne Flynt, *Alabama Baptists: Southern Baptists in the Heart of Dixie* (Tuscaloosa, 1998), 42–47.

91. Raboteau, *Slave Religion*, 314.

92. Rawick, Vol. 6, Series 1, Alabama & Indiana, 417 (Mingo White).

93. Rawick, Vol. 2, Series 1, South Carolina Pt. 1 & 2, 152 (C.B. Burton); See also Ibid., 26, 241, 304, 209 (William Ballard, John Davenport, Wallace Davis, Fannie Griffin).

94. Rawick, Vol. 12, Series 2, Georgia Pt. 1 & 2, 52 (Georgia Baker).

95. Drew, *A Northside View of Slavery*, 338 (Lydia Adams); See also Ibid., 79, 51, 98–99 (Henry Atkinson, Nancy Howard, James Sumler); Albert, *The House of Bondage*, 80 (Octavia Rogers).

96. Henry Bibb, *Narrative of the Life and Adventures of Henry Bibb, an American Slave* (New York, 1850), 39.

97. Blassingame, *Slave Testimony*, 411 (Joseph Smith); See also ibid., 420, 435, 696 (Susan Boggs, Isaac Throgmorton, Lewis Hayden).

98. Perdue, *Weevils in the Wheat*, 224 (Matilda Perry); Likewise, Harriett Tubman refused to join her master's family in prayer. While her white masters held prayer meeting in their home, Harriett removed herself to the landing and prayed independently. Blassingame, *Slave Testimony*, 458 (Harriett Tubman).

99. Rawick, Vol. 6, Series 1, Alabama & Indiana, 193 (Katie Sutton).

100. American Missionary Association, *Twenty-Second Annual Report of the American Missionary Association* (New York, 1868), 36; Alho, *The Religion of the Slaves*, 134.

101. Genovese argues that the slaves understood the failure of hoodoo to work on whites as being the result of natural differences. According to Genovese, " . . . because the one had originated in Europe and the other in Africa . . . this difference in origin somehow meant that they were subject to different natural forces." *Roll Jordan Roll*, 222.

102. Rawick, Vol. 17, Series 2, Florida, 97–98 (Douglas Dorsey); Rawick, Vol. 3, Series 1, South Carolina Pt. 3 & 4, 5 (Cordelia Jackson); See also Perdue, *Weevils in the Wheat*, 322 (Nancy Williams).

103. Rawick, Vol. 12, Series 2, Georgia Pt. 1 & 2, 258. (Minnie Davis); See also Genovese, *Roll Jordan Roll*, 238.

104. Ibid., 329 (Mary Ferguson).

105. Rawick, Vol. 8, Supp. Series 1, Mississippi Pt. 3, 965 (Wash Hayes); See also Pennington, *The Fugitive Blacksmith*, 12; Perdue, *Weevils in the Wheat*, 100. (Cornelius Gardner); Charles C. Jones, *The Religious Instruction of the Negroes in the United States*, 118.

106. Rawick, Vol. 9, Series 2, Arkansas Pt. 3 & 4, 121 (Lee Guidon); See also Rawick, Vol. 3, Series 1, South Carolina Pt. 3 & 4, 239 (Sallie Paul); Rawick, Vol. 12, Series 2, Georgia Pt. 1 & 2, 248 (Easter Huff); William Wells Brown, *Narrative of William Wells Brown: A Fugitive Slave* (Boston, 1847), 36.

107. Rawick, Vol. 16, Series 2, Kansas et al., 22 (Fleming Clark); Rawick, Vol. 12, Series 2, Georgia Pt. 1 & 2, 269 (Mose Davis); Rawick, Vol. 6, Series 1, Alabama & Indiana, 107 (Matthew Hume); Rawick, Vol. 11, Series 2, Arkansas Pt. 7 & Missouri, 267 (Eliza Overton); Bibb, *Narrative of the Life and Adventures of Henry Bibb*, 23; Jacob Stroyer, *My Life in the South* (Salem, Mass., 1898), 50; Rawick, Vol. 12, Series 2, Georgia Pt. 1 & 2, 6 (Elisha Garey).

108. Rawick, Vol. 15, Series 2, North Carolina Pt. 2, 166 (Lily Perry); Rawick, Vol. 16, Series 2, Kansas et al., 29 (Hannah Davidson); Rawick, Vol. 11, Series 2, Arkansas Pt. 7 & Missouri, 40 (George Bollinger); Bruce, *The New Man* , 51; Rawick, Vol. 3, Series 1, South Carolina Pt. 3 & 4, 219 (William Oliver); Lindsay T. Baker and Julie P. Baker, eds. *The WPA Oklahoma Slave Narratives* (Norman, 1996), 342 (Alice Rawlings).

109. Rawick, Vol. 16, Series 2, Kansas et al., 30 (Hannah Davidson); See also Loguen, *The Rev. J. W. Loguen*, 105; Genovese, *Roll Jordan Roll*, 207; Alho, *The Religion of the Slaves*, 164.

110. Rawick, Vol. 3, Series 1, South Carolina Pt. 3 & 4, 210 (Sena Moore).

111. Rawick, Vol. 6, Series 1, Alabama & Indiana, 107 (Matthew Hume).

112. Brown, *Narrative of William Wells Brown*, 37.

113. Rawick, Vol. 3, Supp. Series 1, Georgia Pt. 1, 219 (Arthur Colson); Rawick, Vol. 6, Series 1, Alabama & Indiana, 145 (George Morrison).

114. Perdue, *Weevils in the Wheat*, 287 (Horace Tonsler); See also Rawick, Vol. 12, Series 2, Georgia Pt. 1 & 2, 186 (Ellen Claibourn).

115. Rawick, Vol. 16, Series 2, Kansas et al., 14 (Robert Falls).

116. Rawick, Vol. 10, Supp. Series 1, Mississippi Pt. 5, 2058 (Isaac Stier); See also Rawick, Vol. 12, Series 2, Georgia Pt. 1 & 2, 204 (John Hill); Rawick, Vol. 5, Series 1, Texas Pt. 3 & 4, 96 (Tom Mills); Rawick, Vol. 16, Series 2, Kansas et al., 3–4 (Julia Carey).

117. Rawick, Vol. 13, Series 2, Georgia Pt. 3 & 4, 61 (Ed McCree); Rawick, Vol. 12, Series 2, Georgia Pt. 1 & 2, 5–6 (Elisha Garey); Rawick, Vol. 10, Series 2, Arkansas Pt. 5 & 6, 182 (Tom Neal); Rawick, Vol. 7 Supp. Series 1, Mississippi Pt. 2, 384 (Hannah Chapman); Jan Furman, ed. *Slavery in the Clover Bottoms: John McCline's Narrative of His Life During Slavery and the Civil War* (Knoxville, 1998), 46.

118. Perdue, *Weevils in the Wheat*, 108 (Candis Goodwin).

119. Jermain Wesley. Loguen, *The Rev. J. W. Loguen, as a Slave and as a Freedman* (Syracuse, 1859), 105; See also Blassingame, *The Slave Community*, 130.

120. Rawick, Vol. 12, Series 2, Georgia Pt. 1 & 2, 204 (John Hill).

121. Rawick, Vol. 3, Supp. Series 2, Texas Pt. 2, 576 (William Byrd); See also Rawick, Vol. 5, Supp. Series 1, Indiana & Ohio, 68 (Rachel Duncan).

122. Wightman, *Life of William Capers*, 299.

123. "Address of the Bishops to the Fourth General Conference of the Methodist Episcopal Church, South," *Quarterly Review of the Methodist Episcopal Church, South* (July 1858): 415.

124. Clebsch, "Journal of the Proceedings of an Adjourned Convention of Bishops, Clergymen and Laymen of the Protestant Episcopal Church in the Confederate States of America (1861)," in *Journals of the Protestant Episcopal Church in the Confederate States of America*, 11–42.

125. Charles C. Jones, *Religious Instruction of the Negroes: An Address Delivered before the General Assembly of the Presbyterian Church, at Augusta, Ga, December 10, 1861* (Richmond, 1862), 11.

126. *1860 United States Census* (Washington, D.C.: U.S. Bureau of the Census, 1860). The nine black majority counties used for this average are Camden, Dougherty, McIntosh, Glascock Glynn, Putnam, Burke, Baker, Montgomery.

127. *Proceedings of the Southern Baptist Convention Seventh Biennial Session* (Richmond: 1859), 60. in Southern Baptist Historical Library and Archives, Nashville, Tennessee.

128. *Minutes of the Bethel Baptist Association (Alabama), 1857*, 11. Typescript in Southern Baptist Historical Library and Archives, Nashville, Tennessee.

129. *Minutes of the Forty-First Annual Session of the Alabama Baptist State Convention, 1863*, 1. Typescript from Una Roberts Lawrence Collection in Southern Baptist Historical Library and Archives, Nashville, Tennessee.

130. Genovese, *A Consuming Fire*; See also Daniel W. Stowell, *Rebuilding Zion: The Religious Reconstruction of the South, 1863–1877* (New York, 1998), 38, 180; David B. Cheesebrough, *"God Ordained This War": Sermons on the Sectional Crisis, 1830–1865* (Columbia, 1991), 238–239; Henry B. Foster, *History of the Tuscaloosa County Baptist Association, 1834–1934* (Tuscaloosa, 1934), 87; Boles, *Masters & Slaves in the House of the Lord*, 11; C. Penrose St. Amant, *A Short History of Louisiana Baptists* (Nashville: Broadman Press, 1948), 36–37; Baudier, *The Catholic Church in Louisiana*, 433.

131. Charles C. Jones, *Religious Instruction of the Negroes: An Address*, 12.

132. William E. Montgomery, *Under Their Own Vine and Fig Tree: The African-American Church in the South, 1865–1900* (Baton Rouge, 1993), 40.

"What's Critical About White Studies," by Paul Spickard

1. Jonathan Rutherford, *Forever England: Reflections on Masculinity and Empire* (London, 1997), 5.

This essay is reproduced with some minor modifications from an essay by the same title in *Racial Thinking in the United States: Uncompleted Independence*, ed. Paul Spickard and G. Reginald Daniel (Notre Dame, 2004). Patrick Miller, Nick Spreitzer, Stephen Cornell, Lori Pierce, Laurie Mengel, Reg Daniel, David Torres-Rouff, Ingrid Page, Jonathan Glickstein, and David Libby have all been generous in contributing to my thinking about white studies; none should be held responsible for the final shape of this essay.

2. Noel Ignatiev and John Garvey, eds., *Race Traitor* (New York, 1996), 1–2, 9–12.

3. Of course, one might point out that most studies of United States history and culture for many decades were studies of white people, for people of color were left out. This essay will focus on works that explicitly addressed the white race and its standing in the world.

4. Madison Grant, *The Passing of the Great Race, or The Racial Basis of European History* (New York, 1916; several later editions), ix; Lothrop Stoddard, *The Rising Tide of Color Against White World-Supremacy* (New York, 1920; several later editions). See also Homer Lea, *The Valor of Ignorance* (New York, 1909), and *The Day of the Saxon* (New York, 1912); F. G. Crookshank, *The Mongol In Our Midst* (New York, 1924). For analysis, see Elazar Barkan, *The Retreat from Scientific Racism* (New York, 1992); Ivan Hannaford, *Race: The History of an Idea in the West* (Baltimore, 1996); Daniel J. Kevles, *In the Name of Eugenics: Genetics and the Uses of Human Heredity* (New York, 1985).

5. Richard J. Herrnstein and Charles Murray, *The Bell Curve: Intelligence and Class Structure in American Life* (New York 1994); Peter Brimelow, *Alien Nation: Common Sense About America's Immigration Disaster* (New York, 1996), xxi. See also J. Philippe Rushton, *Race, Evolution, and Behavior* (New Brunswick, N.J., 1997); Dinesh D'Souza, *The End of Racism: Principles for a Multiracial Society* (New York, 1995); Jon Entine, *Taboo: Why Black*

Athletes Dominate Sports and Why We're Afraid to Talk About It (New York, 2000). For correctives, see Steven Fraser, ed., *The Bell Curve Wars: Race, Intelligence, and the Future of America* (New York, 1995); Stephen Jay Gould, *The Mismeasure of Man*, rev. ed. (New York, 1996); William H. Tucker, *The Science and Politics of Racial Research* (Urbana, 1994); Patrick B. Miller, "The Anatomy of Scientific Racism: Racialist Responses to Black Athletic Achievement," in Paul Spickard and W. Jeffrey Burroughs, eds., *We Are a People: Narrative and Multiplicity in Constructing Ethnic Identity* (Philadelphia, 2000), 124–41; Jonathan Marks, *Human Biodiversity: Genes, Race, and History* (New York, 1995).

6. Thomas Sowell, *Ethnic America* (New York, 1981); Nathan Glazer, *Ethnic Dilemmas* (Cambridge, 1983), see esp. "Blacks and Ethnic Groups: The Difference and the Political Difference It Makes," 70–93; Michael Novak, *The Rise of the Unmeltable Ethnics* (New York, 1973).

7. Gordon W. Allport, *The Nature of Prejudice* (Cambridge, 1954); Winthrop D. Jordan, *White Over Black: American Attitudes Toward the Negro, 1550–1812* (Chapel Hill, 1968); Edmund S. Morgan, *American Slavery—American Freedom: The Ordeal of Colonial Virginia* (New York, 1975); Bernard Bailyn, *Voyagers to the West: A Passage in the Peopling of America on the Eve of the Revolution* (New York, 1986); David Hackett Fischer, *Albion's Seed: Four British Folkways in America* (New York, 1989); Richard D. Alba, *Ethnic Identity: The Transformation of White America* (New Haven, 1990). One might even call a book like Langston Hughes's *The Ways of White Folks* (New York, 1934) an example of whiteness studies.

8. His ideas here are essentially those of Edmund Morgan in *American Slavery—American Freedom*. For a different view, see Jordan, *White Over Black*.

9. Alexander Saxton, *The Rise and Fall of the White Republic: Class Politics and Mass Culture in Nineteenth-Century America* (London, 1990), 1–18, 387, and *passim*.

10. Perhaps the pre-eminent attempt to free Marxist interpreters from the assumption that class trumps, in fact is formative of race, is Robert Miles, *Racism After "Race Relations"* (New York, 1993). See also Michael Omi and Howard Winant, *Racial Formation in the United States from the 1960s to the 1990s*, 2nd ed. (New York, 1994).

11. David Roediger, *The Wages of Whiteness: Race and the Making of the American Working Class* (London, 1991), 13, 8. Roediger acknowledges his debt to Du Bois. It is not clear whether he intends to invoke the Biblical contention that the wages of sin is death.

12. Ibid., 13–14.

13. Ibid., 6.

14. Ibid., 173 and *passim*. Roediger later apologized for what he regarded as a mistake in the subtitle: adopting the rhetorical position that whites (and in his reading of his own book, males) were the only members of the working class; *The Wages of Whiteness: Race and the Making of the American Working Class*, rev. ed. (London, 1991), 188–89.

15. David Roediger, *Towards the Abolition of Whiteness: Essays on Race, Politics, and Working Class History* (London, 1994); David R. Roediger, ed., *Black on White: Black Writers on What It Means to Be White* (New York, 1998). See also James R. Barrett and David Roediger, "Inbetween Peoples: Race, Nationality and the 'New Immigrant' Working Class," *Journal of American Ethnic History*, 16:3 (Spring 1997): 3–44.

16. Toni Morrison, *Playing in the Dark: Whiteness and the Literary Imagination* (Cambridge, 1994), 63.

17. Theodore W. Allen, *The Invention of the White Race*, Volume One, *Racial Oppression and Social Control* (London, 1994); Volume Two, *The Origin of Racial Oppression in Anglo-America* (London, 1997). Allen takes issue at length with the interpretations advanced by Jordan in *White Over Black*. I find Jordan's arguments more persuasive, as they are based on a careful reading of the historical sources and advanced with little polemic aforethought. For a nuanced account of the other side of the coin—the making of African American identity—in a similar time period, see Michael A. Gomez, *Exchanging Our Country Marks: The Transformation of African Identities in the Colonial and Antebellum South* (Chapel Hills, 1998).

18. Truth be told, there were not just white and black people in the places Saxton, Roediger, Allen, and Morrison examined, but they tended not to see Native Americans and others.

19. Tomás Almaguer, *Racial Fault Lines: The Historical Origins of White Supremacy in California* (Berkeley, 1994), 209, 104.

20. Neil Foley, *The White Scourge: Mexicans, Blacks, and Poor Whites in Texas Cotton Culture* (Berkeley, 1997).

21. George Lipsitz, "The Possessive Investment in Whiteness: Racialized Social Democracy and the 'White' Problem in American Studies," *American Quarterly*, 47.3 (1995): 369–87; Lipsitz, *The Possessive Investment in Whiteness: How White People Profit from Identity Politics* (Philadelphia, 1998).

22. Lipsitz, *Possessive Investment*, 371.

23. Lipsitz, *Possessive Investment*, 233.

24. Matthew Frye Jacobson, *Whiteness of a Different Color: European Immigrants and the Alchemy of Race* (Cambridge, 1998). The analysis and some of the language used here are drawn from my review of this book for *Social History* (in press).

25. The periods were not that simple, of course; in fact, the processes were so complex that it takes Jacobson every bit of 135 pages just to describe them. Part of his problem is that his evidence does not fit his periodization very well; he is continually forced to explain why key developments happened outside the periods to which they belong thematically. The schema has a simple beauty to it at its most abstract level, but when Jacobson gets down to the details it does not hold together very well.

26. To be fair, neither does this chapter define race. For my take on the meaning of race, see Paul Spickard and W. Jeffrey Burroughs, "We Are a People," in *We Are a People: Narrative and Multiplicity in Constructing Ethnic Identity*, ed. Spickard and Burroughs (Philadelphia, 2000), esp. 2–7.

27. Jacobson, *Whiteness of a Different Color*, 140, italics added.

28. Other examples of excellence in whiteness studies include Philip J. Deloria, *Playing Indian* (New Haven, 1998); Grace Elizabeth Hale, *Making Whiteness: The Culture of Segregation in the South, 1890–1940* (New York, 1998); and Robert G. Lee, *Orientals: Asian Americans in Popular Culture* (Philadelphia, 1999).

29. Kimberlé Crenshaw, et al., eds., *Critical Race Theory* (New York, 1995); Richard Delgado, ed., *Critical Race Theory* (Philadelphia, 1995).

30. Cheryl Harris, "Whiteness as Property," *Harvard Law Review*, 106 (1993); Ian F. Haney López, *White By Law: The Legal Construction of Race* (New York, 1996); Richard Delgado and Jean Stefancic, eds., *Critical White Studies: Looking Behind the Mirror* (Philadelphia, 1997). Harris drew on a number of roots in earlier legal studies of race, including A. Leon Higginbotham, *In the Matter of Color: Race and the American Legal Process* (New York, 1978). The title of this chapter is a play on the name of this movement. Looking beyond merely legal studies, it seeks to determine just what is critical (and what may not be) about White studies.

31. Rutherford, *Forever England*, 5.

32. Rutherford, *Forever England*, 5; Ignatiev and Garvey, *Race Traitor*, 10.

33. James H. Cone, *A Black Theology of Liberation*, 2nd ed. (Maryknoll, N.Y., 1986), vii.

34. I have reported on this exercise in more detail in "Who Is an American? Teaching About Racial and Ethnic Hierarchy," *Immigration and Ethnic History Society Newsletter*, 31.1 (May 1999).

35. Scrapbook in the possession of the author.

36. Noel Ignatiev, *How the Irish Became White* (New York, 1995), 1–2.

37. Karen Brodkin, *How Jews Became White Folks and What That Says About Race in America* (New Brunswick, 1998). The analysis and some of the language used here are drawn from my review of this book for *Social History* (in press).

38. Brodkin, *How Jews Became White Folks*, 22, 138.

39. John Gennari, "Passing for Italian: Crooners and Gangsters in Crossover Culture," *Transition*, 72 (1996): 36–48.

40. Catharine A. MacKinnon, "From Practice to Theory, or What is a White Woman Anyway?" *Yale Journal of Law and Feminism*, 4 (1991): 13–33; Martha R. Mahoney, "Whiteness and Women, In Practice and Theory: A Reply To Catharine MacKinnon," *Yale Journal of Law and Feminism*, 5 (1993): 217–51. For related themes, see also Abby L. Ferber, *White Man Falling: Race, Gender, and White Supremacy* (Lanham, Md., 1998); Ruth Frankenberg, *White Women, Race Matters: The Social Construction of Whiteness* (Minneapolis, 1993); Hauraki Greenland, "Maori Ethnicity as Ideology," in *Nga Take: Ethnic Relations and Racism in Aotearoa/New Zealand*, ed. Paul Spoonley, David Pearson, and Cluny Macpherson (Palmerston North, N.Z., 1991), 90–107; Jane Lazarre, *Beyond the Whiteness of Whiteness: Memoir of a White Mother of Black Sons* (Durham, 1996); Maureen T. Reddy, *Crossing the Color Line: Race, Parenting, and Culture* (New Brunswick, 1994). Lewis makes a reflexive assertion that blacks constitute a race gendered female in "Sex, Race, and Matrices of Desire in an Antiblack World," in *Her Majesty's Other Children: Sketches of Racism from a Neocolonial Age* (Lanham, Md., 1997), 73–88.

41. bell hooks, *Ain't I a Woman: Black Women and Feminism* (Boston, 1981); hooks, *Talking Back: Thinking Feminist, Thinking Black* (Boston, 1989); Hazel V. Carby, "White Woman Listen! Black Feminism and the Boundaries of Sisterhood," in *The Empire Strikes Back: Race and Racism in 70s Britain* (London, 1982); Haunani-Kay Trask, "Pacific Island Women and White Feminism" in *From a Native Daughter: Colonialism and Sovereignty in Hawai'i* (Monroe, Me., 1993), 263–77; Donna Awatere, *Maori Sovereignty* (Auckland, N.Z., 1984), 42 and *passim*.

42. Matt Wray and Annalee Newitz, eds., *White Trash: Race and Class in America* (New York, 1997), back cover.

43. Thandeka, "The Cost of Whiteness," *Tikkun*, 14.3 (May–June 1999): 33–38. See also Thandeka, *Learning to be White: Money, Race, and God in America* (Continuum, 1999).

44. I made this investigation of www.amazon.com connections on July 29, 2000. Jim Goad, *The Redneck Manifesto: How Hillbillies, Hicks, and White Trash Became America's Scapegoats* (New York, 1998); Michael A. Hoffman, *They Were White and They Were Slaves: The Untold Story of the Enslavement of Whites in Early America*, 4th ed. (Independent History, 1993); James Ronald Kennedy, *The South Was Right!*, reprint ed. (1994). Cf. Jeffrey Kaplan, ed., *Encyclopedia of White Power: A Sourcebook on the Radical Racist Right* (Walnut Creek, Calif., 2000).

45. See, for example: Walter Benn Michaels, "Race into Culture: A Critical Genealogy of Cultural Identity," *Critical Inquiry*, 18 (1992): 655–85; Avery Gordon and Christopher Newfield, "Critical Response: White Philosophy," *Critical Inquiry*, 20 (1994): 737–57; Walter Benn Michaels, "Critical Response: The No-Drop Rule," *Critical Inquiry*, 20 (1994): 758–69; Barbara J. Flagg, "'Was Blind, But Now I See': White Race Consciousness and the Requirement of Discriminatory Intent," *Michigan Law Review*, 91 (1993): 953–1017; Micaela di Leonardo, "White Ethnicities, Identity Politics, and Baby Bear's Chair," *Social Text*, 41 (Winter 1994): 174–91; Shelly Fisher Fishkin, "Interrogating 'Whiteness,' Complicating 'Blackness': Remapping American Culture," *American Quarterly*, 47.3 (1995): 428–66; Walter Benn Michaels, *Our America: Nativism, Modernism, and Pluralism* (Durham, 1995); Liam Kennedy, "Alien Nation: White Male Paranoia and Imperial Culture in the United States," *Journal of American Studies*, 30 (1996): 87–100; Mike Hill, ed., *Whiteness: A Critical Reader* (New York, 1997); Michelle Fine, et al., eds., *Off White: Readings on Race, Power, and Society* (New York, 1997); Henry A. Giroux, "Rewriting the Discourse of Racial Identity: Towards a Pedagogy and Politics of Whiteness," *Harvard Educational Review*, 67.2 (1997): 285–320; Howard Winant, "Behind Blue Eyes: Whiteness and Contemporary US Racial Politics," *New Left Review*, number 225 (Sept.–Oct. 1997); Jonathan W. Warren and France Winddance Twine, "White Americans, the New Minority? Non-Blacks and the Ever-Expanding Boundaries of Whiteness," *Journal of Black Studies*, 28.2 (1997): 200–18; Ruth Frankenberg, *Displacing Whiteness: Essays in Social and Cultural Criticism* (Durham, 1997); Richard Dyer, *White* (London, 1997); Joe Kincheloe, et al., eds., *White Reign: Deploying Whiteness in America* (New York, 1998); Dona D. Nelson, *National Manhood: Capitalist Citizenship and the Imagined Fraternity of White Men* (Durham, 1998); John Gabriel, *Whitewash: Racialized Politics and the Media* (New York, 1998); Valerie Babb, *Whiteness Visible: The Meaning of Whiteness in American Literature and Culture* (New York, 1998); Thomas K. Nakayama and Judith N. Martin, eds., *Whiteness: The Communication of Social Identity* (Thousand Oaks, Calif., 1999); Maurice Berger, *White Lies: Race and the Myths of Whiteness* (New York, 1999); Christine Clark and James O'Donnell, eds., *Becoming and Unbecoming White: Owning and Disowning a Racial Identity* (Westport, Conn., 1999); Timothy B. Powell, ed., *Beyond the Binary: Reconstructing Cultural Identity in a Multicultural Context* (New Brunswick, 1999); Chris Weedon, *Feminism, Theory, and the Politics of Difference* (Oxford, 1999); Sarah Barnet-Weiser, *The Most Beautiful Girl in the World: Beauty*

Pageants and National Identity (Berkeley, 1999); Patricia McKee, *Producing American Races: Henry James, William Faulkner, Toni Morrison* (Durham, N.C., 1999); John Hartigan, *Racial Situations: Class Predicaments of Whiteness in Detroit* (Princeton, 1999); Chris J. Cuomo and Kim Q. Hall, eds., *Whiteness: Feminist Philosophical Reflections* (Lanham, MD, 1999); Renee R. Curry, *White Women Writing White: H.D., Elizabeth Bishop, Sylvia Plath* (New York, 2000); Aime M. Carrillo Rowe, "Locating Feminism's Subject: The Paradox of White Feminity and the Struggle to Forge Feminist Alliances," *Communication Theory*, 10.1 (2000): 64–80; Barbara A. Miller, "'Anchoring' White Community: White Women Activists and the Politics of Public Schools," *Identities*, 6.4 (2000): 481–512; John Tehranian, "Performing Whiteness: Naturalization Litigation and the Construct of Racial Identity in America," *Yale Law Journal*, 109.4 (2000): 817ff; Kalpana Seshari Crooks, *Desiring Whiteness: A Lacanian Analysis of Race* (New York, 2000); Nelson M. Rodriguez and Leila E. Villaverde, eds., *Dismantling White Privilege: Pedagogy, Politics, and Whiteness* (New York, 2000); Walter Bronwen, *Outsiders Inside: Whiteness, Place and Irish Women* (New York, 2001).

46. See, for example, *The White Issue*, issue 73 of *Transition* (1996).

47. Richard Delgado makes essentially the same point, expressing amazement at "how white people, even ones of good will, twist discussions concerning race so that the conversation becomes about themselves"; Delgado, *Critical Race Theory*, xiii.

"Lester Young: Master of Jive," by Douglas Henry Daniels

This essay was first published in *American Music* (Fall, 1985). A version of this essay was presented at the American Historical Association Convention in Los Angeles, December 29, 1981. I wish to extend my gratitude to Professors Robert Hill and Ishmael Reed for their suggestions on the earlier version, to Ron Welburn, director of the Jazz Oral History Project, Institute of Jazz Studies, Rutgers University, and to Buck Clayton and Lester Young, Jr., for their aid. The Smithsonian Institution and the Academic Senate and Faculty Career Development Grants of the University of California, Santa Barbara, facilitated research.

1. Amiri Baraka, "Pres Spoke in a Language," *Selected Poetry of Amiri Baraka/Leroi Jones* (New York, 1979), 320; Ted Joans, "Lester Young," in *American Negro Poetry*, ed. Arna Bontemps (New York, 1963), 171–72; Al Young, "Goodbye Porkpie Hat," in *Bodies and Souls* (Berkeley, 1981), 102–3; see also Larry Neal, "Don't Say Goodbye to the Porkpie Hat," *Hoodoo Hollerin' Bebop Ghosts* (Washington, D.C., 1974), 19–24; and John Clellon Holmes, *The Horn* (Berkeley, 1980). The George Morse material in the "Jazz" file of the Institute of Jazz Studies, Rutgers University, Newark, N.J., notes that artist Stuart Davis was influenced by Young. Charles Mingus's composition was recorded on his *Mingus Dynasty* (Columbia G 30628); Rahsaan Roland Kirk's version is on his album *The Return of the 5,000 lb. Man* (Warner Brothers Records B52918).

2. One of the best accounts of the early saxophonists is *Coleman Hawkins: A Documentary*, Riverside LP 12–117/118. On the instrument's early uses and history in jazz, see James Lincoln Collier, *The Making of Jazz: A Comprehensive History* (New York, 1979), 217–37; and Stanley Dance, *The World of Count Basie* (New York, 1980), 106. Young recounts

his experience with the Henderson band in Nat Hentoff, "Pres," *Downbeat* 23 (Mar. 7, 1956): 9; and in François Postif, "Lesterparis '59," *Jazz Monthly* 9 (Feb. 1964): 15ff. The latter interview is available on tape at the Institute of Jazz Studies (IJS), Rutgers University.

3. Leonard Feather, "Prez," *Playboy* 9 (Sept. 1959): 68; "Lester Laid to Rest," *Downbeat* 26 (Apr. 30, 1959); John Hammond, "Two Views of Lester Young: Recollections," *Jazz and Blues* 3 (Aug. 1973): 9. For the Henderson quote, see Dance, Basie, 106. See also Tom Scanlan, "The Impeccable Mr. Wilson," *Downbeat* 26 (Jan. 22, 1959): 20; Ralph J. Gleason, "Jazzman Lester Young Dies," *San Francisco Chronicle*, Mar. 16, 1959, 4; and Mike Nevard, "I'll Take Flip Any Time," *Melody Maker*, 29 (Mar. 21, 1953): 5.

4. Buck Clayton, interview with author, May 21, 1981. See also David Dalby, "The African Element in English," in Thomas Kochman, ed., *Rappin' and Stylin' Out: Communication in Urban Black America* (Urbana, 1972), 170–88; Claude Brown, "The Language of Soul," in Kochman, *Rappin' and Stylin' Out*, 134–40; Robert S. Gold, Jazz Talk (New York, 1975); Earl Conrad, ed., *Dan Burley's Original Handbook of Harlem Jive* (New York, 1944); Clyde Taylor, "The Language of Hip: From Africa to What's Happening Now," *First World* 1 (Jan./Feb. 1977): 25–32.

5. Benny Green, "Lester Young—A Reflection," *Jazz Journal* 12 (May 1959): 9, characterizes Young as "inscrutable." Nat Hentoff and Nat Shapiro, eds., *The Jazz Makers* (New York, 1957): 256, describe him as wearing a "mask"; in the same book, an executive of a booking agency claimed that Young was an "aloof goof" (244); and Bill Coss, "JATP's Chief Executive: The President," *Metronome* 71 (Oct. 1955): 25, refers to him as an "enigma."

6. For references to Young's shyness, see Hentoff and Shapiro, *Jazz Makers*, 243; and "Pres Talks about Himself, Copycats," *Downbeat* 16 (May 6, 1949): 15. For the best statement of his ideas, see Alan Morrison, "You Got to Be Original, Man," *Jazz Record*, no. 46 (July 1946): 7–9; as well as Postif, "Lesterparis '59," 15ff., and the more accurate taped version of this interview at Rutgers University (hereafter cited as Postif, interview). See also Connie Kay, interview with author, June 8, 1981.

7. Barney Kessel, "Lester Young, Part 2," *Guitar Player* 13 (Jan. 1979): 22.

8. Dance, *Basie*, 93.

9. Valerie Wilmer, "The Lee Young Story," clipping in Lester Young file, IJS, Rutgers University; Sir Charles Thompson, Jazz Oral History Project, Rutgers University (hereafter JOHP), reel (vol.) 1, 204–6. (Each interview at Rutgers consists of several reels transcribed into typewritten text. The volume numbers usually correspond to reel numbers.)

10. Dance, *Basie*, 10.

11. Ralph J. Gleason, "Hail to the Chief of Tenor Sax Players," *Rolling Stone* 160 (May 9, 1974): 13.

12. George Hoefer/Robert Reisner material in Lester Young file, IJS, Rutgers University (probably from *Downbeat* 12, 1).

13. Jimmy Heath, interview with author, May 26, 1981; Kessel, "Lester Young, Part 2," 22.

14. Dance, Basie, 103; see also John Chilton, *Billie's Blues: The Billie Holiday Story* (New York, 1978), 44–45, on the lightheartedness of Pres and Holiday.

15. See Cyril Daryll Forde, *African Worlds: Studies in the Cosmological Ideas and Social Values of African Peoples* (New York, 1960).

16. Robert A. Perlongo, "Portrait of Pres," *Metronome* 76 (May 1959): 17–18; Postif, interview.

17. Francis Bebey, *African Music: A People's Art* (Westport, Conn, 1975), 3–5.

18. James A. Harrison, "The Creole Patois of Louisiana," *American Journal of Philology* 3 (1882): 287; Bebey, African Music, 120.

19. Kessel, "Lester Young, Part 1," *Guitar Player* 22 (Dec. 1978): 14; Jimmy Heath, interview with author, May 26, 1981.

20. Duke Ellington, "Swing Is Stagnant," *Downbeat* 6 (Feb. 1939): 2; "The Carnegie Chronicle," *Downbeat* 25 (Nov. 27, 1958): 51; Thompson, JOHP 1:16.

21. Linda Kuehl, liner notes to *The First Verve Session: Billie Holiday*, Verve 2–2503; Connie Kay, interview with author, June 8, 1981; Chris Albertson, taped interview, Rutgers, 1958; Nat Shapiro and Nat Hentoff, *The Jazz Makers* (New York, 1979), 262.

22. Kessel, "Lester Young, Part 2," 22.

23. Ibid.; Perlongo, "Portrait of Pres," 17ff.

24. Buck Clayton, interview with author, May 21, 1981.

25. Jimmy Heath, interview with author, May 26, 1981.

26. P. Harris, "None Better Than Best with a Brush," *Downbeat* 18 (Apr. 20, 1951): 18; Gene Ramey, JOHP 2:34ff.

27. Quoted in Feather, "Prez," 68; Vic Dickenson, JOHP 1:77–78.

28. Jimmy Heath, interview with author, May 26, 1981.

29. Benny Green, "Lester Young," 9.

30. Wilmer, "Lee Young Story," 4; Lee Young, JOHP, is good on the family's back ground; on pig Latin, see Irma Young, interview with author, Sept. 8, 1981 (Irma is Lester and Lee's sister); Graham Colombé, "Jo Jones Speaks Out," *Jazz Journal* 25 (Dec. 1972): 6; S. L. Sergel, ed., *The Language of Show Business* (Chicago: Dramatic Publishing Co., 1973): 42; Bill Ballantine, "Circus Talk," *American Mercury* 76 (May 1953): 22.

31. Postif, Interview.

32. *Tea Pad Songs*, vol. 1 (Stash ST-103) is one album on the Stash label that provides examples. See also Robert Lucas, "The Real Truth about Marijuana," *Ebony* 3 (Sept. 1948): 46–51.

33. Budd Johnson, JOHP 3:6.

34. *Amsterdam News*, June 29, 1940, 32: "The 'Slanguage of Swing" appeared in *Downbeat* 2 (Nov. 1935); a book on jive was advertised in this journal Dec. 1, 1941, 11.

35. Whitney Balliet, *New Yorker*, Feb. 23. 1981, 90ff. Moreover, good discussions are found in Mercer Ellington with Stanley Dance, *Duke Ellington in Person: An Intimate Memoir* (New York, 1978), 55; and Milton "Mezz" Mezzrow and Bernard Wolfe, *Really the Blues* (New York, 1946), 227–28.

36. Kay, interview with author, June 6, 1981.

37. Louis Armstrong, *Satchmo: My Life in New Orleans* (New Yorky, 1964); Dicky Wells and Stanley Dance, *The Night People: Reminiscences of a Jazzman* (Boston, 1971); Billie Holiday with William Dufty, *Lady Sings the Blues* (New York, 1965); Conrad, ed., Dan Burley's *Original Handbook of Harlem Jive*; Burley interviewed Tiny Bradshaw in the *Amsterdam News*, Feb. 24, 1940, 21; *Downbeat* 8 (Dec. 1, 1941): 11; California *Eagle*, Apr. 30,

1942, 3–8, and July 31, 1936, 10. See also Babs Gonzales ("Creator of the Bebop Language"), *I Paid My Dues* (East Orange, N.J., 1967).

38. Ron Welburn, "Ralph Ellison's," 13; Gary Giddings, *Riding on a Blue Note* (New York, 1981), 248–49; Buddy Tate, JOHP, 13; *Eagle*, Sept. 5, 1937, 8.

39. Balliet, *New Yorker*, 98; Jimmy Heath, interview with author, May 26, 1981. Postif, interview; Bud Freeman, *"You Don't Look Like a Musician"* (Detroit, 1974), 27.

40. Max Jones, "Max Jones Spends a Holiday with Billie," *Melody Maker* 30 (Feb. 13, 1954): 7–9.

41. Dance, *Basie*, 93; Thompson, JOHP, 201, 225–26.

42. Jimmy Heath, interview with author, May 26, 1981; Sadik Hakim, interview with author, May 27, 1981.

43. Mezzrow, *Really*, 235; Gara, *Dodds*, 25.

44. *Amsterdam News*, July 6, 1940, 21.

45. Professors Robert Hill, Department of History, University of California, Los Angeles, and Gerard Pigeon, Black Studies Department, University of California, Santa Barbara, informed me of the nickname customs in the West Indies and West Africa and suggested some of the functions of these customs.

46. Balliet, *New Yorker*, 90.

47. Perlongo, "Portrait of Pres," 40. Balliet, *New Yorker*, 90. Sadik Hakim, "My Experiences with Bird and Pres," typewritten manuscript in the author's possession; Sadik Hakim, interview with author, May 27, 1981; Jimmy Heath, interview with author, May 26, 1981.

48. George C. Barker, *Pachuco: An American-Spanish Argot and Its Social Functions in Tucson, Arizona* (Tucson, 1958); Haldeen Braddy, "The Pachucos and Their Argot," *Southern Folklore Quarterly* 24 (Dec. 1960): 255–71; Beatrice Griffith, "The Pachuco Patois," *Common Ground* 7 (Summer 1947): 77–84; and Griffith, *American Me* (Boston, 1948).

49. Douglas Henry Daniels, "Schooling Malcolm: Malcolm Little and Black Culture during the Golden Age of Jazz," *Stepping-stones* (Winter, 1983): 45–60; Jacques E. Levy *Cesar Chavez: Autobiography of La Causa* (New York, 1979).

50. Armstrong, *Satchmo*; Max Jones and John Chilton, *Louis: The Louis Armstrong Story, 1900–1971* (Boston, 1971); Chilton, *Billie's Blues*; Cab Calloway and Bryant Rollins, *Minnie the Moocher & Me* (New York, 1976); Arnold Shaw, *Sinatra: Twentieth Century Romantic* (New York, 1968).

"Holding Center Stage: Race Pride and the Extracurriculum at Historically Black Colleges and Universities," by Patrick B. Miller

1. See August Meier, *Negro Thought in America, 1880–1915: Racial Ideologies in the Age of Booker T. Washington* (Ann Arbor, 1963); James D. Anderson, *The Education of Blacks in the South, 1860–1935* (Chapel Hill, 1988).

2. A starting point for such an account is Raymond Wolters, *The New Negro on Campus: Black College Rebellions of the 1920s* (Princeton, 1975); see also Monroe H. Little,

"The Extra-Curricular Activities of Black College Students, 1868–1940," *Journal of Negro History* 65 (Spring 1980): 135–148.

3. See Paula Giddings, *In Search of Sisterhood: Delta Sigma Theta and the Challenge of the Black Sorority Movement* (New York, 1988), 144–145; Carter G. Woodson, *The Mis-Education of the Negro* (Washington, D.C., 1933).

4. Andrew Ward, *Dark Midnight When I Rise: The Story of the Jubilee Singers, Who Introduced the World to the Music of Black America* (New York, 2000).

5. Richard J. Powell and Jock Reynolds, *To Conserve a Legacy: American Art from Historically Black Colleges and Universities* (Cambridge, 2000), 159–165.

6. On the meanings of "political" acts, see Robin D.G. Kelley, *Race Rebels: Culture, Politics and the Black Working Class* (New York, 1994).

7. Kevin K. Gaines, *Uplifting the Race: Black Leadership, Politics, and Culture in the Twentieth Century* (Chapel Hill, 1996); Louis Harlan, *Booker T. Washington: The Making of a Black Leader, 1856–1901* (New York, 1972); Author's conversation with Cynthia Wilson, Tuskegee University Archives, May 1996.

8. See Wolters, *The New Negro on Campus.*

9. Today, the National Panhellenic Council includes eight organizations. The four fraternities are Alpha Phi Alpha, Kappa Alpha Psi, Omega Psi Phi, and Phi Beta Sigma; the four sororities are Alpha Kappa Alpha, Delta Sigma Theta, Sigma Gamma Rho, and Zeta Phi Beta. Lawrence Otis Graham, *Our Kind of People: Inside America's Black Upper Class* (New York, 1999) 89; Giddings, *In Search of Sisterhood,* 58–60.

10. First quote, Edmonds in Giddings, *In Search of Sisterhood,* 95; second Giddings 54–55; Numa P. G. Adams, "The Place of the Fraternity in Negro College Life," *Howard University Record* 3, (1919): 17; see also Lawrence C. Ross, *The Divine Nine: The History of African American Fraternities and Sororities* (New York, 2000).

11. Graham, *Our Kind of People,* 83–100.

12. Giddings, *In Search of Sisterhood,* 7, 148–153; See also E. Franklin Frazier, *Black Bourgeoisie* (New York, 1957), 83, 94–95, 203.

13. Patrick B. Miller, "Muscular Assimilationism: Sport and the Paradoxes of Racial Reform," in *Race and Sport: The Struggle for Equality On and Off the Field,* ed. Charles K. Ross (Jackson, 2004); L. W. G. Moore, "College Athletics," Fisk University *Herald,* November, 1894.

14. Howard University *Hilltop,* April 29, 1924.

15. See Henderson, *The Negro in Sports* (Washington, D.C., 1939), 100; Chalk, *Black College Sport* (New York, 1976), 199–200; Heintze, *Private Black Colleges in Texas, 1865–1954* (College Station, 1985), 171; Michael Hurd, *Black College Football, 1892–1992: One Hundred Years of History, Education, and Pride* (Virginia Beach, Va., 1993), 28; Arthur Ashe Jr., *A Hard Road to Glory: A History of the African-American Athlete* (New York, 1988), II, 100; Patrick B. Miller, "To 'Bring the Race Along Rapidly': Sport, Student Culture and Educational Mission at Historically Black Colleges During the Interwar Years," *History of Educational Quarterly* 35 (Summer, 1995): 111–133.

16. See Hurd, *Black College Football,* 153–162; Joe Richardson, *A History of Fisk University, 1865–1946* (Tuscaloosa, 1980), 157.

17. *Howard University Record* 16 (December, 1921): 126. Concerning distinctive halftime activities in more recent years, see Michael Hurd and Stan C. Spence, "Halftime: The Band Be Kickin'!" in Hurd, *Black College Football*, 123–129.

18. *Howard Alumni Sentinel* 6 (February, 1923): 13–14. J. R. E. Lee quoted in Leedel W. Neyland, *The History of Florida A & M University* (Gainesville, 1963), 127; Standish quoted in Miriam Jones and Joe Richardson, *Talladega College: The First Century* (Tuscaloosa, 1990), 95.

19. George Streator, "Football in Negro Colleges," *Crisis* 39 (April 1932): 129, 141. The list of the worst offenders included Lincoln (Pa.), Wilberforce, South Carolina State, Allen University, Claflin, and Morris Brown. "Medium, in need of further reform," were Fisk, West Virginia State, Knoxville, and Kentucky State. He ranked Hampton, Howard, Morehouse, Wiley, and Tuskegee as good.

20. Richardson, *A History of Fisk*, 158; Streator, "Negro Football Standards," *Crisis* 38 (March 1931): 85–86; Du Bois, "Athletics in Negro Colleges," in "Postscript," *Crisis* 37 (June 1930): 209. Stevenson, perhaps the greatest black college football player of his era, played for eight seasons in all. See Ashe, *A Hard Road to Glory*, II, 101.

21. Du Bois, "Education and Work," in Julius Lester, ed. *The Seventh Son: The Thought and Writings of W. E. B. Du Bois* (New York, 1971) I, 563. See also Edward P. Davis, "The Function of a Board of Athletic Control," *The Howard Alumnus*, 5 (February, 1927): 115.

22. Allison Davis, "The Second Generation: College Athlete," *Crisis* 35 (March, 1928): 87.

23. Miller, "To 'Bring the Race Along Rapidly'"; see also Miller, "The Anatomy of Scientific Racism: Racialist Responses to Black Athletic Achievement," *Journal of Sport History* 25 (Spring 1998): 119–151.

24. Randolph Edmonds, "Some Whys and Wherefores of College Dramatics," *Crisis* 37 (March 1930): 92, 105.

25. Lillian Voorhees, "Biographical Sketch" (Box 1, Folder 1) Vorhees Papers, Amistad Research Center, New Orleans, LA.

26. Voorhees, "Biographical Sketch."

27. Frank Yerby, "The Little Theatre in the Negro College," M.A. Thesis, Fisk University (Fisk University Archives). Yerby also pointed to the influence of Broadway producer David Belasco on theater directors at HBCUs as well as the folk plays of Paul Green, whose work was highly regarded on black college campuses. It is striking, though, that none of the plays by Willis Richardson or John F. Matheus were listed among those performed by the teachers and directors surveyed by Yerby; to speculate for a moment, the hardest-hitting plays about African American life remained risky at that time. It is noteworthy that Yerby undertook graduate studies—at the urging of that James Weldon Johnson—before he embarked on a long career as a writer, first (and unsuccessfully) of protest fiction, then of widely popular historical novels. See James L. Hill, "Anti-Heroic Perspectives: The Life and Works of Frank Yerby," Ph.D. diss., University of Iowa, 1976.

28. Yerby, "The Little Theatre in the Negro College," 80–89. "Poise, self-confidence, self-control, physical grace, a well modulated voice, and a vivid personality are among the social benefits which [theater directors] believe the student derives from participation in dramatics. On the cultural and intellectual side of the ledger they list increased aesthetic appreciation,

better understanding of the drama as an art form, an urge to self-expression through creative work, a worthy use of leisure time, and a greater appreciation of all forms of art."

29. Tony Scherman, "The Great Debaters" *American Legacy* (Spring 1997): 40–42.

30. Hobart Jarrett, "Adventures in Interracial Debates," *Crisis* 42 (1935): 240; Scherman, "The Great Debaters."

"'Blessed Are the Peacemakers': William Jay and the Drive for International Arbitration," by Stephen P. Budney

1. Richard Cobden, *Speeches of Richard Cobden on Peace, Financial Reform, Colonial Reform, and Other Subjects Delivered During 1849* (London, 1970), 98–99; Merle Curti, *The American Peace Crusade, 1815–1860* (Durham, 1929), 189–90. Curti claims that William Jay devoted himself to the cause of world peace in his biography of his father. I have examined three separate editions of that work and found no such evidence.

2. Richard B. Morris, *The Peacemakers: The Great Powers and American Independence* (New York, 1965), 301–4.

3. Stephen Howarth, *To Shining Sea: A History of the United States Navy, 1775–1991* (New York, 1991). French colonies as well. With some 300 merchant vessels impounded by the British, and lacking a navy of any consequence, America's only recourse was diplomatic protest. Claude G. Bowers, *Jefferson and Hamilton: The Struggle for Democracy in America* (New York, 1925), 246–47; William Jay, *The Life of John Jay: With Selections From His Correspondence and Miscellaneous Papers* (2 vols., New York, 1833), I, 253.

4. Merrill D. Peterson, editor, *Thomas Jefferson, Writings* (New York, 1984), 1030.

5. Bowers, *Jefferson and Hamilton*, 249; Stanley Elkins and Eric McKitrick, *The Age of Federalism: The Early American Republic, 1788–1800* (New York, 1993), 415–422; Frederic Austin Ogg, "Jay's Treaty and the Slavery Interests of the United States," *Annual Report of the American Historical Association* (Washington D.C., 1901), 275–298.

6. John C. Fitzpatrick, editor, *The Writings of George Washington from the Original Manuscript Sources*, 39 vols. (Washington, D.C., 1940), 33, 332.

7. Jay, *Life of John Jay*, I: 357, 361–61.

8. Ibid., I, 311.

9. Curti, *Peace Crusade*, 21–22.

10. Ibid., 42; Charles De Benedetti, *The Peace Reform in American History* (Bloomington, 1980), 38–39; *History of the American Peace Society and Its Work* (Washington DC, 1908), 2–3; *William Ladd, An essay on a Congress of Nations: For the adjustment of Disputes Without Resort to Arms* (New York, 1916), 8–11; Valarie H. Ziegler, *The Advocates of Peace in Antebellum America* (Indianapolis, 1992), 3.

11. Lawrence J. Friedman, *Gregarious Saints; Self and Community in American Abolitionism, 1830–1870* (New York, 1982), 80.

12. Curti, *Peace Crusade*, 14–16; Willliam Jay to Joseph Sturge, July 25, 1841, *A Side Light on Anglo-American Relations, 1839–1858: Furnished by the Correspondence of Lewis Tappan and Others with the American and Foreign Anti-Slavery Society*, edited by Anne Heloise Abel

and Frank J. Klingberg (New York, 1970), 81–2; Edson L. Whitney, *The American Peace Crusade: A Centennial History* (Washington DC, 1928), 64.

13. Ibid., 189–91; William Harbutt Dawson, *Richard Cobden and Foreign Policy: A Critical Exposition with Special Reference to Our Day and its Problems* (London, 1926), 132–40.

14. William Jay, *War and Peace: The Evils of the First and a Plan for Preserving the Last* (New York, 1842).

15. Ibid., 47.

16. Ibid., 52.

17. Ibid., 21–3; Edward D. Jervey and C. Harold Huber, "The Creole Affair," *Journal of Negro History* 50 (October, 1965): 195–204. The debates in Congress may be found in the *Congressional Globe*, Second Session, Twenty-seventh Congress (City of Washington, 1842).

18. Jay, *War and Peace*, 55–6.

19. Ralph Waldo Emerson, *Miscellanies* (New York, 1884), 201.

20. Jay, *War and Peace*, 54.

21. Ibid., 62.

22. Ibid., 65–7.

"Max Weber in New England," by Charles L. Cohen

1. The number of pages Weber allotted to each group provides a simple test for this proposition: he took thirty pages to cover Puritanism, and twenty-six to discuss the other three faiths. See Max Weber, *The Protestant Ethic and the Spirit of Capitalism*, trans. Talcott Parsons (New York, 1958), 98–154.

2. See Reinhard Bendix, *Max Weber: An Intellectual Portrait* (Berkeley and Los Angeles, 1977 ed.), 135; Max Weber, *Economy and Society: An Outline of Interpretive Sociology*, ed. Guenther Roth and Claus Wittich, 3 vols. (New York, 1968), 2:615–23.

3. See among others, David D. Hall, *Worlds of Wonder, Days of Judgment: Popular Religious Belief in Early New England* (New York, 1989); Charles Lloyd Cohen, *God's Caress: The Psychology of Puritan Religious Experience* (New York, 1986); Michael McGiffert, ed., *God's Plot: Puritan Spirituality in Thomas Shepard's Cambridge*, rev. ed. (Amherst, MA, 1994), "Preface," 3–33; Charles Hambrick-Stowe, *The Practice of Piety: Puritan Devotional Disciplines in Seventeenth-Century New England* (Chapel Hill, 1982). For the best evolutionary model of Puritanism, see Stephen Foster, *The Long Argument: English Puritanism and the Shaping of New England Culture, 1570–1700* (Chapel Hill, 1991).

4. E.g., James Truslow Adams, *The Founding of New England* (Boston, 1921), *passim*. Two representative quotations: "This system of negation and protest [i.e., Puritanism] might have done its needed work and passed, had it not had the misfortune, from the moral and intellectual sides, to come to dominate the power of government" (83); "The Puritan, at least, was no more a believer in the political rights of an individual as such, or in democracy, than in religious toleration, and the leaders in Massachusetts denounced both with equal vehemence" (84).

5. Perry Miller, *Errand into the Wilderness* (Cambridge, MA, 1956), vii, viii.

6. Perry Miller, *The New England Mind: From Colony to Province* (New York, 1953), 40–52.

7. Weber, *Economy and Society*, 2.574.

8. See Michael Walzer, *The Revolution of the Saints: A Study in the Origins of Radical Politics* (Cambridge, MA, 1965).

9. See Edmund S. Morgan, ed., *Puritan Political Ideas* (Indianapolis, 1965), esp. xx–xxv; Stephen Foster, *Their Solitary Way: The Puritan Social Ethic in the First Century of Settlement in New England* (New Haven, 1971), 39–40; T. H. Breen, *The Character of the Good Ruler: Puritan Political Ideas in New England 1630–1730* (New York, 1970), *passim*.

10. William Shakespeare, *Richard II*, ed. Kenneth Muir, 2nd rev. ed. (New York, 1999), II.1.50.

11. Charles M. Andrews, *The Colonial Period of American History*, 4 vols. (New Haven, 1934–38), 1.439–41.

12. Weber, *Economy and Society*, 2.594. "Theocracy" is a misnomer. The word's controlling definition is "A form of government in which God (or a deity) is recognized as the king or immediate ruler, and his laws are taken as the statute-book of the kingdom, these laws being usually administered by a priestly order as his ministers and agents; hence (loosely) a system of government by a sacerdotal order, claiming a divine commission; also a state so governed . . . ", *Oxford English Dictionary* (New York, 1971 ed.), s.v. "theocracy." The New England governments were not theocracies: God was the ultimate source of authority but not the immediate ruler; His laws (e.g., in Scripture) were not the basis of statutory law, and ministers did not rule the state (in Massachusetts they were forbidden from sitting on the General Court in 1632). Although they believed that church and state should cooperate closely to secure moral order, Puritans considered the two institutions as separate entities; see Morgan, *Puritan Political Ideas*, xxv–xxxv.

13. Edmund S. Morgan, *Visible Saints: The History of a Puritan Idea* (Ithaca, NY), 80–109; Andrews, *Colonial Period*, 1.435.

14. Weber, *Economy and Society*, 2.593.

15. Talcott Parsons, "Introduction," xxxii, in Max Weber, *The Sociology of Religion*, trans. Talcott Parsons; Parsons, xxxii–xxiii gives three definitions. Weber, *Protestant Ethic*, 117.

16. Weber, *Economy and Society*, 2.630.

17. E. Brooks Holifield, *The Covenant Sealed: The Development of Puritan Sacramental Theology in Old and New England, 1570–1720* (New Haven, 1974), 164–65, 168, 167; for the Willard quotation, see 223; 224.

18. Weber, *Economy and Society*, 2.532.

19. Hall, *Worlds of Wonder*; Richard Godbeer, *The Devil's Dominion: Magic and Religion in Early New England* (New York, 1992).

20. Weber, *Economy and Society*, 2.575.

21. Cohen, *God's Caress*, 116.

22. Weber, *Society and Economy*, 2.514.

23. On literacy, see Kenneth Lockridge, *Literacy in Colonial New England: An Enquiry into the Social Context of Literacy in the Early Modern West* (New York, 1974), 72–101; Hall, *Worlds of Wonder*, 31–43; E. Jennifer Monaghan, "Literacy Instruction and Gender in

Colonial New England," *American Quarterly*, 40 (1988), 18–41. On education, see Samuel Eliot Morison's classic *Harvard in the Seventeenth Century*, 2 vols. (Cambridge, MA, 1936), as well as Lawrence A. Cremin, *American Education: The Colonial Experience 1607–1783* (New York, 1970), *passim*, and James Axtell, *The School Upon a Hill: Education and Society in Colonial New England* (Chapel Hill, 1974).

24. Weber, *Protestant Ethic*, 98, 104, 116.

25. The phrase is Ralph Barton Perry's, *Puritanism and Democracy* (New York, 1944), title of chapter X, p. 245.

26. Weber, *Economy and Society*, 2.575.

27. Cohen, *God's Caress*, 115–16, and see Dewey Wallace, *Puritans and Predestination: Grace in English Protestant Theology 1525–1695* (Chapel Hill, 1982), esp. chap. 3.

28. Cohen, *God's Caress*, 116–17; Wallace, *Puritans and Predestination*, 47.

29. Andrews, *Colonial Period*, 2:151–52.

30. Bernard Bailyn, *The New England Merchants in the Seventeenth Century* (Cambridge, MA, 1955), should be read as qualified by Foster, *Their Solitary Way*, 99–126. See also Darrett B. Rutman, *Winthrop's Boston: A Portrait of a Puritan Town, 1630–1649* (Chapel Hill, 1965), 178–90.

31. Paul Seaver, *Wallington's World: A Puritan Artisan in Seventeenth-Century London* (Stanford, CA, 1985), 112–42; Virginia Anderson, *New England's Generation: The Great Migration and the Formation of Society and Culture in the Seventeenth Century* (New York, 1991), 131–76; Daniel Vickers, "Competence and Competition: Economic Culture in Early America," *William and Mary Quarterly*, 3rd ser., 47 (1990), 3–29.

32. This paragraph is based on Stephen Innes' important book, *Creating the Commonwealth: The Economic Culture of Puritan New England* (New York, 1995), esp. chaps. 3, 5.

33. Weber, *Protestant Ethic*, 183.

34. Mark A. Peterson, *The Price of Redemption: The Spiritual Economy of Puritan New England* (Stanford, 1997); Christine Leigh Heyrman, *Commerce and Culture: The Maritime Communities of Colonial Massachusetts, 1690–1750* (New York, 1984).

35. e.g., John McCusker and Russell Menard, *The Economy of Colonial British America, 1607–1789*, (Chapel Hill, 1985), 91–116, whose index does not even mention "Puritanism."

36. This passage summarizes and elaborates on Edmund S. Morgan, *American Slavery, American Freedom: The Ordeal of Colonial Virginia* (New York, 1975).

37. Barry Levy, *Quakers and the American Family: British Settlement in the Delaware Valley* (New York, 1988).

CONTRIBUTORS

STEPHEN P. BUDNEY is associate professor of history at Pikeville College. He completed his PhD at the University of Mississippi. His dissertation, directed by Winthrop Jordan, is a biography of William Jay and will be published in 2005.

CHARLES L. COHEN is professor of history at the University of Wisconsin–Madison, former director of the religious studies program, and, beginning in 2005, inaugural director of the Lubar Institute for the Study of the Abrahamic Traditions. He received his PhD from the University of California–Berkeley under Winthrop Jordan's direction in 1982.

PATRICIA CLINE COHEN, professor of history at the University of California–Santa Barbara, got her PhD at the University of California–Berkeley under Winthrop Jordan's direction. Her dissertation became her first book: *A Calculating People: The Spread of Numeracy in Early America* (1982). She is also the author of *The Murder of Helen Jewett: The Life and Death of a Prostitute in Nineteenth-Century New York* (1998).

DOUGLAS HENRY DANIELS completed his PhD in history at the University of California–Berkeley in 1975. He took his first research seminar with Winthrop Jordan and was there when Win was dean during the years of tumult—Third World Strike, People's Park, etc. His most recent publication is *Lester Leaps In: The Life and Times of Lester "Pres" Young* (2002); his next book is *One O'clock Jump: The Unforgettable History of the Oklahoma City Blue Devils* (2005).

SUSAN DITTO first came to know Win Jordan as a professor, landlord, faculty advisor, party host, and ultimately as her dissertation director at the University of Mississippi. Since completing her doctorate in 1998 and becoming a visiting assistant professor of history at the University of Mississippi in 2001, she has had the privilege of calling Win a colleague and friend. She has co-edited another collection of essays, *Mississippi Women: Their Histories, Their Lives* (2003) and is currently working on its sequel, *Mississippi Women: The Politics of Gender* (2005).

DANIEL L. FOUNTAIN is a native of Jacksonville, Florida, and earned his doctorate in history from the University of Mississippi in 1999. Winthrop Jordan directed Fountain's dissertation "Long on Religion, Short on Christianity: Slave Religion, 1830–1870." Currently, Fountain is an assistant professor of history with Meredith College in Raleigh, North Carolina.

CHARLES JOYNER is Burroughs Distinguished Professor of Southern History at Coastal Carolina University. He is the author of *Down by the Riverside: A South Carolina Slave Community* (1984) and *Shared Traditions: Southern History and Folk Culture* (1999).

DAVID J. LIBBY is an independent scholar working at a commercial publisher in San Antonio Texas. As a doctoral student under Winthrop Jordan's guidance, David house-sat with Charlie (Win's dog), sought Cora Jordan's legal aid, and impersonated Win for every incoming group of grad students. He completed his PhD at the University of Mississippi in 1997. His dissertation has been published as *Slavery and Frontier Mississippi, 1720–1835* (2004).

PATRICK B. MILLER teaches African American History and Race Relations at Northeastern Illinois University in Chicago. He has also taught at the University of Münster and the University of Bayreuth as a Fulbright Senior Lecturer. At the University of California–Berkeley, during the late 1970s, he was among many of Winthrop Jordan's admiring graduate students and teaching assistants. Miller is co-author, most recently, of *The Unlevel Playing Field: A Documentary History of the African American Experience in Sport* (2003).

SHEILA L. SKEMP is professor of history at the University of Mississippi. She is the author or editor of six books, including *Race and Family in the Colonial South* (1988), coedited with Winthrop Jordan.

Paul Spickard teaches history, Asian American studies, and religion at the University of California–Santa Barbara. He encountered Winthrop Jordan in his first graduate seminar at Berkeley in 1974. He has heard Win's voice in his head, chiding him about sloppy writing, whenever he has put pen to paper or fingers to keys since. He is author or editor of a dozen books, among them *Mixed Blood: Intermarriage and Ethnic Identity in Twentieth-Century America* (1989) and *Race and Nation: Ethnic Systems in the Modern World* (2004).

Ronald G. Walters is professor of history at Johns Hopkins University, where he has taught since 1970. He received his PhD in 1971 from Berkeley where the best thing he did was to have Winthrop Jordan as director of the dissertation that eventually became *The Antislavery Appeal: American Abolitionism after 1830* (1976).

INDEX

abolitionism, xviii, xxii, 3–24, 164, 165; and pacifism, 164–69. *See also Liberator, The*; slaves and slavery; Society of Friends
Adams, John Quincy, 28, 164
Adams, Louisa, 89
Adams, Lydia, 99
adultery, 16, 28, 53–56. *See also* divorce; sex and sexuality
Advocate of Moral Reform, 37
affirmative action, 110, 115
Africans and African Americans, xxi, 57–58, 62–63, 107, 109, 110, 111, 112, 115, 116, 119, 120, 121; and the arts, 126–40, 143, 152–55; and debating, 155–57; elitism among, 146; in fraternities and sororities, 144–47, 150–51, 216n; and Italians, 122–23; lynching of, 62–63; musical traditions, 130, 132–33; oral traditions, 130–40, 155; and sports, 147–52; on white privilege, 112–13. *See also* Civil Rights Movement; clothing; historically black colleges and universities (HCBUs); jazz; Jim Crow; jive; race and racism; slaves and slavery; women, African American; women, slave
"Afternoon of a Basie-ite," 139
Alba, Richard D., 110
Albertson, Chris, 139
Albion's Seed, 110
Alien Nation, 110
Allen, Theodore, 113, 114, 124
Allport, Gordon W., 110
Almaguer, Thomás, 113–14

American Missionary Association (AMA), 99–100, 153
American Peace Society, 161, 164, 165. *See also* Ladd, William
American Slavery—American Freedom, 110
Amsterdam News (New York), 134, 136, 138
Andrews, Stephen Pearl, 14, 18, 21–22
architecture. *See* housing
Armstrong, Louis, 127, 132, 134, 138, 140; band, 134
Armstrong, Phebe and George, 55–56
Asians and Asian Americans, 107, 108, 109, 113, 115, 116–17, 119, 121. *See also* race and racism
Atlanta University, 141; athletics at, 148–49; social organizations at, 146. *See also* historically black colleges and universities (HBCUs)
Austin, Hannah, 97
Awatere, Donna, 123

Bailey, Gamaliel, 15
Bailyn, Bernard, 110
Baker, Georgia, 99
Ball, Charles, 96, 98
Baptists, 53, 85, 86, 91–92, 97, 98, 107, 148, 170; Southern Baptist Convention, 86–88, 92, 103–4. *See also* religion
Baraka, Amiri, 126
Barker, Louisa, 7, 9
Barnett, Spencer, 91
Basie, Count, 126–27, 128–29, 135; band, 128, 129, 132
Baxter, Richard, 170, 177
Beare, Charlotte, 32–33, 34, 36

Becton, John, 90
Bell Curve, The, 110
Berkeley, University of California at.
    See University of California at Berkeley
Berkeley, William, 181
Best, Denzil, 132
Bethune, Mary McLeod, 153–54
Bevel, James, 107, 124
Bibb, Henry, 99
Bienville, Jean Baptiste le Moyne Sieur de,
    70, 73–74
Binns, Arie, 94
Birney, James G., 9, 12, 13–14
birth control, 21–22, 48–49, 50, 189n.
    See also sex and sexuality
Black on White, 112
Bledsoe, Susan, 90–91
Bodnar, John, 110
Boggan, Manda, 90
Bonner, Siney, 91
Bourne, George, 7, 11
Bracey, Callie, 90
Brimelow, Peter, 110
Bristow, Josephine, 89
Brodkin, Karen, 121–22, 124
Brown, Betty, 89
Brown, John, 108
Brown, William Wells, 101
Brown Thrush, The, 153
Brown University, xiii, xxi
Brown v. Board of Education, 156
Burley, Dan, 136
Burton, C. B., 99
Butler, Mrs. Clement Moore, 29–30, 32,
    34, 35, 36
Byrd, William, 102

Calloway, Cab, 127, 136, 140
Cannon, Sylvia, 90
Cantor, Eddie, 129
Capers, Rev. William, 103
Carby, Hazel, 123
Carney, Harry, 131
Cashin, Lillian, 152, 154

Catholicism, 27, 43, 87, 98, 101, 120, 177;
    anti-, 11, 175. *See also* religion
Chavez, Cesar, 140
Cheatam, Henry, 91
Chepart, Sieur de, 75–76, 77
Chesnut, Mary Boykin, 94
Chicago, Ill., 135, 146, 156
Child, Lydia Maria, 5–6
children, 5, 15, 133, 182; abolitionist
    concerns for, 8, 18, 20–21; of Puritans,
    176; of slaves, 71, 87, 97; of yeoman
    farmers, 44, 46–51, 55, 57, 58–60, 63
Churchman, The, 37
Civil Rights Movement, xiv, 117, 147,
    155, 156
Civil War, American, 6, 60, 99, 104.
    See also Lost Cause
Clark, Flemming, 89
Clayton, Wilbur "Buck," 127, 132
clothing, 121; porkpie hat, 126, 129, 135;
    and sexual harassment, 33; slave, 102;
    zoot suit, 140
Cobden, Richard, 161, 165, 169
Colson, Arthur, 101
Company of the Indies, 70–71, 72, 73–75,
    79, 82
Cone, James, 118
Congress of Nations, 164, 167, 169
Conway, Moncure, 23
Cooper, Anna Julia, 112
corn shucking, 51–52, 95
Cravath, Erastus Milo, 148
Creole, 166–67
Crisis, 150–51, 152, 156
cruelty, 4, 23, 54, 56–57
Crutcher, Frances E. and George T., 54–55
Curti, Merle, 163

Darwin, Charles, and Darwinism, 22,
    23, 143
Davidson, Hannah, 100
Davis, Allison, 151
Davis, David Brion, xv
Davis, Stuart, 126

Delgado, Richard, 118
de Soto, Hernando, 67, 68
Dickenson, Vic, 132
divorce, 18, 53–57. *See also* adultery;
    cruelty; law; marriage
Dodds, Warren "Baby," 129
Dodson, Owen, 153
Domestic and Indian Mission Board, 87
Douglass, Frederick, 97–98
Du Bois, W. E. B., 111, 143, 154, 157; on
    education, 141–42; on sports, 150
Dunbar, Paul Lawrence, 153; societies, 143
du Roullet, Regis, 80–81, 82

Eaton, John and Fannie, 60
Eaton, Tobe and Nancy, 59–60
Edison, Harry "Sweets," 127, 129, 138
Edmonds, Helen, 146
Edmonds, Randolph, 151–52, 154
Edmondston, Catherine, 93–94
Ellington, Duke, 127, 131, 132; band, 130
Ellison, Ralph, 136
Emancipator, 13
Emerson, Ralph Waldo, 168; Award, xiii
England and the British, xx, 23, 143, 167,
    182; Civil War, 179; colonialism, 70, 71,
    76, 166, 181; and the "Oxford Move-
    ment," 27, 29; Parliament, 161, 169;
    Puritanism, 170–71, 172, 173, 178–80;
    and race, 108, 113, 118, 119, 120, 122;
    slave trade, 69, 80, 82, 165, 166; and the
    United States, xxii, 162–64, 166–67
Episcopalianism, 27–28, 29, 32, 37, 42–43,
    88, 103, 172. *See also* religion
Ethnic America, 110
Ethnic Dilemmas, 110
Ethnic Identity, 110
eugenics, 21–22

Falls, Robert, 101
family, 9, 15–16, 173; Puritan, 179; Quaker,
    182; slave, 100, 101; white middle class,
    19; yeoman, 46–51, 53, 54, 58–60.
    See also divorce; marriage

Farley, Joseph, 91
Farmer, James, 156
Faulkner, William, 52, 113
Ferguson, Mary, 100
Fields, W. C., 129
Fisher, David Hackett, 110
Fisk University, 141, 146, 157; athletics at,
    147, 148; and the Fisk Jubilee Singers,
    143; theater program at, 152–54.
    See also historically black colleges
    and universities (HBCUs)
Foley, Neil, 114–15
Follen, Charles, 20
Foster, Abby Kelley, 5
France and the French, 166; in colonial
    Louisiana, 67–83; and the Jay Treaty,
    162–63
Frankenberg, Ruth, 124
Free Soil Party, 169
Ft. Rosalie, 70, 73, 75. *See also* Natchez,
    Miss.
Fusco, Coco, 112

Gaillard, Elizabeth, 54
Garrison, William Lloyd, and
    Garrisonians, xviii, 3–5, 6, 10, 14, 18,
    20, 21, 23. *See also* abolitionism;
    Liberator, The
Garvey, John, 108–9, 118
Gaye, Marvin, 122
Gennari, John, 122–23
Giddings, Paula, 146
Gilpin, Charles, 152; players, 154
Glazer, Nathan, 110
Gleason, Ralph J., 127
Goad, Jim, 124
"Goodbye, Pork Pie Hat," 126
Goodell, William, 14, 17, 19, 20
Goodwin, Candis and Jake, 101–2
Goodwin, Lorendo, 98
Gordon, Dexter, 132, 136
Gordon, Lewis, 112
Graham, Sylvester, 19–21
Grandberry, Ella, 90–91, 92

Grant, Madison, 109, 110
Green, Beriah, 12–13, 17
Green, O. W., 91
Gregory, T. Montgomery, 152
Griffin, Mrs. Lou, 91
Grimké, Angelina, 13, 19, 20. *See also* Weld, Theodore Dwight
Grimké, Sarah, 12, 19, 20

Hall, David, 90
Hamilton, Alexander, 162, 163
Harris, Cheryl, 117
Harrison, James A., 130
Hawkins, Coleman, 126, 131, 132, 137
Hawkins, Tom, 97
Hayes, Wash, 100
health reform, 19–21
Heath, Jimmy, 131, 132, 133, 136
Henderson, Fletcher, 126
Herrnstein, Richard, 109–10
Heyrman, Christine, 180–81
Higginson, Thomas Wentworth, 8, 14, 20–21, 184n
Hispanics and Hispanic Americans, 109, 113, 114–15, 116, 119, 121, 140. *See also* race and racism
historically black colleges and universities (HBCUs): the arts at, 143, 151–55, 217–18n; athletics at, 147–51; debate teams of, 155–56; Greek organizations at, 144–47, 157; and racial uplift, 141–44, 145–46, 152, 156–58. *See also* Africans and African Americans; Atlanta University; Fisk University; Howard University; Tuskegee Institute
Hoffman, Michael, 124
Holiday, Billie, 122, 127, 131, 138, 140; origin of "Lady Day" nickname, 137
Holifield, Brooks, 175
Holmes, John Clellon, 126
homosexuality, 54. *See also* sex and sexuality
hooks, bell, 123

housing, 115; boarding houses, 8; yeoman, 44–48, 58–60, 63
Houston, Charles Hamilton, 156
Howard University, 141, 150; athletics at, 147, 148–49; debate team of, 156; Greek organizations at, 144–45, 146; theater program at, 152. *See also* historically black colleges and universities (HBCUs)
How Jews Became White Folks and What That Says About Race in America, 121–22
How the Irish Became White, 120–21
Hubert, Marc-Antoine, 70
Hunter, Olive, 153
Hughes, Langston, 146
Hume, Matthew, 101

"I Didn't Know What Time It Was," 128, 139
Ignatiev, Noel, 108–9, 118, 120–21, 124
Innes, Stephen, 179, 182
Invention of the White Race, 113
"I Only Have Eyes for You," 139
"I Struck a Match in the Dark," 129

Jackson, Andrew, and sexual politics, 15, 28
Jackson, Silas, 90
Jacobs, Harriet, 98
Jacobson, Matthew Frye, 115–17, 124, 209n
Jarrett, Hobart, 156
Jaspar, Sandy, 90
Jay, John, 162–64; and the Jay Treaty, xxii, 161–62, 163, 167
Jay, William, 161–69
jazz, 127, 171; and aristocracy, 137–38; fans, 140; humor in, 128–29; as language, 128, 130–33, 136; marijuana use and, 134. *See also* Africans and African Americans, musical traditions; Africans and African Americans, oral traditions;

jive; New York, N.Y., Harlem; Young,
    Lester "Pres"
Jim Crow, 129, 142, 156, 157–58. *See also*
    African Americans; Civil Rights;
    lynching; minstrelsy
jive, 127, 130, 133–40; handbook of,
    136; resemblance to pachuco, 140.
    See also jazz
Joans, Ted, 126
Jones, Charles Colcock (C. C.), 94–95,
    103, 104
Jones, Emma, 90
Jones, Jo, 129, 131, 133, 134, 135
Jones, Leroi, 126
Jordan, Winthrop D., xiii, 110; as a
    colonial historian, xiii, xxi; professional
    impact, xv, xvi, xxii; publications,
    xiv–xv; on race, xiv, xx; on sexuality,
    xviii; on slavery, xix; teaching career,
    xiv, xvi–xviii. *See also Tumult and
    Silence at Second Creek*; *White Over
    Black*
"Just You, Just Me," 139

Kansas City, Mo., 128, 132, 135, 140
Kay, Connie, 128, 131, 135
Kenley, Phoebe, 56
Kennedy, James Ronald, 124
Kersey, Kenny, 129
Kessel, Barney, 128, 131
King, Martin Luther, Jr., 107, 155
Kirk, Rahsaan Roland, 126

Ladd, William, 161, 164, 167, 168
la Salle, René Robert Sieur de, 67
law, 34–35, 44, 61–62, 191n; buggery, 54;
    family, 49, 53; fencing, 57–58;
    international, 163, 167–69; literacy,
    93–94; martial, 166; obscenity, 44,
    61; and race, 115–16, 117–18. *See also*
    divorce; rape
LeConnait, Mother Hyacinth, 87
Lee, Randall, 91

Lee, Spike, 147
Lewis, Dio, 20
Lewis, John, 135, 136
Liberator, The, 8, 18, 185n. *See also*
    abolitionism; Garrison, William Lloyd
Lipsitz, George, 115, 117, 124
Loguen, J. W., 102
London Peace Society, 165
López, Ian Haney, 118
Los Angeles, Calif., 140
Lost Cause, 61
Louisiana, xx, 87, 88; colonial, 67–83;
    Creole language in, 130. *See also*
    Company of the Indies; Natchez,
    Miss.; New Orleans, La.
lynching, 62–63, 145. *See also* rape

MacKinnon, Catharine, 123
Mahoney, Martha, 123
marriage, 28, 101, 151, 182; companionate,
    47, 48, 54; interracial, 6; and passion,
    13–14, 17–18; plural, 21; slavery as threat
    to, 15–16; yeoman, 48, 49, 52, 53, 54–56.
    See also adultery; divorce; family
Marshall, Thurgood, 156
Mason, Isaac, 98
masturbation, 18, 20. *See also* sex and
    sexuality
McDowall, Rev. John, 17
Menken, H. L., 171
Methodists, 86, 88, 98, 103. *See also* religion
Mexicans. *See* Hispanics and Hispanic
    Americans
Mezzrow, Mezz, 138
Miley, Bubber, 130
Miller, Perry, 171–72
Milling, Cureton, 97
Mingus, Charles, 126
minstrelsy, 39–42, 129, 143. *See also*
    Jim Crow
miscegenation, 6–11, 16, 22, 62, 97, 185n.
    See also race and racism; sex and
    sexuality

Mississippi, xiv, xv, xix, 44–63, 89, 90, 91,
    100. *See also* Mississippi River; Natchez,
    Miss.; University of Mississippi
Mississippi River, 67, 68. *See also*
    Louisiana; Mississippi; Natchez, Miss.
Moody, Loring, 23
Moore, Sena, 100–1
Moravians, 93
Morgan, Edmund S., 110
Morrison, George, 101
Morrison, Toni, 110, 112–13
Mott, Lucretia, 17
Murphy, Sally, 90
Murray, Charles, 109–10

Nanton, Joseph "Tricky Sam," 130
Natchez, Miss., xv, xx, 67–68, 70–71,
    73–76. *See also* Ft. Rosalie; Louisiana,
    colonial; Mississippi; Native
    Americans, Natchez
Native Americans, 111, 113, 115, 116;
    Chaouacha, 79; Chickasaw, 69, 77, 82;
    Choctaw, 67, 68–70, 73, 78–82;
    Natchez, 67–68, 69, 70, 73, 75–79; and
    matrilineal culture, 68–69, 80; and
    slavery, 69–70, 73, 76–83. *See also*
    Natchez, Miss.; race and racism; slaves
    and slavery
Nature of Prejudice, The, 110
New England, xvi, 10, 20, 148, 170–82.
    See also Puritans and Puritanism
Newitz, Annalee, 123, 124
New Orleans, La., 68, 75, 77, 81, 130, 136,
    153, 157, 166. *See also* jazz; Louisiana;
    Mississippi River
New South, 44, 61, 148
New York, N.Y., 8, 17, 163; black elite in,
    140, 146; Harlem in, 134–35, 136, 137,
    152; peace movement in, 164–65; sexual
    harassment scandal in, 25, 29, 36, 38–39,
    42; theater in, 153, 154. *See also* jazz
Novak, Michael, 110
Noyes, John Humphrey, 21

Oliver, Joe "King," 126, 130–31
Olmsted, Frederick Law, 51
Onderdonk, Rev. Benjamin T., xviii–xix,
    25–43
Oneida community, 21, 24, 42
Organization of American Historians, xvi
O'Sullivan, John, 168

Parker, Charlie, 127
Parker, Theodore, 12, 22
Passing of the Great Race, The, 109
Pennington, James, 89
Périer, Etienne Boucher de, 75, 76, 79
Perlongo, Robert, 130
Perry, Matilda, 99
Peterson, Mark, 180
Phelps, A. A., 9
Philadelphia, Pa., 29, 39, 88
Pillsbury, Parker, 23
Playing in the Dark, 112–13
"Polka Dots and Moonbeams," 139
Possessive Investment in Whiteness, The, 115
Presbyterians, 97
privacy, xix, 26, 44–48, 51, 58–60, 62, 63.
    See also sex and sexuality
prostitution, 8, 14, 17–18, 49–50. *See also*
    sex and sexuality; women
Protestant Ethic, The, 180. *See also* Puritans
    and Puritanism; Weber, Max
Puritans and Puritanism, xvi, xxii, 8,
    220n; and capitalism, 172, 178–82;
    declension theory of, 172; and the
    occult, 174–76; and predestination,
    170, 172–73, 176, 177–78, 179; and the
    Protestant work ethic, 170, 171, 177,
    178, 182. *See also* New England;
    religion; Weber, Max

Quakers. *See* Society of Friends
quilting bees, 52

race and racism, xx–xxi, 22, 28, 39–42, 62;
    and class, 110–14, 123–24; critical theory

of, 117–18; and gender, 123; hierarchy of, 118–19; Jews and, 116, 119, 121–22; Winthrop Jordan on, xiii, xiv; and pride, 141–58; and religion, 98–100; and whiteness, 107–25. *See also* Africans and African Americans; Asians and Asian Americans; Hispanics and Hispanic Americans; miscegenation; sex and sexuality; slaves and slavery
Race Traitor, 121
Racial Fault Lines, 113–14
Ramey, Gene, 132
Randolph, Rev. Peter, 97
Rankin, John, 7, 8, 9
rape, 7, 26, 37–38, 49–50, 61–63. *See also* law; lynching; sex and sexuality
Redneck Manifesto, 124
"Reefer Man, The," 134
religion, xxii, 11, 22, 27, 28, 29, 35, 42, 43; and abolitionism, 3–24, 164; civil, 62; evangelical, 26, 56, 58, 60–61, 87–88, 95–96; and the peace movement, 163–69; and the Second Great Awakening, 25; and sexuality, 12–14, 17–18, 37, 39; slave, 84–104; and slaveholding, xviii, 12–13, 99. *See also* Baptists; Catholicism; Episcopalianism; Methodists; Moravians; Presbyterians; Puritans and Puritanism; Society of Friends
Richmond, Rev. James, 31, 33, 35–36, 38
Rise and Fall of the White Republic, The, 110–11, 113
Rise of the Unmeltable Ethnics, The, 110
Rising Tide of Color Against White World-Supremacy, The, 109
Robeson, Paul, 154; Drama Club, 153
Roediger, David, 110, 111–12, 113, 114, 124
Rolfe, John, 181
Rollins, Sonny, 129
Rowles, Jimmy, 138
Rudderow, Helen, 31–32, 33, 34, 35
Rudderow, Jane, 31–32, 34

"Runnin' Wild," 128
Rural Southerner, The, 48
Rutherford, Jonathan, 108, 109, 118

Saxton, Alexander, 110–14
School Daze, 147
Scott, Anna, 91
Sewell, Alice, 97
sex and sexuality, xviii–xix, 63; and abolitionism, 3–24, 186n; and evangelicalism, 26; and health, 20; and household economy, 15, 48, 58; and livestock, 44, 50, 54, 57, 58, 61; and race, 6, 7, 9–10, 39–42; as sin, 12–14, 17–18, 26, 35, 37, 39; and slavery, 6, 7, 8, 9–11, 13, 15, 97–98; and the yeomanry, 44–63, 192n; and youth, 39, 47, 49–52. *See also* adultery; birth control; homosexuality; masturbation; miscegenation; privacy; prostitution; rape; sexual harassment; virginity
sexual harassment, 25–43. *See also* sex and sexuality
Sharp, Rev. James E., 86
Shepherd, Ella, 143
Simpkins, Millie, 91
Sinatra, Frank, 122, 123, 140
Singleton, Zutty, 138
slaves and slavery, xviii, xix–xx, 46, 48, 111, 113, 115, 120, 169, 181; Bambarra designation, 72, 76–77, 197n; Caribbean, xiv, 70, 165, 166–67; families, 15–16; French concepts of, 72, 196n; Winthrop Jordan on, xiii, xiv–xv; literacy restrictions under, 85, 92–95; in Louisiana, 67–83; and music, 91, 95, 132, 143, 155; narratives, xv, 98, 99; Native Americans as, 70; Native American views of, 69–70, 76, 81–82; and power, 4–6; rebellions, xiv–xv, 72, 76–77, 88–89, 92, 96, 166–67, 199n; and religion, 84–104; Senegambian, 68, 71–72, 76; and sex, 6, 7, 8, 9–11, 13, 14,

15, 98; trans-Atlantic trade in, 70–72, 165, 168. *See also* abolitionism; Africans and African Americans; race and racism; women, slave

"Sometimes I Feel Like a Motherless Child," 133

Smith, Ervin, 94

Smith, Gerrit, 6–7

Smith, Joseph, 99

Society of Friends (Quakers), xvii–xviii, 53, 165, 169, 182. *See also* abolitionism; religion

Souls of Black Folk, 141

Southern Christian Leadership Conference (SCLC), 107

South Was Right!, The, 124

Sowell, Thomas, 110

Spencer, Herbert, 23

Standish, Clara, 149

Stanton, Elizabeth Cady, 17, 21, 22, 23

Stanton, Henry B., 5, 20

Stefancic, Jean, 118

Stier, Isaac, 101

Stoddard, Lothrop, 109

Stoddard, Solomon, 175

Stowe, Harriet Beecher, 19, 22

Streator, George, 150

Sturge, Joseph, 165

Sugg, Hattie, 89

Sunderland, LaRoy, 9, 20

Sutton, Kattie, 99

"Sweet Sue," 134

Swisshelm, Jane, 3–4

Tappan, Arthur, 17, 165

Tappan, Lewis, 18, 20, 165

Tate, Buddy, 135, 136

Taylor, Joe Gray, 88

temperance, 17, 21, 29, 35–36, 164, 166, 168

Thandeka, 124

Theatre Owners Booking Association (TOBA) circuit, 133

They Were White and They Were Slaves, 124

Thompson, Sir Charles, 128, 131; origin of nickname, 137

Tidwell, Emma, 97

Tolson, Melvin B., 156

Tonsler, Horace, 101

Towards the Abolition of Whiteness, 112

Trall, Russell, 20

Transplanted, The, 110

Trask, Haunani-Kay, 123

Tumult and Silence at Second Creek: An Inquiry into a Civil War Slave Conspiracy, xiv–xv, xix–xx. *See also* Jordan, Winthrop D.

Turner, Nat, 88. *See also* slaves and slavery

Tuskegee Institute, 143–44; athletics at, 148–49

University of California at Berkeley, xiii, xiv, xv, xvi, xxi, 146

University of Mississippi, xiv, xv, xvi, xvii

Van Dyke, Charlie, 84

Verot, Bishop Augustin, 88–89

"Viper's Song, A," 134

virginity, 8, 17, 36, 49–50, 52, 61. *See also* sex and sexuality

Voorhees, Lillian, 152–54

Voyagers to the West, 110

Wadley, Sarah Lois, 44–47

Wages of Whiteness, 111–12, 113, 117

Walker, Amasa, 20

Walker, Minksie, 94

War and Peace, 165–66, 167, 169

Warren, Earle, 129

Washington, Booker T., 142; Atlanta Exposition Address, 144

Washington, George, 162, 163; as a jive term, 139

Washington, Madison, 166

Waskam, Eliza, 56–57

Weber, Max, xxii; and American historians, 170–73, 180, 182; and capitalism, 172, 178, 179, 182; and predestination, 170, 172–73, 176, 177, 179; and the Protestant work ethic, 170, 171, 177–78. *See also* Puritans and Puritanism

Webster, Ben, 126

Webster, Daniel, 164

Webster-Ashburton Treaty, 167

Weld, Theodore Dwight, xviii, 4, 5, 12, 17, 18, 184n; marriage to Angelina Grimké, 13–14, 20. *See also* Grimké, Angelina

Wells, Dicky, 137

Whipple, Charles K., 4, 5

White, George, 143

White, Mingo, 92, 99

White By Law, 117–18

Whiteness of a Different Color, 115–17

White Over Black: American Attitudes Toward the Negro, 1550–1812, xiii, xiv–xv, xvi, xviii, xxii, 110. *See also* Jordan, Winthrop D.

White Scourge, The, 114, 117

White Trash, 123

Whitman, Walt, 168

Wightman, William, 103

Willard, Samuel, 175

Willbanks, Green, 91

Williams, Bert, 129

Williams, James, 91

Willis, Nathaniel P., 36–37, 39

Wilson, Teddy, 127

Woolman, John, 6

Woman's Rights Movement, 19, 123, 145

women, 17, 138–39; African American, 39–42, 123, 145–46, 151, 157; as captives, 76, 77, 78, 79; in colonial Louisiana, 71, 73; slave, 7, 8, 11, 98, 101–2, 191n; slaveholding, 7, 8; white middle class, 9, 12, 15, 19, 28, 33–34, 36, 38, 40, 47, 61; yeoman farming, 48–49, 51–53, 55–57, 61–63. *See also* birth control; prostitution; rape; sex and sexuality; sexual harassment; virginity; Women's Rights Movement

Wray, Matt, 123, 124

Wright, Henry C., 8, 14, 17–18, 21, 22, 97

X, Malcolm, 140

Yerby, Frank, 154, 217–18n

Young, Al, 126

Young, Lee, 128, 133–34, 136

Young, Lester "Pres," xvi, xxi; childhood, 133, 136; contributions to jazz music, 126–27; humor of, 128–29; and language, 127–28, 131–32, 133–40; origin of nickname, 137. *See also* jazz; jive

Young, Willis "Billy" H., 133

www.ingramcontent.com/pod-product-compliance
Lightning Source LLC
Chambersburg PA
CBHW030646270326
41929CB00007B/234